*Dedicated to Sophie Partridge, Tim Gebbels
and members of the Graeae family who have long gone
but have played a crucial part in the company's history.*

Reasons to be

A unique insight into the UK flagship disabled-led theatre company.

GRAEae
[grey-eye]

A work in progress

WEL COME

The idea for the book came about when we received funding from Arts Council England to revive our production *Reasons to be Cheerful*.

This production commemorates our wonderful patron the late Ian Dury and has enabled us to go back to being bold, brash, and anarchic: the Graeae of olden days only on bigger stages. The show is joyous and gives people a reason to be cheerful and it got me thinking about the reasons for Graeae's existence. I put a call out to various members of the Graeae family asking them to think about their reasons for Graeae, their reflections, and memories of the journey they have been on with the company. Some replied with their top ten memories and others gave a more detailed study of the work.

I have tried to weave these testimonials into a narrative that outlines our artistic development and learning.

I have loved spending time with our founder Nabil Shaban, and my predecessor Ewan Marshall, discovering the trials and tribulations of the early stages of the company.

This is a book to dip in and out of and I hope there is something in here for anyone who likes theatre, disability arts, history, politics and stories.

Jenny Sealey MBE
CEO/Artistic Director
Graeae Theatre

December, 2017

THE 1980s

[1980 + Graeae]

Graeae founded by Nabil Shaban and Richard Tomlinson.

[1980 + Sideshow]

Graeae's first production, devised by Richard Tomlinson and the company.

[1981 + Graeae]

Graeae are offered an office, rehearsal space and facilities by an Arts Centre in Aldershot and were able to set up base for about eighteen months.

[1981 + 3D]

Devised by Richard Tomlinson and the company. Directed by Nic Fine.

[1981 + BBC2 Arena]

Documentary on the work of the company.

[1982 + M3 Junction 4]

Co-directed by Richard Tomlinson and Nic Fine.

[1982 + People's Minds]

Channel 4 documentary about the making of the show.

[1983 + The Endless Variety Show]

Written by Chris Speyer. Directed by Geof Armstrong.

[1983 + Not Too Much To Ask]

Written by Patsy Rodenburg. Directed by Caroline Noh.

[1983 + Casting Out]

Written and directed by Nigel Jamieson.

[1984 + Cocktail Cabaret]
Devised by the company. Directed by Caroline Noh.

[1984 + Practically Perfect]
Written by Ashley Grey. Directed by Geof Armstrong.
Theatre in Education show.

[1984 + Choices]
Central TV Programme about the Theatre in Education
work of the company.

[1986 + Working Hearts]
Written by Noel Greig. Directed by Maggie Ford.

[1987 + Equality Street]
Devised by Ashley Grey and Geof Armstrong.
Theatre in Education show.

[1987 + Private View]
Written by Tasha Fairbanks. Directed by Anna Furse.
Graeae's first womens' project. National and
International Tour.

[1988 + The Cornflake Box]
Written by Elspeth Morrison. Directed by Brian Thomas.
Graeae's first community play.

[1989 + Why]
Written by Geof Armstrong and Yvonne Lynch.
Directed by Ewan Marshall. Theatre in Education show.

THE  1990s

[1990 + Why]

Written by Geof Armstrong and Yvonne Lynch.
Directed by Ewan Marshall. Theatre in Education show.
Adapted for a National Tour.

[1991 + Chances Are]

Written by Jo Verrent. Directed by Annie Smol.
Theatre in Education Show. National Tour.

[1992 + Hound]

Written by Maria Oshodi. Directed by Ewan Marshall.
10th Anniversary National Tour. ITV 'Link' programme
on the play.

[1992 + A Kind of Immigrant]

Written by Firdaus Kanga. Directed by Ewan Marshall.
National tour.

[1993 + Soft Vengeance]

Written by Albie Sachs. Adapted for stage by
April De Angelis. Directed by Ewan Marshall.
National and International Tour.

[1994 + Playback]

Forum Theatre in Education programme.
Directed by Colette Conroy.

[1994 + Ubu]

Written by Alfred Jarry. Adapted by Trevor Lloyd.
Directed by Ewan Marshall.

[1995/6 + Playback 2 U]
Forum Theatre in Education programme.

[1996 + Flesh Fly]
Adapted from Ben Jonson's *Volpone* by Trevor Lloyd.
Directed by Ewan Marshall.

[1996 + Sympathy for the Devil]
Written by Roy Winston. Directed by Ray Harrison
Graham. A co-production with Basic Theatre Co.

[1997 + What the Butler Saw]
Written by Joe Orton. Directed by Ewan Marshall.

[1998 + Two]
Written by Jim Cartwright. Directed by Jenny Sealey.

[1998 + Alice]
A free adaptation by Noel Greig of *Alice in Wonderland*
by Lewis Carroll. Directed by Jenny Sealey and Geoff
Bullen. A co-production with Nottingham Playhouse
and Nottingham Roundabout TIE.

[1999 + A Lovely Sunday for Creve Coeur]
Written by Tennessee Williams. Directed by Jenny Sealey.

[1999 + Fittings: The Last Freak Show]
Written by Mike Kenny. Co-directed by Jenny Sealey
and Garry Robson. Co-production with Fittings
Multimedia Arts.

THE 2000s

[2000 + The Fall of the House of Usher]

Written by Steven Berkoff. Directed and designed by Jenny Sealey. Movement direction by Liam Steel.

[2000 + Graeae]

Missing Piece Training Course launches.

[2000 + Woyzeck]

Written by Georg Büchner. Directed by Philip Osment. Missing Piece 1 Training. London Tour.

[2000 + Message in a Bottle]

Written by Michèle Taylor. Directed by Peter Rumney. Missing Piece 1 Training. London Tour.

[2001 + Blood Wedding]

Written by Federico García Lorca. Directed by Philip Osment. Missing Piece 2 Training. North West Tour.

[2001 + The Changeling]

Written by Thomas Middleton and William Rowley. A new adaptation by Claire McIntyre. National Tour. Directed by Jenny Sealey and Amit Sharma.

[2002 + peeling]

Written by Kaite O'Reilly. Directed and designed by Jenny Sealey.

[2002 + The Trouble with Richard]

Written and directed by Jamie Beddard. Forum Tour.

[2002 + Wild Lunch VI]

Paines Plough and Graeae's first collaboration. A series of professional lunchtime readings of new work by disabled and non-disabled writers at The Young Vic.

[2003 + Diary of an Action Man]

Written by Mike Kenny. Directed by Jenny Sealey.

[2003 + Mother Courage and her Children]

Written by Bertolt Brecht in a new translation by Lee Hall. Directed by Janwillhem Van Den Bosch. Missing Piece 3 Training. London Tour.

[2003 + Vagina Monologues]

Written by Eve Ensler. A V day celebration performed by 30 D/deaf and disabled women with eleven women sign language interpreters and audio describers.

[2004 + On Blindness]

Written by Glyn Cannon. A unique and eagerly awaited collaboration between Graeae, Paines Plough and Frantic Assembly.

[2004 + Bent]

Written by Martin Sherman. Directed by Jenny Sealey.

[2005 + George Dandin]

Written by Molière. Translated and directed by Philip Osment. Missing Piece 4 Training. London Tour.

[2006 + Blasted]

Written by Sarah Kane. Directed by Jenny Sealey.

[2007 + Whiter than Snow]

Written by Mike Kenny. Directed by Jenny Sealey.

[2007 + Flower Girls]

Written by Richard Cameron. Directed by Jenny Sealey and Pete Rowe.

[2008 + Static]

Written by Dan Rebellato. Directed by Jenny Sealey and Graham Eatough with Suspect Culture.

[2009 + Graeae]

Graeae moves to Bradbury Studios.

[2009 + Just Me, Bell]

Written by Sophie Partridge. Directed by Rachel Bagshaw.

THE  2010s

[2010 + Signs of a Star Shaped Diva]
Written by Nona Shepphard. Directed by Nona Shepphard and Jenny Sealey. Starring Caroline Parker.

[2010 + The Garden]
Written by Alex Bulmer. Directed by Jenny Sealey and Grant Mouldey.

[2010 + The Rhinestone Rollers]
Directed by Rachel Bagshaw. Choreography by Marc Brew.

[2010 + Reasons to be Cheerful]
Book by Paul Sirett. Music by Ian Dury and the Blockheads. A co-production with Theatre Royal Stratford East and New Wolsey Theatre. Directed by Jenny Sealey

[2011 + The Iron Man]
Written by Ted Hughes. Adapted for Graeae by Paul Sirett. Directed by Jenny Sealey and Amit Sharma.

[2012 + Graeae]
Jenny Sealey and Bradley Hemmings co-direct the London 2012 Paralympic Games Opening Ceremony.

[2012 + Reasons to be Cheerful]
The first revival. National and International Tour.

[2013 + Graeae]
Write to Play launches.

[2013 + The Rollettes: Deck the Stalls]
Directed by Mik Scarlet, Laura Dajao and Amit Sharma.

[2014 + The Threepenny Opera]
Written by Bertolt Brecht. Directed by Jenny Sealey and Pete Rowe. A co-production with New Wolsey Theatre.

[2014 + The Rollettes: Ready to Rumble]
Graeae's Youth Programme. Directed by John Kelly and Jodi-Alissa Bickerton.

[2015 + Graeae]
Ensemble training programme launches.

[2016 + The Solid Life of Sugar Water]
Written by Jack Thorne. Directed by Amit Sharma. A co-production with Theatre Royal Plymouth, playing at the National Theatre, a first in the company's history.

[2016 + Graeae]
Graeae's first ever exhibition, in partnership with the Central Illustration Agency, entitled *Reframing the Myth*, held at *The Guardian* building in King's Cross.

[2016 + Stepping Stones]
Written by Mike Kenny. Directed by Jenny Sealey. Schools Tour as part of the Ensemble training programme.

[2016 + The Rollettes: Buccaneers Final Frontiers]
Directed by Daryl Beeton.

[2016 + The Rollettes: The Astro Elves Save Christmas]
Directed by Daryl Beeton.

[2017 + The House of Bernarda Alba]
Written by Lorca. Translated by Jo Clifford.
Directed by Jenny Sealey with Nickie Miles-Wildin.
A Royal Exchange Theatre Manchester co-production

[2017 + Cosmic Scallies]
Written by Jackie Hagan. Directed by Amit Sharma.
The first time Graeae produces a play by one of their
Write to Play graduates.

[2017 + Reasons to be Cheerful]
Graeae's cult musical revamped revival tours for
the last time.

[2018 + Graeae]
Oberon Books publishes *Reasons to be Graeae:
A work in progress.*

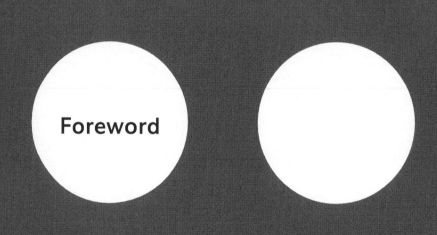

Foreword

Mat Fraser
Actor, Writer and Drummer

My mum invited me to a play called *Ubu* at the Ovalhouse Theatre, South London in 1994, by a disabled theatre company called Graeae. I had 'come out' as a disabled person in 1992 at thirty years old; I yearned to do something aligned with my disability politics and love of performing.

As the son of two actors, I wanted to act but I had been put off badly by kids laughing at me in the school play audition at thirteen years old, the only disabled kid in my school. I had carried with me from then on the idea that disabled people on stage were nothing more than an embarrassment to most others. Acting was not a possible career for someone with as visibly different a body as mine.

Then I saw Jamie Beddard, a man with a good dose of cerebral palsy, shouting on stage at everyone else and showing his arse. He was spitting cake at a wheelchair using woman, Mandy Colleran, who was mocking him and a Deaf woman, Caroline Parker, who was signing. All manner of radically different things unfolded as the whole company romped their way through the most bawdy, anarchic, messy play I had ever seen. And the sold out, mostly non-disabled audience, loved it. No embarrassment but laughter, cheers, applause, and enjoyment.

I've often tried to describe the feeling that came over me then, a disabled wannabe actor imprisoned by a notion of, 'body not good enough'. My whole life exploded as I realised there was a place for me to be, to be equal, understood, etc. I had a non-religious epiphany that night.

[Foreword + Mat Fraser]

I decided to leave my band the next morning and try to get an audition with Graeae. I was lucky that Ewan Marshall (then artistic director) saw potential in me. I became a member of the company, doing a three-month schools tour of forum theatre with Colette Conroy. I finally got a part in their production of Joe Orton's *What The Butler Saw* with Dave Kent, Ilan Dwek, Daryl Beeton, and Jacqui Beckford in 1996-7.

From there, I got an Equity card and worked off and on with Graeae for a few years before branching off to do my own work. This disabled theatre company had given me the confidence to perform and a belief that I, as a disabled person, had equal value as an arts creative.

Graeae grew over the next few years, got better funding, and Jenny Sealey took over as artistic director in 1997. Her influence included forming relationships with mainstream theatres, training hungry disabled people in basic theatre skills, and bringing in more and more what we might term, 'inclusive design', i.e. building accessibility into the show itself, from the writing stage where possible. Any Graeae show these days has BSL and audio description/stage text built into the script and other areas where possible.

From Nabil Shaban forming Graeae in 1981 to now as I write this in 2017, the growth, output, professionalism, profile, and international relationships with other theatres and groups has grown to make Graeae the leader in disability-led theatre. I live in the US and there is nothing like Graeae here, although there are some that try to emulate it.

Changes to the ethos, such as making the company inclusive in its casting; working on co-productions with mainstream theatres; and making more commercially accessible work have all proved to be successful in raising Graeae's profile. They are now rightly the most well-known disability-led theatre company in the world. Perhaps more successful is that their influence has reached deep into mainstream UK theatre, which has seen much change although it needs to see and hear a LOT more!

Jack Thorne's commissioned play *The Solid Life of Sugar Water* directed by Amit Sharma at the National Theatre, and *The House of Bernarda Alba* directed by Jenny Sealey at the Royal Exchange Theatre, Manchester, are two examples of the heights of the commercial, inclusive theatre profile that Graeae has attained in recent years. I feel super proud of their achievements and influence in UK mainstream theatre—*Ramps on the Moon* could not have happened without all of Graeae's work, for example. My last performance work with them was as the drummer on the original tour of *Reason to be Cheerful* in 2010. I look forward to my next project with them because, as with all the disabled and non-disabled people who have passed through this great company, I will always be a member of their family.

Perseus himself could never have imagined the power those three women crips—the Graeae Sisters had, with only one eye and one tooth between them—when they became the theatre company that saved and made my artistic life, as they have for so many other disabled and non-disabled theatre practitioners.

[Foreword + Mat Fraser]

How It All Began
Maria Oshodi
Geof Armstrong
Steve Mannix

Elspeth Morrison
Rachel Hurst
Prof. Anna Furse
Caroline Noh

Beginnings

Jamie Beddard
Daryl Beeton
Dr. Colette Conroy

How It All Began

Nabil Shaban, Graeae Founder: 1981–1983
Interview with Jenny Sealey

NS You probably already know that the story of Graeae's origin has several beginnings. The roots of the company go right back to my time at Derwen College and Hereward College where Richard Tomlinson was a tutor. Richard was non-disabled, but he came from a theatrical background. He was a posh bloke, however he was a man of the 1960s. That decade created lecturers who were radically left-wing and who spread out across the UK so that by the early 1970s people like Richard Tomlinson existed. Meanwhile there was me, a natural born rebel with an acting bug who refused to take no for an answer.

JS Where do you think that bug came from?

NS It came from my desire to tell stories. It came from my desire to be something else. To be other characters, to dress up, to live in a world of fantasy, to escape my condition.

JS Was that about escaping your past identity? Your early stages of life were quite traumatic, weren't they?

NS I don't think that my early life was any more traumatic than it is for any other disabled person. But I had a very vivid imagination—I enjoyed telling stories and entertaining. From photographs of me at that time it seems that I always had a smile on my face. And I like to stand up for the underdog, it appears. So, in the children's home, I was usually the adults' worst enemy because I was nearly always taking the side of my peers and nearly got expelled on many occasions. But the school appreciated my ability to create theatre and liked me organising drama so the staff forgave me a lot.

When I went to Derwen College, I still wanted to be an actor. Every drama school in the country had already refused me by the age of sixteen. They just didn't want to know. I had also been rejected by amateur dramatics! The British Drama League were determined not to allow a person with a wheelchair to take part in their amateur summer schools.

At Derwen I continued to gather together fellow inmates as I had at school, and did at least two or three productions in the three years I was there. Then I arrived at Hereward College. Richard Tomlinson was on the interview panel and asked me one question and that was about my interest in theatre; he'd seen it listed as a hobby in my application. I elaborated on why I was interested and said I hoped that if I came to Hereward, I would get involved with their drama groups in the evenings. He was pleased about that. Anyway, I got accepted at Hereward.

JS   What course did you enrol in?

NS   I did an Ordinary National Diploma in Business Studies. Totally unrelated to drama. Richard wasn't even one of my lecturers. He was somewhere else teaching History and English, but he had a mania for the theatre. The thing about Richard was that he believed that disabled people had important stories to tell about their experiences of being disabled, about their lives, and in every context with every issue. He had a real curiosity about it. He was aware that it would occasionally verge on voyeurism, but so what really—we had to start somewhere! He wanted to create a series of shows where disabled people were telling their stories.

We worked together on a play I entitled *Ready Salted Crips*, coining the nickname 'crips' and took it on tour around Warwickshire—it was a phenomenal success, playing to full houses wherever we went. Richard became excited about the potential of the show and decided we must set up a theatre company to provide opportunities for disabled performers and to educate, demystify, and destroy myths regarding disabled people.

In 1975, I was accepted to Surrey University and Richard had plans to move to Illinois University to work with disabled students. Before we both left Hereward, we decided to do one last project together, called *Sideshow*. After that show finished he said to me, 'Do you fancy setting up a theatre company of disabled people?' I said, 'Well, yes ... but I'm not interested if it means you just want me to be an administrator. I'm an actor; I want to perform. And if we're going to have a theatre company, don't expect me to just be a manager. I want to be on that stage!' He replied, 'Of course! I couldn't do it without you as an actor.' I said, 'Fair enough.' And he said, 'How are we going to go about it?' and I said, 'I haven't a clue!'

I was a friend of Michael Flanders who was the only disabled wheelchair performer in the 1960s. He was a comedy singer; he sang songs about hippos! He said to me, 'If you want to get on the stage, you have to create your own work and you have to create work which is unique; that no one has seen before. Stop trying to write what other people write. Stop trying to make adaptations of plays that other people can do better than you. Your life and every other disabled person's life is unique and it's important that you tell those stories. That's what you should focus on.'

Richard and I agreed that this is what it should all be about but we still didn't know what to do. But we were in no great hurry. When I got to Surrey University, I didn't stop being a student actor. So, although my degree had nothing to do with theatre …

JS   And what degree was that?

NS   I did a degree in psychology, philosophy, and sociology.

JS   You've got a massive brain, haven't you?

NS   Nah! I originally went to do economics, sociology, and statistics. But after two weeks, I realised that I was not a capitalist!

JS   [Laughs]

NS   Anyway, Richard and I kept in touch. He had very rich friends because he was a posho, which meant that he knew how to get bits and pieces of money. Also, his wife and mother-in-law were actors and they were nicely connected!

[Beginnings + How It All Began]

We needed a name that would say everything we wanted to say about our disabled theatre company. We both agreed that we needed a name that was connected to mythology, to the breaking up of myths and misconceptions. We were toying with mythical creatures that had a disability connection. Obviously, we came up with ridiculous things like Cyclops Theatre Company, or Centaur Theatre Company, or Minotaur Theatre Company.

JS   Those are all very male names.

NS   Exactly. Then I remembered a myth about the three Graeae sisters who were related to the Gorgons and had one eye between them. I didn't know then about the tooth, that was something Richard discovered later in the process. So, Richard did a little research ...

JS   ... and that's when Graeae was born.

NS   Absolutely.

JS   I love telling the Graeae story. Nobody can ever pronounce Graeae correctly the first time, but it's the best name for a theatre company.

NS   Well you see, one of the reasons why it's so good is that it's hard to say.

JS   But once people get the message, it stays with them.

NS   Exactly, it's an automatic controversy!

JS   Meanwhile, what happened once you had decided on a name for the company?

NS   Richard discovered that 1981 had been designated the International Year of Disabled People. And I went, 'Aha! Right, in that case we should have Graeae up and running by 1981.'

JS   An ambitious target to aim for.

NS   Exactly. We needed to be a bandwagon for people to jump onto. Because the fact was, we knew that by 1981 there wouldn't be any other disabled theatre companies around. Everyone would want to do their bit for disabled people because it would be kind of trendy and fashionable at that point. So if we could have Graeae running by 1981, we would be inundated with offers. That was the master plan: be established by 1981.

The next thing that Richard tells me is that in 1980 there is going to be an international conference on rehabilitation and disability in Winnipeg, Canada. He reckoned that if we could have a show ready to perform in Canada in 1980, it would be a perfect launch pad for 1981. I agreed—1980 was the ultimate deadline. The next thing he had to do was write a load of bullshit and claim to the organisers of the conference ...

JS   ... that you were a bona fide, fully established theatre company.

NS   Absolutely. So, this is 1978 right, when we are putting this plot—this conspiracy—together.

JS   This is like a once upon a time story, isn't it?

NS   Richard writes a proposal letter to the organisers of the conference and of course claims that we have a theatre company, that we have a script, and that it would be good if they would invite us to perform. Well, what do they know? They wrote back and said yes. So, Richard comes back to me and says, 'We've been invited' and I go, 'Oh fuck! We better do it then!' We ended up not just performing at the conference in Canada, we also toured to the United States, starting at Illinois University where we did twenty-seven shows in twenty-three days.

JS   You must have performed to a lot of people during that trip.

NS   It was a tough baptism of fire. Back home, recruiting actors for the Graeae's first proper touring show, *Sideshow*, was a hard slog. We were setting up lots of audition workshops at PHAB clubs (Physically Handicapped and Able Bodied), day centres, and any other kind of place where there was a collection of disabled people. By the summer of 1979 we had a cast of six people including myself.

JS   But no D/deaf people.

NS   Our stage manager was Deaf, so tokenism! We only had two non-disabled people: Richard and the assistant stage manager. We had a blind woman, Elaine; a woman with muscular dystrophy; and a woman with spina bifida, called Alex. Plus myself, Jag Plah, and a guy called Will Kennan.

Graeae began as a professional company in May, 1981. Our premier was at Surrey University, after which we travelled to America. When we got back, we needed to organise a tour of Britain. Since we were all amateurs, we were only available for performances on Fridays, Saturdays, and Sundays. We had to divide up the country, to cover as much ground as possible. That way, we could perform at three different venues in a weekend.

One of the first theatres I rang was Ovalhouse. I explained to them that we had a show, described it to them and so on. They said it sounded interesting. We agreed a date and they said, 'So what about £100?' And I went, 'What?! A hundred pounds?' I was thinking we ain't got a hundred fucking quid! You see, I was used to the idea that you paid to go and perform. I was thinking where am I going to get £100 from? I said, 'Oh. A hundred pounds?' And there's a pause and she responds, 'Alright, £200'. They wanted to give *me* £200! I was like, 'Oh yeah, £200. That sounds reasonable. Yeah, we'll take that!!!'

JS   Good old Ovalhouse. That was where we mounted my first London production with Graeae. It's been an important part of Graeae's history.

NS   Oh, absolutely. They were there right at the beginning. Jacksons Lane was another one.

JS   Ovalhouse, Jacksons Lane, Riverside. Great venues. If you had to name the favourite play you did with Graeae, what would it be?

NS   It's probably *Volpone*.

JS   We have a picture in the Graeae living room of you all trussed up with an orange in your mouth from that production. When I take people round the building, giving the Graeae history, I love showing them that image and telling them this is Nabil, founding member of Graeae. It provokes such a reaction and consolidates the Graeae story, the political ambition, our maverick spin and uniqueness, if you know what I mean. Why did you leave?

NS   Simply because I was lucky; I was offered another acting job, at the National Theatre. I've worked at the National twice, you know: in 1998 and 2001!

JS   Are you surprised that Graeae is still around almost thirty-five years on?

NS   Yes. I had hoped that it would no longer be necessary by now. I had hoped that after thirty-five years, disabled performers and artists would be integrated into mainstream theatre, TV, film, and entertainment. That disabled people who want to be actors would not have continuing barriers to becoming professional actors and receiving proper training. That doesn't mean I think Graeae isn't offering proper training because they certainly are doing so, but any disabled person who has a talent should be able to get into any drama school or college without any prejudice.

JS   Why do you think we are still around?

NS   Because the mainstream industry in all honesty does not want us on their stages or on their screens. They still want to reserve the entertainment industry for the privileged. They don't want non-disabled audiences to be frightened of disabled and deformed bodies.

JS   And how does that make you feel?

[32]

NS I still feel very angry. Not with Graeae. Thank god Graeae has managed to continue to this day. But, thirty-five years later, opportunities for disabled performers should have multiplied. We should be seeing and hearing disabled and D/deaf performers in the media everywhere on a regular basis. The National Theatre, for example, should not be complacent about the fact that only occasionally is someone like me on their stage.

I believe that Arts Council England and other arts funding bodies in Britain should adopt my policy on disabled performers. I believe that all cultural institutions—theatres especially—should employ disabled performers as a matter of course. That if any theatre, whether it's the National, Birmingham Rep, or wherever, that if any mainstream venue fails to maintain a 10% quota of disabled performers every year, they should have 10% of their budget cut. Theatres should be forced; it's not enough to just have the occasional crutch or D/deaf person or blind person on the stage in crowd scenes. The theatres must commit to 10% of all leading roles being given to disabled performers.

We could also have got a lot further if Equity had done their job and were on our side. They should seek to penalise any film, TV, or theatre company that employs non-disabled people in specific disabled roles.

JS Some people might say that Graeae has failed. I suppose it still bothers me, that drama schools are only just thinking about these issues again now. The fact that only now, after thirty-five years, we have the Ramps on the Moon project for regional repertory theatres. A project that arose from Graeae touring *Reasons to be Cheerful* with a big cast, and a mixed bag of people.

Sarah Holmes at New Wolsey Theatre and Stuart Rogers at Birmingham Rep applied to the Arts Council for Ramps on the Moon. The project means that once per year each of the six big regional rep theatres gets the opportunity to have a big inclusive cast for one production. Which is great, a real move in the right direction.

NS It's a start, but is it enough of a start? We need more than a ramp, we need a launch pad. My personal feeling, that those six theatres should be doing at least one play with an inclusive cast each year anyway.

I believe, and it's probably very oblique of me to believe this, that the State wants to eliminate disabled people from society. The Right-Wing State, that is. Because of the capitalist imperative, because of the profit imperative, they do not want any more resources to go to disabled people. They do not want any uneconomic consumers to be allowed to drain the economy of resources. Which is why we are seeing all these attacks on disability allowances and benefits. Why they are making it increasingly difficult for disabled people to survive in the outside world and trying to push them back into institutions? This is what we're up against and quite frankly in some ways I'm surprised that Graeae has managed to weather this onslaught and survive.

JS   I think we need a whole book on just you, your life and politics Mr Shaban!

Do you realise we have been chatting for over three hours! All of this has got to be transcribed so I can edit it!

Nabil—thank you for your time and thank you for starting Graeae.

Next Steps

Ewan Marshall, Artistic Director: 1992–1997
Interview with Jenny Sealey

JS   What made you apply for a job at Graeae?

EM   I wanted a directing job and I knew about Graeae; I had previously done a bit of part-time work for the company. But I think the most important thing that drove me to apply was an accident I had when I was eighteen. I wanted to be an actor. It was my first day at drama college and I had an accident on my motorbike. I was badly injured and I spent quite a few months in recovery. The whole world completely changed. After that it was all about everyone saying, 'Well, you aren't going to be an actor anymore. You aren't going to do drama anymore' and in fact someone from the hospital said, 'A lot of people with your injuries become radio operators for the police.'

Lying in bed one morning, I watched an *Arena* programme on this theatre company. It was profiling a company called Graeae who were a company of disabled actors. I remember how compelling and brilliant an actor called Nabil Shaban was and, after seeing that programme Graeae became an inspiration to me. The job of artistic director came up at a time when I was looking for that kind of position and it just seemed like a fantastic opportunity. Emotionally, the company meant a great deal to me.

JS   Can you remember your first day? Where was the Graeae office when you started?

EM   It was in Bayham Street, Camden. It was a portacabin, full of bits of old set and only two desks, maybe even one desk. I remember on the first day Steve Mannix and I went out to buy a carpet. I loved that portacabin!

JS   I bought a Cafetiere on my first day. Only instant coffee was available and I drink posh coffee. That rule has stayed ever since.

JS   Your first play was *Hound*. Did you commission or inherit it?

EM   *Hound* was a shock to me because nobody had mentioned at the interview that there was already a play that was waiting to be directed. It was quite a big thing for them to not mention, and quite a big thing for me to not have asked. The company had no regular Arts Council funding at that time so the only way you could put a play on was through project funding. Maria Oshodi's play *Hound* had been successful in getting project funding.

When I read the script, I was very worried I wouldn't be able to cast it because it was so specific in gender, ethnicity, and age. *Hound* is about the experience of blind people undergoing guide dog training and is very much informed by Maria's experience training her guide dog. I realised that I was accustomed to working as the only disabled person in a theatre company and I had little awareness of other disabled actors. It was, as I found out, a very small pool of people. I admit that I got to a point where I was following blind people in the street. I remember this young woman going past me with a guide dog—she was the perfect age, a young black woman with a guide dog. I literally followed her as she walked into the Society for the Blind! I had a conversation with her. She didn't end up being in the play but she did direct me to the right place. Though I don't think following women in the street is a very healthy activity, it was successful later. Someone walked past me one day and I thought god, they're really, really striking. They've got something about them, I wonder if they can act? And it turned out that Jamie Beddard could act very well.

JS   That's how you met Jamie Beddard?

EM   He walked past me on the Southbank, though I didn't actually meet him then. He applied to join the company and I recognised his photo when we were looking for actors. I was so pleased to see his application.

JS   *Hound* was quite successful, wasn't it?

EM   I think it had a mixed reception. I'm proud of the work we did on it but I always felt that it could be dismissed as 'worthy' too easily. Some people liked it and some people just didn't.

JS	Graeae had been through an agitprop period under Nabil Shaban. When you arrived and directed *Hound*, it set the company on a whole new path, producing extant plays and new writing.
EM	The real issue when I joined Graeae was that they wouldn't tour to any space that wasn't accessible. This meant that almost all arts centres and theatres were off the agenda. I said however bad the access is, we must go to them otherwise we'll never be taken seriously as a theatre company. That was important—the theatre company had to be a good theatre company that people wanted to come and see. These brilliant, skilled, funny, bright, knowledgeable disabled people were just everything to me and I wanted to create the best theatre for them. And that meant taking risks.
JS	The production of *Ubu* was a great risk!
EM	It was interesting to explore a punk play. It is the most punk piece of theatre I know. It's a skit of *Macbeth*, written by a French schoolboy a hundred or so years ago; it's surreal and wild. *Ubu* is wonderfully grotesque and indeed non-disabled people look at us as grotesque. By producing and performing in this play, we were subverting that view of disabled people. It's the most empowering kind of work and it suddenly lit a fuse. The show went down really well—word of mouth and reviews were extremely good—and people wanted to come and see the company. Lots of the ideas for the show came from the actors who were working on it, and this was the first time we incorporated a sign language interpreter into the action.

JS   I saw it at the Mansfield Arts Centre and I have a vivid memory of signer Vikki Gee Dare with a birdcage over her head. One of the performers, Sara Beer, started speaking in Welsh and Vikki signed, 'Speaking in Welsh. Don't understand'. Jo Verrent and I, the only Deafies in the audience, fell about laughing and then we realised no one else was laughing. It felt like a real treat just for us. That is something I have absolutely stolen from you, the idea that everyone gets the information at some point, but at different times. For example, a D/deaf audience might be a beat behind or maybe there is something just for the D/deaf audience members.

EM   Yeah. Having obviously D/deaf actors in the show gave me the confidence to play with this. I remember at the time there was a very strong lobby from traditionalists who insisted an interpreter should be positioned at the side of the stage and you were messing around if you did anything else.

With *Ubu* we suddenly became a cool company. I remember Mat Fraser being in the audience of the show and saying afterwards, 'That's it! I want to be in this company! I want to be an actor!' It was an extremely enjoyable show to tour with; it went down fantastically well in Germany.

JS   You've directed a whole series of firsts and a healthy eclectic mix between plays which are about being disabled and plays that that have no disability reference at all. Of all the plays that you did at Graeae which are the ones you are most proud of?

EM   *Ubu* created the biggest change for the company and set us on the map. *Flesh Fly* (an adaptation of Ben Jonson's *Volpone*) was a better crafted piece of theatre. We were just a bunch of disabled people doing a piece of classical text and finding our way to own it and, as always with Graeae, to subvert it and be suitably maverick.

JS   A few last questions. What would you say are the major battles you've fought during your career?

EM   The biggest battle was to get the board of trustees to accept that we wanted to be established in the wider theatre circuit and that D/deaf and disabled audiences can be part of a wider audience. We wanted to be the best theatre company around and for lots of people to see our work; to be a player on the UK and the international theatre map.

JS   You had great successes in achieving that goal and the profile of Graeae has continued to grow. It was in an amazing state when I took over, so I will always thank you for that.

EM   You have been building strongly on integrated sign language and audio description in performances, as well as thinking about all forms of access; imbedding access into the heart of what the theatre company does. How do you feel about working on co-productions with other venues and companies?

JS   I like it better when I can direct the co-production. Call it an ego or a control issue but, as a Deaf director, I have a certain sensibility. I see things in my mind's eye but I like to play first to see if my instinct is right or not. Co-directing with someone is always harder because you have different styles, two egos rubbing along together, two people telling the actors different things. It's hard, but you do learn a lot. You learn a lot about yourself and what an egotistical bugger you are!

But also, I worry about conforming to the norm and not being able to utilise all those things that are so intrinsic to being D/deaf and disabled. My experience with our group of actors is so rich and they offer such tricks and quirks which are authentically theirs. For example, in rehearsals for *The Threepenny Opera*, Max Runham would take off his arm and use it to scratch his back. How could I not have that in the show? It was Brecht after all. Or in 2012, when all the circus performers came down off their apparatus, saying, 'Jen, pass my leg. No not that one, the one over there', or I would play, 'hide the leg.' On the afternoon of the London 2012 Paralympic Games Opening Ceremony (POC), I was looking for our designer as I had a beautiful metal prosthetic which was one of my performer's spare legs and was to be put on the *Spasticus Autistics* set. I kept asking the crew if they had seen anyone hopping. You should have seen their faces!

EM   I am thinking about the disabled people I worked with, how it changed me and what I learnt about directing at Graeae.

JS   Do you still feel that you are a part of Graeae?

EM   Completely, completely.

JS	Do you think there will always be a need for Graeae or, now that the big theatres are taking on accessible and inclusive theatre-making practices, do you think Graeae will lose its brand?
EM	No. Because you will always have what is absolutely the best thing about Graeae: a group of like-minded people getting together and doing something extraordinary, steeped in a real disability sensibility which gives it our unique spin.

Past Plays

Interview with Sarah Scott (SS), Ewan Marshall (EM),
Ray Harrison Graham (RG) and Jenny Sealey (JS)

JS	Thank you Sarah, Ray and Ewan for joining me for a trip down memory lane!
	First question. How many plays have you done together?
SS	We did *Soft Vengeance*.
RG	And *Sympathy for the Devil*.
JS	Doing both those plays were a real first for Graeae. In terms of the issues, the casting, the signing, the conventions—and both were political.
SS	What was just before *Soft Vengeance*?
EM	*A Kind of Immigrant*. Firdaus Kanga was an Indian writer. He wrote this novel, *Trying to Grow*, about growing up with brittle bones. It was a fantastic novel, so I commissioned him to do it as a play, which was tougher because it was so personal and political.

JS	The wider politics being the relationship between two gay disabled men.
EM	It was a coming out play.
JS	I think Graeae is always political as putting D/deaf and disabled people on stage is political. But you put other big politics into the mix.
EM	With *Soft Vengeance*, I knew the book *The Jail Diary* by Albie Sachs, which is about when he was detained without trial for ninety days, then another ninety days. He spent months in solitary confinement. And then a few years later, he's blown up in Maputo and wrote *A Soft Vengeance of a Freedom Fighter*. It was a very good book because of the struggle against apartheid, his role in all this and of course the disability politics of somebody, who has an acquired disability talking about it very eloquently. It resonated with me as somebody who had lost an arm.
RG	Do you remember the phone message I sent you? I sent a fake message pretending to be an agent.
	You had told me about your motorbike accident. I made up some name and asked, 'When did you last see your arm?' You did laugh back then. It was so awful.
EM	So awful but so funny.
SS	So awful. And nothing to do with *Soft Vengeance*!
RG	Nothing at all. But the reason I've mentioned it is because it's to do with the way we relate to things with humour.

JS	Ewan, how did you make the decision to be in it and direct it.
EM	I was having a real problem with impairment-specific casting. In *A Kind of Immigrant*, you absolutely had to have someone with brittle bones so Firdaus was also in it. In *Soft Vengeance*, I got a group of actors I wanted to work with Ray, Sarah, Deborah Williams and Dave Kent.
RG	I wanted Ewan to play the lead so that I would be his conscience, his black conscience. But you wouldn't do it.
EM	And I still wouldn't do it now, and it worked really well and it's a very simple thing. I hate saying it but you are a better actor than I am, Ray! So we have this black guy playing this white guy and the white one-armed guy is his conscience. It was kind of the day and night Albie. It was April De Angelis, a new writing talent, whose it idea it was to have two Albies. A reviewer in the *Evening Standard* said—'... this casting ... I don't, I can't even begin to explain it, but it works really well'
SS	The production had so many layers that you wouldn't have got if you had gone straight with it.
EM	Albie Sachs liked a black guy playing him and understood having someone one-armed like him as also being part of the authentic picture.
RG	Sure he did! The casting allowed us to show a multitude of layers about apartheid and disability.
JS	If a white non-disabled middle-class director was directing, how would they cast it?

RG	They would cast it straight.
EM	You would be Zuma. You wouldn't even be Albie. Albie would be white.
	And they would have someone hiding their arm. As it is in the film. And they would not have had another black woman in it let alone one with a hand missing like Deborah. It was Deborah's first play, you know? With Graeae.
	She was fantastic. When she auditioned for me, she did her speech and I said, 'That was very good.' and she said 'I know.'
JS	Makes me realise how lucky we are at Graeae because we can be mavericks. We can break all the rules. Casting is a wonderful thing to play with. All of that I think is from the real desire to not be normal.
SS	Yes! Yes you are right.
JS	Did you, Ray and Sarah, both sign in the play?
RG	We had the big scene where we had to light the candles and we signed the whole scene.
EM	Yours was the only scene that was signed. That was the last play we ever did where there wasn't a level of signing that was constant in the play.
JS	Did you have an interpreter for every show?
EM	Every venue, we would have one night signed but remember we were only project funded then.
JS	Oh bloody hell.

EM   Yeah it was after this production we finally became part of the Arts Council England (ACE) portfolio.

SS   We did get money from British Council to go to Minsk, Belarus. Get that. British Council sent us to Belarus in 1993 with a D/deaf, disabled and ethnically mixed cast.

RG   Me and Debs got spat at in the streets. But when I finished the main speech April wrote, I got a standing ovation. Even though they didn't understand much English.

SS   They all stood up, an audience of thousands in this huge theatre.

JS   That is one of those moments that theatre changes lives. They stood up feeling the power of what you were saying.

RG   I think they understood the fight and they understood the car bomb. I think they understood the fight to continue.

EM   The Berlin Wall had come down. They were newly independent and there was this sort of thing going on ... and of course the Ukraine was the centre of so many massacres and the Holocaust. They had horrendous things going on. They were occupied for a long time so they totally identified with that.

RG   We did Battersea, Colchester and Leicester.

EM   Did we go to Sadler's Wells?

JS   I saw it at Sadler's on the night before my thirtieth birthday in 1993.

EM   Richard Wilson, a patron of Graeae and Albie Sachs were there too! I wish he had seen *Sympathy*.

RG   *Sympathy for the Devil* was a black play and black audiences loved it. They loved the whole play, the black humour, but at the end I turned on the audience said 'Thank you for your applause but you're too late. We've gone through this life with you hating us, disliking us, telling us to take off hearing aids, hiding us under beds and putting us through all of this. And now you are going to applaud because you had a good night out?' It was hard for me to turn on my own community and get them to think about this.

JS   You wrote this. What was the writing process like?

RG   It was difficult because it was very personal. It dealt with family issues of disability and sexual abuse. It was painful to write but it needed to be said. This is what the final speech is about.

JS   Did your family see it?

RG   Yes.

JS   Shit. How was that?

RG   My sister obviously cried like hell. My other family just said, 'You're sailing too close to the wind. This is too close. Too close,' and I said, 'It has to be. If you don't sail close to the wind, what's the point?'

EM   It was an important play and it reminds me how few disabled people from BAME backgrounds are in theatre.

SS   When I worked at the Arts Council, I was given some funds to do some development work to engage with the disabled people from the BAME community

JS	Why do think there's a lack of BAME disability arts?

RG	To give yourself up as a disabled person is a big thing. To say, 'I am disabled and I am here'. Because it's so ... it's looked down on so badly. So people don't.

JS	Ewan you commissioned it and produced and Sarah you were administrating it yes?

SS	I remember typing—a lot.

RG	I couldn't type.

SS	I would get all his writings and I would type it. I suppose I was like a company manager.

JS	Did Jacqui Beckford sign every show?

RG	No. Couldn't afford it in those days. It was only specific performances.

JS	Did we have Access to Work [ATW] though?

SS	I remember getting ATW for a phone coupler. It was mainly for equipment back then.

JS	Let's not get me started on the whole ATW thing! Any other thoughts/final words?

RG	*Soft Vengeance* was important because I was part of the ANC and it was a chance to say Free Mandela. I was part of the non-stop protest outside South African House. I got arrested a few times. And, *Sympathy* was a chance to say what I felt all my life. Stop it. Stop pretending. It's happening to young D/deaf and disabled black people. Those two plays had a big impact on me.

SS	I loved being part of the whole disability movement and we were pushing against society. It was energising, exciting and necessary.
JS	How did you get involved? You were in *Children of a Lesser God*, so what was your journey to Graeae?
SS	Soon after *Children of a Lesser God*, I started work at the Unicorn Theatre for children and their development officer of Little Deaf Unicorn from 1984 till 1995. In '86, Elspeth Morrison who worked at Artsline and published the *Disability Arts in London* (DAIL) magazine wrote to me and it is through her, I became connected to the disability arts movement.
JS	I used to stuff *DAIL* into envelopes for Elspeth.
EM	So did I. I was hopeless at it!
JS	We had Graeae, *DAIL*, Artsline, and London Disability Arts Forum. Wow, we were lucky then!
	I love that we were all there fighting and I love the connection of the whole disability arts movement, which I, Jenny, feel very much a part of. But the disability arts movement sometimes sees Graeae as something separate because we also play to mainstream audiences in mainstream (accessible) theatres. I want everyone to know who Graeae is and see the talent within our community. Sometimes I feel like I'm caught between a rock and a hard place.
SS	I am sure you do. It will never work for everybody. It just won't. Just keep doing good stuff.
EM	And keep fighting!

[Beginnings + How It All Began]

JS	One last thing. I'm still harbouring resentment ... I auditioned for Ewan twice. He never gave me a job!!
RG	He took his time with me too. Was it a black thing?
EM	Racist. Misogynist!!!!
JS	And on that note, a million thanks for your time.

A New Phase

Jenny Sealey, CEO/Artistic Director: 1997–Present

My first encounter with Graeae was in 1987. The company was auditioning for *A Private View* by Tasha Fairbanks, directed by Anna Furse. I arrived in a large room to find a splendour of diverse women. Across the room, I saw Caroline Parker wearing flippers (we had to bring an object to the audition) and a million colours as she always does. She was chatting and signing with a confident fluidity. I became Deaf when I was seven years old and spent my education being the only Deaf person in my class. I had to teach myself to lip-read and consistently felt like I was playing catch up. I often felt like I was on the outside of a world that I was never actually allowed to enter. Seeing Caroline and the other women was like an epiphany. I knew I had finally found where I belonged.

I got the job and experienced my first Graeae rehearsal period (without an interpreter) and tour, which was extraordinary, not least meeting D/deaf and disabled people up and down the country but it was also my political awakening realising the depth of inequality, marginalisation and discrimination of our community. Fast forward to 1997, when I saw an advert in *The Stage* for artistic director of Graeae Theatre Company. I was directing multisensory productions for young people with profound and multiple disabilities for Interplay Theatre and devising work for the D/deaf community in the Midlands. I talked to David Johnston, artistic director of Nottingham Roundabout who was sort of my mentor who said 'I think you are a better director than you are an actor and I will be very cross if you do not go for this!' I sat with my partner Danny Braverman and went through the job description again and again until I had the confidence to believe I could do it. I got an interview and was asked to give a presentation about my ambitions for the company and to direct some Graeae actors using a text of my choice.

The interview panel consisted of Elpseth Morrison (trustee), Rachel Hurst (chair), and Kevin Dunn (administrative director). The actors I was asked to work with included Jamie Beddard, Liam O'Carroll, and Sarah Beauvoisin, with sign language interpreter Jenny Towland. The selected text was from Mike Kenny's *Stepping Stones* which is written in Haiku form and had originally been commissioned for Interplay. I had to work quickly to establish a system to line-feed Liam (a blind actor), hold a script for Sarah (a Deaf BSL actor), and place Jenny so that she could sign for Jamie (differing voice pattern and difficult for both Sarah and I to lip-read). The sweat was cascading down my back and every so often I would take a furtive glance at the panel. It was most unnerving that Rachel Hurst, in her majestic power chair, had a white Scottie dog on her lap which she stroked rhythmically, like Blofeld in the James Bond movies.

I somehow got through that first task. The actors left and I sat in front of the panel, slightly out of breath, dress stuck to my back, hands clammy and shaky as I began my presentation. The remainder of the process was a blur.

Interview over. I had given it my best shot.

I arrived home that night to a fax with Elspeth's spidery writing. It said, 'Well done, the job is yours, but don't tell anyone just yet!' I was working that night, dressed as an old lady and performing a signed song version of the Spice Girls *Wannabe* with my Deaf girls (Caroline Parker, Jo Verrent, Ali Briggs, and Iona Fletcher) at the Nottingham Playhouse bar. I blurted out the news to Ali (who was dressed as a nun for the gig). She gave a few Hail Marys, hugged me and said, 'You'd better give me a job!' So, my partner Danny started his job at Theatre Royal Stratford East, our three-year-old son Jonah started nursery and I started at Graeae!

What happened next was an extraordinary series of firsts. It was the first time I had been an artistic director, managed a team (other than actors and a creative team), set budgets, led on productions, approved contracts, restructured a company, given a verbal warning and dismissal, written big funding applications, managed a board, recruited staff ... The list goes on but it is the artistic firsts I've experienced here that have really kept the creative flame of Graeae burning.

Maria Oshodi

Writer and Artistic Director, Extant Theatre

Ten Graeae Moments

1. Thinking back ... I remember wanting to write something about my recent experience and how it felt to be processed for the first time by one of the main sight loss charities—also the Graeae board at the time wanted to commission me to write something, so my play *Hound* came into being in this way.

2. There was no artistic director in situ at Graeae at the time and I remember going for meetings with Steve Mannix, the company's general manager in the Graeae office which was a portacabin in Mornington Crescent.

3. Ewan Marshall then came on board as the company artistic director and was handed me and my play as his first job, something perhaps we both had a little reticence about, not knowing each other much.

4. I remember it was hard finding enough trained blind actors to cast in the play—at one point Ewan found himself following a woman of colour with a guide dog who was coming out of the RNIB, just to see whether she could be a possible candidate for the part of Aisha.

5. It felt both concerning—and a minor triumph—that the play was perceived as being worthy enough to have been boycotted by a major charity.

[Beginnings + Maria Oshodi]

6 ⠿ Dave Kent, who played Joe would always bring his guide dog on stage for the first scene, which was a bonus for the set design and went against the age old maxim of never working with animals!

7 ⠿ There were some great mesh dog headdresses that were designed for the actors to wear in the show's formation training routines. About a year or so after the tour ended I heard there had been a break in at Graeae ... the next day, while at a performance of the comedy crew 'The Posse', the three comedians came on stage wearing the 'Hound' masks. I was relieved to hear when I reported this to Graeae, that the masks had been lent and not spirited away as bootie.

8 ⠿ I interviewed over twenty blind and visually impaired people for the research for this play, so was pleased there was so much positive feedback from this audience at the time. However I am still surprised when visually impaired people sometimes say that they remember it, or on reading it, tell me that it has had an impact on them.

9 ⠿ I remember a reviewer on the former Radio 4 arts programme 'Kaleidoscope' (which was replaced by the current Front Row) saying that the play had moments of superb quality writing, which at the time felt a nice reward for all the hard work that went into it!

10 ⠿ Jenny's wonderful warm hugs!

Geof Armstrong

Director, Arcadea

To say that my life changed when I joined Graeae in 1982 would be an understatement of huge proportions. Consequently, whenever I'm asked about the time I spent with this amazing theatre company, I truly struggle for the words that would do justice to how profound an effect Graeae has had on every aspect of my life then and since.

Chance, timing, and some extraordinary people brought me to the company at a time when the social model of disability was emerging as the *de facto* approach to understanding physical and intellectual impairment and the disability movement was beginning (quite rightly) to throw its rattles and anything else it could find out of the pram.

It was early and formative days for Graeae and it was with the company's second national tour of *M3 Junction 4* that I had my first true taste of national touring. Wherever we went, from the Isle of Skye to Dorset, there was a buzz. A bunch of disabled actors, sometimes exhausted, sometimes laughing, bundling out of the tour van always caused a stir amongst venue staff and often, just a touch of anxiety as no one really knew if the venue was up to scratch or what we were really up to. But we were nearly always met with respect. The biggest welcome, the most interest, and the deepest understanding of what the company was setting out to do came from the disabled people we met along the way.

[Beginnings + Geof Armstrong]

Disabled audience members and cast would chat to each other in excited amazement after the shows. Five disabled people had just spent sixty-five or so minutes on stage telling a tale of cruelty, segregation, normalisation, and despair without anyone telling us what to do. Though, if we were in a bar having a drink and it was way past disabled people's bedtime (usually around 9.30 pm then), there was often frustration as various carers would drag people off mid-conversation as their shift was nearly over.

> I think we all knew that change was coming and it was with the following show that, for Graeae, this change began to take place. The Endless Variety Show that I was commissioned to direct—a sweet little piece of children's theatre written by an amazing TIE writer Chris Speyer—returned to the theme of normalisation and its cost to the individual and society. It wasn't overtly about disability but rather about diversity. It set out to position disability alongside other major and enduring social movements such as feminism and gay rights.

> It wasn't so much the show though, it was the cast and staff that began the seismic change that turned Graeae from a theatre company for disabled people into a theatre company of disabled people; in particular, cast member Sian Vasey. Few, if any, would question that Graeae's founders Nabil Shaban and Richard Tomlinson had a huge idea and made it real. For that, countless disabled creatives and audience members have benefited enormously. But what I believe they didn't see coming, along with most of us, was the huge change that the social model and the disability movement was about to unleash. And Sian brought that bang centre stage to Graeae.

Sian was a powerful advocate for disability rights and was fully up to speed with, and deeply embedded in, the young disability movement. Which, as we know, has self-determination at its heart; for disability organisations this translated into user-led.

While what followed was a natural and inevitable transition that was undertaken with grace and goodwill, it was no less agonising for everyone that had been, or was involved with the company at the time. It was also a precursor of what was going to happen to many disability organisations, large and small, across the country in the following years.

This was a defining moment in the company's history and, as with so many aspects of Graeae, it sent a clear message to disabled people, the arts community, and beyond: that we are passionate, creative, talented human beings that want to be in control of our own destinies. It sounds obvious now but back then this was a highly controversial idea.

For myself, the politics and aesthetics of Graeae sit equally side-by-side. Yes, the company creates great work and is a stunning and vital platform for disabled writers, actors, directors, musicians, managers, etc. But beyond the brilliant theatre and the fantastic opportunities it creates, is the fact that it belongs to disabled people and is a beacon of hope for every disabled person, their friends, families, and comrades that fight for a fair and inclusive society.

The company and those like it are needed now as much as they were then. As we endure years of austerity, watch our dignity being stripped away, and our rights diminished, these beacons of hope and the outrage they illuminate have to shine brighter now than ever they have.

[Beginnings + Geof Armstrong]

Steve Mannix

Chief Executive, Colchester Mercury

First of all, what an honour it is to be asked to write about the early days of Graeae. It's a strange thing to be asked to reflect on those days. In my mind, it's like yesterday but in reality, twenty-eight years have gone by since I first started to work with the company.

As many of us look back at the struggles and fights that we had then, it doesn't seem that different to today. We've come full circle. The issues are still there—manifesting themselves in different ways maybe, but they are there—rights, independent living, access, inclusion, respect, having your voice heard. They are all still as relevant today as they were then.

We all believed in those early days that one day there would be no need for a company like Graeae. Our mantra was that our role was to make ourselves, and the need for the company, redundant. The world would accept the social model in the not-too-distant future, would be inclusive, and would respect the rights agenda. We all knew there was a lot to do but boy, little did we know!

So, depending on your age dear reader, this short chapter will either jog lots of memories for you of days spent on demos and sit-ins, or your own personal fights with various authorities, or you might read this chapter and shout, 'really?' Yes—it's all true and not just me looking back with a 'rose tinted' view. Honest!

My first encounter with Graeae and the disability arts movement was through working at the Albany Empire in Deptford, London in the early to mid-eighties. The Albany at the time was known as one of the key venues in London to host political work, alongside other venues such as Ovalhouse, Chats Palace, and the Tom Allen Centre in Stratford. We hosted the launch of London Disability Arts Forum. Heart n Soul started life as a workshop with Shape at Lewisham Academy of Music and Graeae visited to perform several shows and host residencies with local disabled young people. The work of the company was accepted alongside other 'movements' of the time.

I then went to work in America for a while. I received a phone call from Graeae when I got back to see if I might be free to take on some admin work. I was enjoying freelancing at the time so I thought nothing of it; I'd had a great time working with the company at the Albany. They were all great fun— why not, I thought!

I met several of the board members to chat about the job and what they needed. Things were clearly not in a good state as they handed me a couple of boxes of paperwork. We agreed I would do a couple of days per week on a temporary basis to help them out. To quote one of the board members at the time, 'you're not a cripple but a poof so the next best thing—at least you know about oppression' and as they say, the rest is history ...

Oh, the glamour of that period was self-evident from my first day. The company was based in two small rooms in a portacabin off Camden High Street, shared with a family welfare organisation.

[Beginnings + Steve Mannix]

It was just about accessible, boiling hot in the summer, freezing cold in the winter—like working in a tin box. Though a tin box might have been more watertight; when it rained we had to get out the buckets to catch the leaks.

At one end of the office were all of the pieces of set, props, and costumes, piled high to the ceiling. You could just make out two desks at the other end, one with an old Amstrad 9512 (for those of you who are younger, google it—they are probably vintage now), a typewriter, a phone, and a filing cabinet. Beyond that, another room piled high with boxes and boxes of 'stuff'—that was it! It was Maggie Hampton as the education co-ordinator, the freelance stage manager, and me.

Maggie is profoundly Deaf and a sign language user. I'll be forever grateful to Maggie for her patience and kindness, for teaching me to sign (still very badly I'm afraid), and for making me laugh and giggle as we faced it all together.

I giggle to myself today when I set up inductions for new staff members, or get them to read handover notes, or guides to online filing systems. There was nothing. I mean nothing—nothing!

My first board meeting was coming up a few weeks later. I diligently tried to get papers together and put together the accounts (note young people: from manual double-entry paper ledgers that I found hidden amongst the props). The day came and I was sitting in the glamourous surroundings of said portacabin waiting for the board to arrive ...

Let me set the scene. There I was. Twenty-six years old and keen. Pencil sharpened, agenda to hand, waiting for what was, at the time, one of the most eminent groups of disability activists in the country (in future years they would all go on to receive OBEs, MBEs, knighthoods, or take their place in the House of Lords) ... and me.

> I got a call from a phone box on Oxford Street (oh, the days before mobiles!). The call was from a member of the board. The conversation went:
>
> 'Can you drive?'
>
> 'Yes,' I replied, having only passed my test a few months earlier.
>
> 'Can you drive a van?'
>
> 'Yes,' I replied. 'Once or twice' would have been more honest.
>
> 'You'd better bring the van down here now.'
>
> 'Oh. But I'm really sorry, I can't. There's a board meeting tonight,' says the dutiful administrator.
>
> 'Well, there won't be any board meeting tonight. Most of them are chained to a bus across Oxford Street.'
>
> I did as I was told and drove down to Oxford Street in an old shaky Lords Taverner van. I spent the rest of the day at the centre of the demo, or between Oxford Street and Charing Cross Police Station as the police had no accessible transport to issue the obligatory cautions they were doling out to my employers (aka the Graeae board).

[Beginnings + Steve Mannix]

I'd read about political theatre at college, seen lots of the agitprop and issue-based shows that prevailed in the eighties but there I was, immersed in it. Theory had become reality. The months and years went by and it seemed normal to finish writing a funding application, or booking a tour in the morning, and then driving us all to a demo: Children in Need, Thames Telethon, the Arts Council, Westminster, and most London borough councils. You name it, we were there *en masse*. We'd have a company meeting in the pub afterwards and then live to fight another day.

The company was annually funded at the time by Camden Council and London Borough Grants Scheme (which had taken on the responsibilities of the old Greater London Council), with a small project grant from Greater London Arts (the independent Arts Council London of the time). Just a few months into my job, the funders asked for a meeting with the board and I. We knew something was up in our heart of hearts when they all arrived together at our now clean and tidy portacabin (we'd even laid on tea and biscuits, I seem to recall).

The meeting didn't take long. They informed us that our funding was to be withdrawn. We were all shocked of course but (in a wise move) the chair asked for some time together before responding. They came back into the room a while later and together we put forward our case. We asked for some time to present a new business plan and vision for the company. Then they asked for some time alone. It felt like we were awaiting a judgement. We were allowed back into the room to be told they would give us three months but not to get our hopes up. They promptly left and I was sent round to the off-licence for a few bottles—the planning for our future commenced right there and then.

The plan emerged over the following weeks. The Amstrad got a lot of use as did the fax and the minicom. But we did it. They accepted the plan and we set about advertising for Graeae's first full-time artistic director. Ewan Marshall arrived a few months later to start the company on its next exciting phase.

However, while it was pleasing to see us compared to similar national touring companies of the time such as Black Theatre Co-op, Paines Plough, Women's Theatre Group, and Gay Sweatshop, unlike them we didn't receive regular ACE funding for another five years. We somehow managed on project funding, the generosity of several trusts and foundations (including George Michael), and the fees we could generate. We received our first commission from Warwick Arts Centre—and the amazing mentoring of its then-director Jodi Myers, who years later joined the Graeae board—to support a tour to small-scale venues across the UK who were eager to see the work of the company. We were even able to tour internationally to Berlin, Minsk, and Ireland with the support of the British Council.

There was no avoiding the fact—it was hard work for everyone. The company would be on the road for twelve to sixteen weeks at a time. It was hard to not only present the show with all of the usual logistics of touring but also with the access needs of the actors. Just for the company to go and have a meal and a drink after the show was a challenge. Although we did our best, there were some difficult access moments and there was little, if any, awareness. I still have nightmares about getting phone calls from the stage management team telling me about their encounters. I remember that we made the front page of the *Liverpool*

[Beginnings + Steve Mannix]

Echo as a performer had got stuck in the lift at the old Everyman Theatre in Liverpool and the fire brigade had to be called to rescue her. Great for ticket sales, horrible for the individual concerned. But, in true Graeae style, we laughed at the time and have continued to do so all these years later. My respect for all artists, performers, and stage managers went up so much during those years and remains high to this day.

> We graduated from the small portacabin in Camden to Interchange Studios (basically a larger portacabin) and started to have visions for the company having its own fully accessible transport and its own 'home'. We managed to convince Mercedes-Benz to design a fully accessible van for the company before I left—the first in the UK. It was to be many years before the new building was realised.
>
> Those early days of the company were a bit anarchic (even for me!) and yes, a bit chaotic but we got there in the end. They were full of fun, laughter, and true politics. I made life-long friendships with those I can truly call comrades. We all learnt together in the face of real opposition and adversity. Don't forget—there was no rule book and no legislation (the DDA, Equalities Act, Disability Rights Commission, and other advances of the nineties were a decade away). We laughed and we cried.
>
> When I see the company touring internationally today, taking centre stage in Edinburgh or at the National Theatre, the efforts of all of us in those days seem worthwhile. That's why we were there and what we were fighting for and why, years later,

I was so proud to be chair for ten years and help the company move into its purpose-built home and not be relegated to the sidelines in a leaking, cold portacabin!

Here's to many more decades!

[Beginnings + Steve Mannix]

Elspeth Morrison

Voice Coach

I first saw Graeae at Theatre Workshop in Hamilton Place, Edinburgh a long time ago. Actor Jag Plah threw his crutches on the floor and as they lay there static said, 'See? They're useless without me!' That stayed with me—that anarchic and atypical view coming from the mouth of an actual disabled person.

My main encounters with disabled people until then had been via the hushed tones of my mother who volunteered to work with those, 'poor souls with special knees at the handicapped school'. At least, that is how my young brain understood it. Moreover, there was Lindsay Olaf who lived around the corner and was 'polio in a wheelchair'. I thought this must be a good thing as it seemed to mean you could have a nice patchwork blanket across your knees, a fancy selection of nail varnishes, and a flask of sweet tea with you at all times.

I signed up for a writers' workshop led by Monstrous Regiment and Graeae at Jacksons Lane, North London in my mid-twenties. It was for disabled and non-disabled women. The dynamic Ashley Grey and Pat Place were the organisers for Graeae. I was put in the disabled camp. I was mildly perplexed, being of the firm belief that all disabled people came with their own wheels and probably couldn't talk. This group came in all shapes, sizes, mobilities, and communications. I thought it was normal for me to be a bit of an outsider who had spent a goodly amount of primary school in hospital and walked with a limp. This was the beginning of me embracing my otherness and liking it. Here, I met Sian Vasey. She used a wheelchair and spoke. A lot. We bonded. Her acting experience had been as a 'Dollop' in the company's *The Endless Variety Show* in 1983 and subsequently she became chair of the board. She introduced me to Graeae and before you could say 'supercrip', I was being fêted with mounds of official looking papers and invited to join the board. I liked that. It sounded grand and city-like.

> The initial meetings were in a portacabin in Camden. One of my first meetings involved a discussion about what to do about a relationship that had gone wrong between two of the actors in the company. One of whom, mid-argument, had tried to jump out of a moving vehicle. Which one to sack? Oh. This was going to be interesting. And then there was an admin person who would file anything awkward in the dustbin. An actual dustbin but at least the same one. So when this person 'left', the most important documents were still there, just with some chip papers on top.

> And whoever said disabled people don't know how to party? One of the greatest contributions to the social life of anyone attached to Graeae in the early days was one Geof Armstrong. This feisty, one-and-a-half-legged Geordie made sure that everyone could get down the pub. People who had never been down the pub, people who you would never expect to see down the pub, were in the pub boozing and carousing until lock in and beyond. Dial-a-Ride and regimented early nights be damned.

[Beginnings + Elspeth Morrison]

There were fantastic advocates for Graeae in the eighties and nineties, such as the wonderful Sue Timothy from the London Arts Board who supported the development of the work. She understood that artistic product does not always pop out fully formed. I remember having a warm red wine and a fag with her after one show (indoors—this was in pre-history), where we both agreed the next artistic endeavour would be ... err ... better!

Then there was the time I worked as tour manager with *A Private View* in Malaysia. The actors were Jenny Sealey (yes, the very same before she became the artistic director), Letty Kay, Kaite O'Reilly, Merry Cross (who we used to call 'Jolly Angry'; she was not, but it was too good a pun to miss), and Anna Furse, the director. We made the front page of the *Borneo Times*. We played to all sorts of bemused corporate audiences with delicate wordplay from Tasha Fairbanks about art and relationships. We played to not so many actual disabled people (this wasn't a crip-led gig) but met all sorts of deranged expats desperate for something other than heat, booze, and other people's spouses. They gave us white bread sandwiches in one place, with fillings of Brussels sprouts, carrots, cabbage, and potatoes. A message had been mangled about dietary requirements so we missed a night of the deliciousness that Malaysia has to offer and instead got a unique interpretation of 'English' food.

I left the board when the amount of paperwork per meeting became taller than me. Being a board member is a tricky balancing act—you are not there on a daily basis but are being guided to take decisions that affect the people who are there every day.

Kevin Dunn, Cathy Gross, Carolyn Lucas, Michael Hempstead, Steve Mannix, Roger Nelson, Judith Kilvington, plus an army of other grounded admin heroes provided the bridge during my time.

I have returned to work with Graeae in a practical way, as a voice coach on *The Fall of the House of Usher*; *peeling*; and most recently, *Cosmic Scallies*.

Does it have an end? It had a beginning. In spite of other companies coming and going, Graeae is still with us.

Rachel Hurst

Activist and Former Chair, Graeae Theatre

My involvement with Graeae has been long (since 1985), sometimes rocky, but always life enhancing. In the early days, when working professionally at anything was not the experience of many disabled people, there were difficulties to overcome: office staff using dustbins as filing cabinets, inaccessible venues and transport, inexperience, and unrealistic expectations: the usual growing pains. But Graeae was always exciting and a vitally important part of the journey for social change to ensure rights and justice for disabled people.

I was invited to become a trustee of Graeae in 1989 in order to help cope with a necessary, but difficult, dismissal. It was an honour and a privilege to watch the steady development of Graeae's performances, training, educational programmes, and international reputation after that hiccup was successfully managed. I was particularly pleased about the training. I had spent my early years in the professional mainstream theatre and had always been worried about those aspiring disabled actors who thought that a wish to do something was enough to do it well (I did not include actors with great talent and drive to excel, such as Nabil Shaban, in my worries!). Mainstream drama colleges were not open to disabled people—Graeae had to offer its own. And it has done so with great results, as evidenced by the many Graeae actors now seen in TV dramas and advertisements.

Graeae's performances are now true live theatre; not just experimental or alternative theatre but dynamic, artistic, dramatic expressions of life. What better to illustrate this than the London 2012 Paralympic Games Opening Ceremony, co-directed by Jenny with many past and present performers.

I watched the Ceremony with tears pouring down my cheeks (I have become very sentimental in my old age), knowing that theatre really was a force for change in the difficult struggle to recognise disabled people as equal and rightful members of society. A struggle that continues but is enhanced by Graeae's contribution.

[Beginnings + Rachel Hurst]

Professor Anna Furse

Artistic Director, Athletes of the Heart and Director of
MA in Performance Making, Goldsmiths University

Directing *A Private View* for Graeae was one of those life-changing experiences for me and perhaps all of us. It was the company's first womens' project and I was thrilled to be invited into it as a non-disabled director. An irrepressible young woman who had caught my eye when I was researching Deaf dance and theatre in London, Jenny Sealey, was cast, together with Kaite O'Reilly, Letty Kaye and Merry Cross. The highlight was our British Council tour to Malaysia for the Year of the Disabled in a country where the word for disabled was 'dirty', and families hid their disabled relatives.

Some areas we performed in were strictly religious, and there was some censorship: diplomacy required us to convert the lesbian relationship between Jenny and Kaite into besties. In this repressive country at the time we were out there, far out. While our material was challenging, our presence in public attracted gawping crowds, who would part as we wheeled through. Wherever we went we had VIP treatment: red carpets, garlands, and many official dinners. At this time Graeae were still very keen for the message to get across and I remember a script meeting where we discussed whether we should mention accesible toilets to make a point. The writer Tash Fairbanks and I stood firm for letting the piece be other than didactic: a bit dotty and zany and actually hardly referring to disability at all. It was more about showing what these women could do and not what they couldn't.

The play was written specifically for the actresses. It was set in an art studio and there was a heist. Looking back it was incredibly naïve but also brave and ahead of its time. Four disabled women on a very small stage, being witty, glamorous, nasty, sexy, argumentative and human. For me the project—and working on a Graeae training project during this same period—expanded my consciousness forever. Known to be a very physical and visual director, I adapted my habitual practice, determined not to compromise but to discover instead what they needed. I pushed. They wanted to be pushed.

And together, with bags of passion and commitment, I think we found complex and new ways to move and communicate on stage at a time when a disabled production was rare enough, let alone one with four feisty disabled actresses strutting their stuff.

[Beginnings + Professor Anna Furse]

Caroline Noh

Performing Arts Consultant, Director and Voice Coach

Ten Graeae Moments

1. ⠿

To receive the appointment as the first artistic director for Graeae Theatre Company in 1984 was indeed the most challenging work in my career to date (see www.carolinenoh.com). I was therefore accepting the challenge to explore the unchartered territory in touring theatre history with a company of disabled actors. Guaranteed to be unique interpretations of whatever the artistic focus to be chosen.

2. ⠿

I chose to adapt a classic—Charlotte Brontë's *Villette*—chosen because it was penned over many of her final years capturing her life of limitation and adventure, education and imagination, when Charlotte's sight was diminishing. To have a blind actor, Ailsa Fairley play the part was extraordinary. *Not Much To Ask* became the title for the show and it was successfully performed to local critical acclaim at many venues including the London run at Riverside Studios. Patsy Rodenburg adapted the script and worked one-on-one with each actor as vocal coach. This was an exceptional and unique experience of lifting words off the page into character representation and believable acting. The audiences were spellbound. The acting was superb. This became theatre at its best, an inspiring story to tell both within a contemporary context and rooted in historical facts.

3 ⠒

As artistic director I was privileged to work with extraordinary 'unskilled workers', with very limited training or professional experience to date. The auditions were unique. A couple of two-week intensive actor-training summer schools were based at Goldsmiths College, London, which very few non-disabled people participated in; the emphasis was to involve/engage a disabled person whenever possible. With great success, I brought together a fine company of tutors, actors and trainees, who came from all over the UK to make it happen. See feature in *Drama: The Quarterly Theatre Review* (First Quarter, 1985, No. 155.)

4 ⠒

The design team for *Not Much To Ask* was put together by the wizard Peter Mumford, who brought set, lighting and costumes to the table. With the demands of one-night-stands, two-night-stays, five-night-runs in the many and various venues up and down the UK, the reliability of construction, deconstruction and durability were paramount. Pete was able to create ways of working with the touring management team and stage management to answer and accommodate the unique demands the production presented. The set representing the Victorian storyline changing to the twentieth century Day Centre, complete with electric wheelchair access and Day-Glo effect, was brilliant in elevating Graeae Theatre Company's artistic reputation.

5 :::

The score/music for *Not Much To Ask* was composed and adapted by Isobel Ward. To work with such an extraordinary talented woman who was only in recent times diagnosed with a debilitating disease and therefore only just getting used to being referred to as disabled, composed an original score in Victorian style interwoven with *Reasons to be Cheerful*. For Ian Dury to waive all copyright fees and to allow the original tracks to be used and his voice to be featured, it brought the production very much into the here-and-now for audiences, making the score such a vital part of the theatre experience.

6 :::

I directed *Cocktail Cabaret*—an original musical production by Isobel Ward and Mark Glentworth with the script compiled from contributions of people the company met along the road. The workshops shared in institutions or schools for special needs was bringing theatre experiences to different groups, mostly remote, in environments with very limited artistic inclusion. I particularly remember the lyrics and script as words coming from a woman who could not speak, yet could tell a story on the page by typing with a pen strapped to her forehead. The wonders of modern technology then, 1984! This production was a celebration of multi-talented people, sharing their many creative abilities, as well as meeting the unique demands and restrictions placed on them by the touring circuit in Scotland and England. Designed by Celeste Dandecker who later suggested to me it was taking inspiration from working with Graeae that she went on later to establish the unique Candoco Dance Company bringing together the non-disabled and disabled worlds so brilliantly.

7 ⠿

Cocktail Cabaret inspired the British Theatre Awards to give a special award. The Garrison Club, London, where the ceremony for presenting the award would take place had many, many steps to ascend. Undeterred we found an army of muscular males either side of each wheelchair, straight and safe carrying, getting each company member in a wheelchair to the allocated room. When Sir John Gielgud presented the award I ensured it was to actor Tim Gibbins who energetically accepted for Graeae from his wheelchair which, at the time was a rare sight.

8 ⠺

Access, trailblazing and sledgehammers ... Not only did the company have to work to allow disabled audience access, more importantly, the company needed access to the dressing rooms, green rooms and back stage in venues that had never dealt with electric or manual wheelchair users ever. Yes, it was truly unique to enable this to happen. In the wake of Graeae's visits, venues would literally be accessible for the first time, and moving forward welcomed and expanded the theatre experience for disabled audiences and actors alike. These issues are still as vital to the existence of the company today, in 2018.

[Beginnings + Caroline Noh]

9 ⠩ To meet the unique demands of touring I introduced a new company role—tour manager. The board of trustees were willing to accept this new post as necessary to meet the unforeseen demands ahead, as one-night-stands became the where-to-stay and the accessibilty question had to be anticipated for the entire company well in advance of taking to the road. This proved to be an invaluable contribution to the smooth running of a heavy schedule of performances, workshops, interviews and publicity events.

10 ⠼⠚ The production of Frankenstein was a bringing together of a very talented company and also featured disabled people working backstage too. When Sir Peter Blake agreed to provide the artwork for the poster and publicity, this demonstrated how Graeae was attracting the involvement of extraordinary artists. Again the fee was waived and for the struggling finances Graeae was always presented with, this was worth its weight in gold. *The Sunday Times* ran a feature for the entire production.

Jamie Beddard

Co-Artistic Director, Extraordinary Bodies

Graeae has had a tremendous influence on where I am today, professionally and personally, some twenty-five years after first connecting with the company. The arts were never on my radar as a disabled young person and I drifted from school, to university, to a nondescript sociology degree, to the streets of Kilburn where I became an ineffective and dissatisfied youth worker. The BBC called out of the blue seeking disabled actors for the film *Skallagrigg*; they could not find any disabled performers and had stumbled across my name. I went to White City out of curiosity rather than any aspiration to become an actor. With nothing to lose, I slightly over-egged my talent and experience—I had none—and the following day, to my amazement and apprehension, was offered the role. I was on a film set a month later, had my name on a dressing room door, people attending to my every need, and I was hanging out with my hero, Ian Dury. I had run away to join the circus.

I contacted Graeae and found like-minded folk pursuing careers of which I had never dreamt, hell-bent on challenging the status quo and making their mark. It was incredibly liberating. Before, I had sought to avoid the 'stare' of others, to seek anonymity, to conform as best I could, to do jobs I felt little affinity with. Now I was among ballsy disabled directors and actors, subverting norms, owning the stare and stage, and telling new, vital stories. I had found a home.

Ewan Marshall, (then artistic director) offered me a week of workshopping for *Ubu* (to be adapted by Trevor Lloyd) and, much like the play itself, a riotous, anarchic, and debauched journey ensued. 'Excess is not enough' became our moniker. A week of buffoonery, challenging taboos, food fights, turning worlds upside down, and rudimentary thesp exercises followed. We were a company of 'rough diamonds', young and enthusiastic but with little formal training or experience between us. *Ubu* went into full production and stories and adventures abounded, many lost in the fog of time and excess. I was semi-clad in the poster; a graffitied posterior, wearing crown and furs with fag in hand. Newham Council banned the offending poster because of the cigarette. The team all gathered on stage for a photo-call before our opening night at the Tom Allen Arts Centre. The stage collapsed. It was hastily rebuilt and the show duly opened; just another hurdle for this intrepid band of imposters. We shocked and entertained audiences, we danced badly, we laughed, we confused critics, we farted, we argued, we drank too much, we went to Berlin, we formed lifelong friendships, and we made a brilliant show. I had become part of a community, understood the power of the arts and the importance of placing disabled people centre-stage.

I have come in and out of Graeae as a performer, associate director, writer, and workshop leader since those heady days. The company are now widely known and established, with their own Bradbury Studios and an ever-growing list of D/deaf and disabled alumnae artists who got their break through Graeae. If *Skallagrigg* was cast now, I would be out of the picture as the BBC would have a wealth of talent from which to cherry-pick.

Graeae has been crucial in creating and developing this supply line. The work, ethos, and influence of the company continue to burn brightly but the people underpin everything. Particularly in a year in which we lost two of our most important comrades, Tim Gebbels and Sophie Partridge, the network of people I have met through Graeae has sustained me.

We are not a family, but are bloody close.

[Beginnings + Jamie Beddard]

Daryl Beeton

Theatre-Maker, Actor and Director

I first became aware of Graeae in 1995, during my second year at university. I was doing work experience at a theatre in Stockport and one of my tasks was stuffing thousands of envelopes with flyers for a show called *Ubu*. There was a naked man on the cover of the flyer with his bum out. I remember thinking at the time that it was a cheap way to sell a show, like a page 3 girl in *The Sun*—all tits and no substance. I hadn't even realised the guy, Jamie Beddard, was disabled. I didn't even stay to see the show. Ewan Marshall, then the artistic director of Graeae, came to our final degree show. Afterwards, Ewan invited me to see Graeae's latest production of *Fleshfly* (*Volpone*) with yet another disabled, semi-naked man on the front. This time it was Graeae's founder, Nabil Shaban. I had only just begun to self-identify as disabled and it was a complete shock to the system! I had never seen theatre like it!

Two shows that I was involved with at Graeae dramatically impacted my professional career. The first was *What the Butler Saw* by Joe Orton, which opened up a new creative and theatrical language to me that is now core to all of my work; the second was *Alice* adapted by Noel Greig, which became the catalyst for my love of theatre for young audiences.

We need to rewind back to 1997. I was twenty-two. It was a few years after seeing the semi-naked men on Graeae flyers when I was cast in *What the Butler Saw*. This time though, I was the semi-naked guy on the Graeae flyer. I was dressed in the tiniest of black briefs and covered head-to-toe in tattoos (a nod to Joe Orton being sent to prison for defacing library books with images of tattooed men). The tattoos took five hours to paint on, one hour to take the photos, and then just ten minutes to wash off. That night I ended up sleeping with the guy who'd spent five hours painting my most intimate body parts. This was the start of my relationship with Graeae that I have always loved and cherished.

> *What the Butler Saw* opened my eyes to a new way of using disability as a playful and creative language of communication, which I continue to grip and hold tight within my work as a director and performer to this day. The show was unapologetic, anarchic, farcical, rude, sexual, and in your face! All of which blurred from on stage to off stage as the tour progressed. Graeae gave me the confidence as a disabled performer to literally cast off my clothes and be proud of my body. This show was my baptism of fire into the world of small-scale touring. It was twelve solid weeks on the road where we would create harmonies to well-known songs in the back of the tour van, get angry and political at inaccessible pubs, and share rooms in dodgy B&Bs.
>
> The tour also opened my eyes to the absolute diversity of this country and its people. We would perform in small theatres in random locations all over the place, meeting a wide breadth of audiences. Some audience members knew the work of Graeae and some were expecting to watch, 'a nice play about the handicapped'. We would play to an audience of 200 one night and four the next. It never allowed us to get comfortable or complacent. This is still how I approach working with the actors I direct today. Theatre needs to

exist in the here and now. Play with, but respect, your audiences and you can take them on any journey. We should never assume we know our audiences because of where we performed the day before. Audiences are as diverse as the people on a Graeae stage, so let's embrace that.

> *What the Butler Saw* was a great platform for me as a performer and led to many other acting jobs for many other companies. I have done many a tour since then but none have ever been so liberating, sexually awakening, or fucking enjoyable as that tour. It's like a first love. That younger version of me learnt how to unload a set and do get-ins at venues with only ten minutes before curtain up, how to tightly pack the large set into a tiny van that shouldn't be physically possible, and how doing shows hungover is not a good idea! *What the Butler Saw* taught me how to truly tour and I will never forget it!

> Roll forward a year to the summer of 1998. This was the year of Euro '98 and the year of *Alice*.

> *Alice* was completely different: there was no sex, no touring, and no nakedness. I had swapped my tiny boxer shorts for a full-body Victorian bathing suit and, on top of that, there was a new artistic director, Jenny. I didn't know her but we were both from Nottingham so I thought she must be alright! *Alice* was my first experience of theatre for young audiences and we went mainstream.

> *Alice* was important for me and for Graeae because it was the first time we had put disabled performers on the main stage of a regional theatre. I learnt that not all the experimental approaches to theatre-making that were possible in small-

scale touring where you were in a different venue every couple of nights, worked in a mainstream theatre where you were performing in the same venue for two weeks and had to sell thousands of tickets to audiences who were used to something different.

We didn't get everything right but what I did discover was that young audiences are the most honest. They don't have the theatre etiquette of adults and have no fear in proclaiming very loudly, 'I'm bored'. What this did teach me was to really listen to an audience and adapt my performance accordingly. These young audiences had no preconceptions about disability. They accepted our difference on stage and moved on without spending the entire show trying to work out the non-existent metaphor our impairment brought to the character. Their approach was, 'he walks funny ... oh, now he's doing a silly dance' and they moved on and just listened to the story being told. Because of *Alice*, I embraced the world of theatre for young audiences as a place that challenged my storytelling. I wouldn't have ended up becoming artistic director of a theatre company for young audiences, Kazzum, if it weren't for *Alice*.

I've worked for Graeae on and off for twenty years (most recently as associate director on the revival of *Reasons to be Cheerful*). As much as the company has grown and evolved, the one thing that has never changed since my first day is the ongoing discussions and debates about the multiple layers of access and how they can be used as tools for creative exploration, or as a route to a creative cul-de-sac. **It's a fine balancing act to make it all work, a subject that has never stopped being explored and challenged and, thanks to Graeae, I love it!**

[Beginnings + Daryl Beeton]

Dr. Colette Conroy

PhD FHEA Director of Research and Postgraduate Research Director, Hull University

The Impossibilities—A Very Short History

I have earned my living from theatre since I was seventeen, initially working backstage and then becoming a student at university. I graduated in 1994 and started to work with Ewan Marshall at Graeae in the autumn of that year as assistant director on *Ubu*. The following January, I was a director on the *Revenge of the Graeae* festival of women writers and, in that summer, I was appointed as the first associate director of the company. This was more than twenty years ago. Things change quickly and time speeds up. I am now an academic in my mid-forties. Graeae has its place in the history and the future of theatre and I'd like to explain why this is important.

I have watched Graeae's work over twenty years and, yes, the company has changed. Graeae has also changed theatre. Writing this piece has made me remember a lot of experiences that formed the way I think today. As well as the major touring productions, I remember unlauded parts of the company's work: performances in schools and youth clubs across the UK; working with young disabled people who had never encountered a disabled actor before; forum theatre performances involving families and social care providers; the painstaking development of conventions of simultaneous BSL performance; several really strange devising processes with other companies ... None of these events was recorded, analysed, or reviewed and have disappeared from history. In a way, that's not important. As theatre-makers, we create ephemeral experiences that speak to our audiences. Some of these conversations are tiny revolutions that leave their traces even when they are gone from memories.

> The process of engaging with theatre making and training institutions in the mid-nineties was one of hitting obstacles but making it work anyway. In a world where Kafka's *Castle* appeared to be a familiar and realistic landscape, the multiple voices of well-meaning individuals wove an impasse that could not be shifted by argument alone. Below is a list of the arguments I encountered from across a range of institutions at the interface of mainstream theatre and Graeae in the years from 1994 to 1997. No individual articulated all of these perspectives but the effect of the whole list created a mountain of impossibility that seemed pretty nearly insurmountable.
>
> The impossibility of actor training for disabled people within conservatoires.
>
> The impossibility of allowing untrained disabled actors to perform on stage.
>
> The impossibility of adapting theatre buildings for disabled performers.
>
> The impossibility of attracting audiences to disability theatre.
>
> The impossibility of finding parts for disabled actors.
>
> The impossibility of disabled actors passing as non-disabled characters.

[Beginnings + Dr. Colette Conroy]

The impossibility of earning a living as disabled actors within a realist mode of performance.

> The impossibility of putting disabled (untrained) and non-disabled (trained) actors together onstage.

> The process of shifting these perspectives in the UK was partly achieved over the last twenty years, with these perspectives seeming in hindsight to be outmoded and perhaps silly. The generations of artists in disability culture movements have smashed up these attitudes by ignoring them, weaving round them or, as is often the case, crashing right through them. If you are a disabled director or performer in 2017, you will (I know) still encounter these beliefs. However, we can often see them for what they are: fearful excuses. The history of disabled arts and culture makers offers evidence that individuals who work together for change have changed things in the past. Bearing this in mind, draw strength from the fact that you can change things in the future. The irksome thing is that things don't stay changed.

> If we listen to the voices of impossibility, we can see a set of assumptions about theatre as a social structure. For those who embrace the impossibilities, theatre is purely conventional. Theatre is handed to us as part of a large bucket of tradition in which there are rules for who represents whom, what stories are important, and what the world looks like both inside and outside the theatre. You need not accept this.

Theatre is a distinctly strange cultural phenomenon. We use it to externalise and rehearse ideas, to look at ourselves, distorted through different lenses. We use it to try out ideas that are difficult to think about in other contexts. Our social ideas about who is qualified to perform in this thinking machine are parallel to cultural beliefs about who may or may not hold power in wider society. Opening this out to excluded groups isn't just a series of small tweaks, a process of opening the door to one or two different individuals at a time and labelling it 'diversity'. If you change the people who make theatre, and if you change the people who go to see theatre, you'll change theatre. I'm seeing theatre as the sum total of all of us—makers and audiences. If you create theatre that is original, moving, and exciting then you'll make theatre want to change.

The history we need to write is one of stubbornness and brilliance. If we only regret the inflexible structures of theatre, its inaccessibility or its exclusiveness, we position ourselves as helpless functionaries of a pre-existing system. Studying the achievements of disabled cultural activists and artists over the last three decades is important in breaking through this deadlock.

Graeae's history reveals to us in a vivid and understandable way that every work we watch or make is the embodied presence of theatre in the world. We can choose to participate in work in which the relationship of artist and audience is invented and positioned anew each time.

[Beginnings + Dr. Colette Conroy]

Jenny Sealey

Kaite O'Reilly

Pete Rowe

Jeni Draper

Claire Saddleton

Caroline Parker

Cherylee Houston

Nadia Albina

**A Series
of Firsts**

Jodi-Alissa
Bickerton

Judith Kilvington

Roger Nelson

Jenny Sealey

CEO/Artistic Director, Graeae Theatre

A Series of Firsts

● *Two* **by Jim Cartwright (1998)** This was the first play I directed at Graeae. I wanted a vehicle for Garry Robson and Caroline Parker, both of whom I had directed at Interplay. The play could have been written for them, but my team of two became four as sign language interpreters Vikki Gee Dare and Rob Chalk came on board. This is the first time I had embarked on the process of translating a script into BSL at the same time as I was discovering the characters. It felt necessary to continually work as a full team because everyone had to own the characters and the choice of sign, rhythm, pace, and physicality.

The choice of signs was informed by both the actors discovering their intentions and the emotional drive and energy of the writing. Once we had our physical and emotional landscape fixed in spoken and signed languages, we then focused on how these two languages would co-exist in the space. The simplest way was to mirror the spoken with the signed vocabulary; one couple on one table dressed identically to the other couple on the other table. This worked for some of the couples in the piece, but with others it didn't work the way we had hoped. So, we broke the usual conventions and had Caroline signing (and quite rightly as she is a Deaf sign language user) and Vikki (who is also an actor) do the voice over.

[92]

This way of working was intense, juggling with a diversity of needs and sometimes level of accessibility in a scene could take precedence over the actors' explorations of their relationships with each other. When we did only focus on Garry and Caroline the interpreter/actors were always present as any change in emotional intention or delivery impacted them too.

The essence of *Two* was teamwork, collaboration, and a desire to take risks. We had to dare to be abstract and break conventions. My learning curve was monumental, not just because of the directing and the process but because I had never led on the mechanics of a national tour, or worked with a press and marketing agent, nor even had a review. The *Time Out* review for the show is one I have treasured forever and whenever I have directed a 'turkey' and had awful reviews, I dig this one out to reassure and remind myself of my foundations, which helps me get back up and start again.

With *Two*, we got the access for BSL users right, but not for D/deaf audiences who do not sign. The script was clear in what the characters were saying to each other, but how it was executed meant that there was not enough visual detail text-wise to create a fully equal experience for blind and visually impaired people. Learning this was to be another first for me.

● **Fittings: The Last Freak Show by Mike Kenny (1999)**
In this collaboration with Fittings Multimedia Arts we were the larger company and led on the production. It was a tented tour with an art installation of bespoke walking sticks and related impairment attachments and aides.

The play opens on the eve of the millennium with a group of Freaks wondering what was going to happen next.

GUSTAV 'Beauty is truth, truth beauty. That's all you know on earth. And all you need to know ...', you have my permission to stare ... You've paid your money ... You'd probably stare anyway, wouldn't you? Whether I gave you permission or not.

A freak show is a safe place. For us. When the punters have gone home who cares if you've got one leg more or less? The more the merrier. And we're free to hate each other if we want to.

I love this show. They're my people. But it won't last. Times change. We'll have to close. Can't compete, you see. You can get midget porn and people fucking amputees on the net. Takes two minutes to find in the comfort of your own home.

There was a time we got called monsters, from the Latin *monstra* ... to warn, show, or sign. We were taken seriously. We were up there with unicorns. Now we're errors. Mistakes. Blunders. Nobody's going to pay to look at that.

I'd rather be a monster.

This review from Lyn Gardner tells it as it was:

'It is New Year's Eve, 1999 and in the Millennium Dome in Greenwich it is the end of an era for Gustav Drool and his freak show. The trouble is that Aqua the mermaid, Avia the woman with wings, and Christian the wobbly boy are no longer such a draw when you can turn on the TV any time and watch *The Jerry Springer Show*. Besides, as we all so fervently seem to believe on the cusp of the millennium, the future is going to be just perfect. No room for Drool and his gang.

But Drool is in combative mood and he's down fighting at the last chance saloon: exploiting his performers' weakness, manipulating their emotions, and spurring them on to ever greater acts of degradation. And wouldn't you just know it, Drool is one of them. We all are. Drool knows all our weak spots, our prejudices and fears. 'Who needs a hall of mirrors when you've got us?'

The Graeae company is in combative mood, too, for this potentially groundbreaking examination of disability issues. But while it lights the fuse it doesn't quite have the courage to detonate the bomb. The failure of nerve comes less from Mike Kenny's script, which often displays an aggressive beauty as well as an ironic turn of phrase, and more from the structure of the performance. What could be better in a piece about our perceptions of people's physical form and beauty than to smash our traditional perceptions of theatre?

The frustrating thing about Jenny Sealey's production is that it goes so far, but not far enough: the circus tent, the video screen and the installation all hint at striving towards something more radical, but the different elements of the show are not imaginatively integrated and what we end up with is a bit of this and a bit of that and an awful lot of sitting on hard seats in rows.

Still, this is the kind of failure that I can admire and for all its weaknesses you can't but applaud the cussedness of the enterprise. And in Gustav Drool, Kenny and actor Garry Robson have created a monstrous character, the cripple who cripples others.'

[A Series of Firsts + Jenny Sealey]

Lyn's review was accurate. We were, however, the talk of Edinburgh because a lagered-up stag party and a religious group were in the same audience one night. We thought the lads would leave but they stayed to the end applauding wildly, while the other lot left after forty minutes!

● **The Fall of the House of Usher by Edgar Allan Poe, adapted by Steven Berkoff (2000)** This was perhaps the most dramatic first for Graeae as this new and radical approach to the process changed how we made theatre forever more and coined the term 'aesthetics of access'.

We had almost depleted our resources on *The Last Freak Show* as tented tours often throw up unexpected financial curve balls, not least having to hire a cherry picker to prevent the tent sinking into a muddy field at Three Mills in Bow, London.

To honour our ACE commitments, we were required to mount a second show but, given limited finance, it would have to be a show with a small cast. I am hugely indebted to whoever signposted me to Steven Berkoff's adaptation of Edgar Allen Poe's *Usher*. This gothic three-hander immediately captured my imagination and reading Berkoff's beautiful, evocative, and descriptive stage directions triggered my light bulb moment. The playbook includes a commentary of the entire play which includes the direction:

> *He reaches up and tears down a dripping silken fabric which could have previously suggested the fabrics of the house and now becomes both an image of her winding sheet and soft cocoon as if the bed had come to her and she spins around this until mummified.*

Did I dare use this text as live audio description spoken by the actors? I held my nerve and wrote to Berkoff who wrote back, 'this is an extremely good idea and I wish I had thought of it myself'.

I cast Simon Startin as the tortured Roderick Usher; Pamela Mungroo as his equally disturbed sister; and David Toole as Edgar, a sinister but seductive friend. The sheer intensity of this *ménage à trois* left me with little doubt that placing a sign language interpreter—even in role of the butler—was not theatrically, emotionally, or spatially right. The design for the show (which I created myself, to save costs) was a huge wrought iron bed flanked by two old fashioned wheelchairs. Above the bed hung a wrought iron mirror which served as a surface on which to project the image of Ilan Dwek, a Deaf BSL user who became our fourth character—a macabre figure interpreting and sometimes commenting on the spoken language.

All the sign language was to be pre-recorded which created a great deal of pressure on the rehearsal process. This was done as late as possible so the actors had time to cement their emotional rhythms and delivery before filming began.

Ilan led on the BSL translation alongside Liz Graham, our rehearsal sign language interpreter. Both knew the script inside-out. Ilan sat facing Liz for the filming. Liz cued Ilan to sign so we could film in time to the rhythm of the speaker. It was a painstaking process.

I edited the signed film footage with a company called Blast Theory. Liam Steel, our movement director, continued to push the choreographic language, and the more we found ways to intensify the relationships between characters, the more we had to re-edit the film (we ran out of time to re-film Ilan). This was actually artistically liberating because it forced us to think about how we could play with form slowing down signs, making them repeat over and over again, or have Ilan mimic the actions of the onstage actors, as sometimes the visual picture spoke more powerfully than the few words the actors uttered at that point.

The process demanded real commitment from the actors as the production had the discipline and rigour of a dance piece; this was particularly tough for them as their characters inevitably developed during the tour. Their challenge was to embed new discoveries within the given parameters, without becoming out of sync with the signing.

The stage directions and signing reinforced the gothic horror of the incestuous relationship between Roderick and Madeline, it lit her illness in a different way. *'Magdalena swirls in violet blue light'*; she knew what was happening to her and owned it, which in turn made her more vulnerable to Roderick's hold over her.

The experience of using pre-recorded sign language and live audio description to layer the play, and the endless creative possibilities this presented has informed everything we have done since. It has allowed us to build on the knowledge that placing both signing and audio description at the heart and start of a production pushes the theatrical authenticity beyond what is imaginable.

●   **peeling by Kaite O'Reilly (2002)** I had been doing some work for ENO on their accessible performances. As I stood on their vast stage, I had a strong image of some of my Graeae women on high chairs at the back of the stage as part of a large chorus. I shared this image with writer Kaite O'Reilly and asked her to create something both epic and domestic, with an additional challenge to include audio description as part of the relationship between the characters. As a visually impaired writer, this was right up her street.

Lisa Hammond, Sophie Partridge, and Caroline Parker explored the beginnings of Kaite's epic—a new version of *The Trojan Women* and were instrumental in the research and development of the piece. Improvisations included a day where Kaite and I left the women alone for a few hours with several trashy magazines and some topic headings: being D/deaf and disabled women, their families, their role in theatre, and some wool (I think). We recorded all this on a dictaphone and Kaite was able to lift the bones of their characters from this material and create *peeling*.

The relationship between the three characters—Alfa, Beaty, and Coral—was a love-hate relationship. The audio description was spoken by the characters and beautifully enhanced the way they would bite and tear at each other.

BEATY Coral's eyes roll contemptuously to the heavens.

ALFA (to Beaty) WILL YOU STOP IT!!!!????

BEATY Flames blaze in angry eyes. Alfa's mouth scowls, the lips pucker. (*as self*) Really quite ugly, actually ...

Sometimes the audio would say what was actually happening:

BEATY Alfa appears from behind her dress, with some carrots, a bowl, and her blender.

And sometimes a mixture of both.

BEATY She looks at me, then out towards the auditorium.

ALFA Have they forgotten about us?

Have they all gone home?

BEATY Beaty takes Alfa's bag of knitting and empties it of finished garments. She begins laying the clothing on the floor, adding her own contribution: tiny white matinee jackets; a new-born baby's vest; booties ...

[A Series of Firsts + Jenny Sealey]

Another first with *peeling* was exploring BSL syntax as a spoken language. As the world of the women became deconstructed, so did their communication. This was theatricalised by Alfa signing the final speech about women and children, with Beaty and Coral voicing over in the BSL word order. This created a beautiful eerie poetic word/soundscape. One example is:

ALFA   Children pfhoo

The sign for 'pfhoo' is a right hand sweep across the lips as they mouth the word with breath. Pfhoo means none, nothing. Beaty and Coral said the word pfhoo. This convention within the setting was emotionally right but, as always with new forms, it was a gamble. We did not want to represent BSL as a deconstruction of language.

I designed the set with my first image of the ENO stage in mind, except the high chairs became crinoline frames of various sizes. A ramp led into Sophie's frame and steps with small gaps between each rung led into Lisa's (who is of short stature, so she could climb easily). Each frame held two costume dresses designed by Kevin Freeman: a slate grey dress with geometric neck and sleeves marked the brutality of the epic, then Caroline and Lisa unpicked the skirts from all three frames, revealing blood red silk and taffeta underneath. They all changed their bodices from grey to red and later to vests; each fastening was unique to their physicality as was their way of undoing clothing. I had an idea of pre-recording three different signers and projecting them onto the skirts but, thankfully, there wasn't enough money as this would have been a technical nightmare. More importantly, there were some key moments in the play about Alfa *not* being able to communicate with the others, or them deliberately not communicating with her. If I had included signers, the empathy from the D/deaf community for Alfa would be lost because it would all be equally accessible.

We created and projected PowerPoint slides of the text for the first time, using a different font and colour for each actor and a generic font for the Trojan Woman chorus. I was mindful that not all D/deaf people find reading easy and that perhaps the poetry could alienate them (I find this myself when I see Shakespearean or large swathes of text on a screen). To combat this, Mark Haig, a film maker who I adore working with, made short films after each of the 'epic' moments, with images that encapsulated the essence of the text. We chose music from Shostakovich, Evelyn Glennie, and other, more obscure musicians. The images were timed with the music and created a wonderful holding form— the film would finish, lights crossed, and lo! We were back with the women.

There were so many firsts with *peeling* that still inform how we work with writers, how we create and project text on stage, and how we employ film as another medium to make information accessible. We dared to play with the concept that everyone gets most of the information but not always at the same time (I never say that audiences will receive all the information, as I know that I have not yet created the ultimate all-singing, all-dancing, fully accessible production).

The actors found this play hard due to their investment in the R&D period; the final product was either too close to home or poles apart from their initial input and they felt conflicted about what was finally written. It was the first time we had created a play that was open about physical and communicative impairment and, for the most part, disabled actors want to embody characters that are not like them. The revival was then, in some ways, easier for two new actors, Ali Briggs and Lizzie Smoczkiewicz, to take on. The brilliant Sophie Partridge continued to play Coral, who has one of my favourite moments in the text:

CORAL   Make do and mend.

Preferably with cat gut.

My body is criss-crossed with scars like a railway track. Like Crewe station, seen from the air: single tracks, with no apparent destination; major interlocking junctions, where intercity, sleepers, and local lines all connect. Puckering scar tissue, hand-sewn with careless, clumsy stitches. I like to finger it, trace the journeys. That unborn skin: smooth, intimate—the coral-pink colour of mice feet.

It's beautiful.

I love it.

Given the choice, I'd never have it any other way, now.

Not everyone liked *peeling*. Rhoda Koenig titled her loathing review for *The Independent* 'Dramatically Handicapped' and in the first paragraph included the following:

It is presented by the Graeae Theatre Company, whose performers are all handicapped, and the actresses in *peeling* share their characters' disabilities. Beaty (Lisa Hammond) is four-feet tall; Coral (Sophie Partridge) has tiny limbs and a torso about the same size as her head; Alfa (Caroline Parker) is Deaf.

And our response:

Sir,

We are writing in response to your review of *peeling* at Soho Theatre in London (9 April). This is the tenth press review we have received in the past week, and incidentally the first bad one. However, our response is not borne out of sour grapes since over the years, critics have found it difficult to be negative about the work of Graeae for fear of upsetting 'right on' sensibilities around disability. We have always joked how refreshing a poor review would be, as it would suggest implicit acceptance that our artistic endeavours were finally uppermost in all considerations. Criticism based on artistic merit—as with all other companies—is preferable to the malevolent pre-disposition to, 'pat us on the back'. We have produced one or two turkeys in our time, and fully deserve to be lambasted for these efforts.

However, when the liberal broadsheets use, at best, sloppy reporting, and at worse, highly offensive language that perpetuates all the worst excesses of daily ignorance, it is time to reply. Rhoda Koenig argues that she cannot judge what might be the value of the show to a disabled audience. Who is she reviewing for? Presumably, solely the 'usual suspects'; a middle-class non-disabled audience, rather than the cultural cross-section *The Independent* apparently seeks to cater for. If this is the case, perhaps there could be an adjacent review catering for the 'handicapped people' (her words, not mine). Taken to its logical conclusion it would suggest that Rhoda Koenig can only review for Rhoda Koenig.

Unfortunately, this is not the case and our performers have been subject to crass, ignorant, and untrue assertions on their peripheral role in society and physicality: one apparently has 'tiny limbs and a torso about the same size as her head'—factually inaccurate and hideously offensive. Of course,

[A Series of Firsts + Jenny Sealey]

reviewers may want to make relevant reference to the actors' physicality, but using language that does not offend nor detract from the value of the criticisms is surely in everyone's interest.

On the first day of the new-look *The Independent* espousing, 'a broader view' such journalism merely perpetuates tired old stereotypes. A bad review is fair enough, but is it really too much to expect those writing professionally in your normally thoughtful paper to pay some regard to the power of the language they choose?

Yours faithfully,

Jenny Sealey, Artistic Director
Jamie Beddard, Associate Director

Kaite O'Reilly
Playwright and Dramaturg

There's not many who have been to Malaysia, least of all with a troupe of arty female crips touring Tash Fairbanks' *A Private View* to Kuala Lumpur in the late 1980s. Hot out of college and increasing my Sign Supported English (SSE) knowledge by the hour, I performed in spoken English with SSE in Graeae's women's theatre company, touring Malaysia in their Year of the Disabled, dressed as what director Anna Furse described as 'a space leprechaun' (we did disability arts and culture different back in those days). Jenny Sealey, who played my artist lover in the production, fared considerably better with dreadlocked blonde extensions, rakishly wielding a paintbrush between her toes as we shared stages across the South China Sea with Letty Kaye and Merry Cross. It was rough, it was rude, but for our audiences it was revolutionary.

Graeae then, as now, was fuelled by politics, passion, and a politely punkish energy. Quietly defiant, we subverted our hosts' patronising behaviour, fielded the too personal questions, and steered the medical model labels towards the social model, making the case for equality, inclusion, and diversity long before the terms were ubiquitous. We also, memorably, had to liberate the wings of a theatre in Penang from multiple commodes—more than one apiece—in order to get on stage. This embarrassment of riches in portable loos exemplifies for me our time on the road and the interactions we faced almost daily—uninformed but well-meaning autonomous acts intended for our comfort but which merely created further barriers and made doing our work impossible. Tact, a sense of humour, and inventive responses stalled what could have been multiple international incidents. It's an approach I still recognise in the work Jen makes today.

It was strange being on tour with Graeae in 1988. We made the front page of the *Straits Times*, there were receptions and banquets in our honour, yet the word on the toilet doors we used translated as 'blemished, unclean'.

I think in Malaysia, as well as the UK tours that followed, we managed to weather with grace the various storms blown up by narrow preconceptions, low expectations, and plain prejudice. I think it made us more determined to succeed, to subvert, to innovate, and to create an equal space for ourselves on stage and in the public sphere, away from the institutions and cultural ghettos in which we were usually hidden away. Combined with the years I trained with Augusto Boal, it was a brilliant apprenticeship.

Fast forward a dozen years, and I was an established dramatist working internationally and Jenny had become the artistic director of Graeae. Curious about what work we might make together informed by our impairments and individual explorations into the aesthetics of access, she commissioned me to write what became *peeling* (2002/03). This marked a quantum leap in my development, working with the outstanding cast of Lisa Hammond, Caroline Parker, and the late, great Sophie Partridge, whom we all still miss each day. With this fabulous cast and innovative design and direction from Madam Sealey, *peeling* became a landmark production, winning best play of the year awards along with critical acclaim. It was a definitive moment, Ruth Bailey claimed in *Disability Now*; a production where disability arts and culture finally came of age, the first time that D/deaf and disabled theatre practitioners were reviewed seriously by the mainstream national press, and as serious professional artists.

Graeae have long understood the necessity of providing training for emerging artists. Even in 2017 there is still a lamentable dearth of courses and opportunities for atypical practitioners. Graeae has been inspirational and pioneering over the years, providing training for actors, directors, and playwrights, trying to shift the cultural and professional training paradigm through these important actions. It's my great pleasure to have been instrumental in schemes developing future generations of D/deaf and disabled writers, working alongside Jonathan Meth and Sarah Dickenson of writernet. For the 1999 Disabled Writers Mentoring Scheme, an initiative between Graeae, writernet, and Theatre North, I was a mentor along with Mark Ravenhill, Sarah Woods, Lucinda Coxon, and Patrick Marber amongst others. It was important that the initiative was of the highest quality, with well-known mentors who were award winners and troublemakers, who would demand much from their mentees and not patronise them with low expectations. This project laid the foundations for *disPlay4*, 'an eighteen-month journey towards production and beyond' as Jonathan Meth coined it, a collaboration between Graeae, writernet, Soho Theatre, and Theatre Royal Stratford East.

[A Series of Firsts + Kaite O'Reilly]

I was the project's dramaturg, designing and co-ordinating the programme, leading the workshops, and organising guest tutors, then dramaturging the rehearsed readings of the scripts at Soho Theatre.

Relationships and connections were forged during this time, but I couldn't help feeling, as Graeae launched yet another writing programme, *Write To Play* nearly fifteen years after *disPlay4*, that we're endlessly reinventing the wheel. Graeae is clearly in this game for the long-haul but, three decades on from my first encounter with the company, I can't help feeling frustrated at how very little has changed since I donned that fecking space leprechaun costume ...

There are many reasons for this, many whys and wherefores I am no doubt ignorant of, but from my experience there is a lack of infrastructure within the creative industries to support emerging D/deaf and disabled artists, and few pathways to professional opportunities other than the endless offerings of training and workshops. I don't want to denigrate these—as emphasised earlier, we need them, they are important and appreciated given our history of being denied access to formal education and training—but future generations of new writers and practitioners cannot thrive in a climate where they are endlessly the apprentices. We need more commissions and work that goes into production, and more faith in our perspectives and abilities. Productions carry risk financially and artistically—the work has to be to a high standard, which is why the training opportunities are deemed necessary—but if we can't graduate into professional productions, we are kept constantly as the underlings, the talented amateurs ever waiting for the break.

I also feel there is sometimes a type of interest in disability experience from the so-called 'mainstream' which I would describe as prurient, a particular framing which can be problematic, adhering to the old paradigms of normalcy and 'the other'. I have written about this at length elsewhere and, although things are thankfully starting to shift, there are attitudes, fears, and narratives that are ingrained, assumptions and prejudices which create the barriers so many face. I can personally vouch for the difficulty of pitching projects to theatre and media companies, and the sudden lack of interest when I resist the victim story, or inspirational porn, which often seem to be the desired narratives about disabled or D/deaf protagonists.

We need more outlets for alternative stories, forms, and theatre languages. Graeae is but one small company with its own artistic programme and 'house style'. We need other companies commissioning new writing from D/deaf and disabled artists, work destined for everyone but, in my ideal scenario, also retaining the innovation, politics, and chutzpah of D/deaf arts and disability culture.

This, I feel, is where commissioning initiatives and festivals like Unlimited and DaDaFest have been massively important. Through my close relationship with these two organisations, I have witnessed their impact on developing artists and the embedding of their work into mainstream venues at home and internationally.

[A Series of Firsts + Kaite O'Reilly]

But things are changing, albeit slowly ... We need to have resilience and patience and punkishness alongside endless energy to keep banging on those doors, seeking entrance, engagement, and equality. Thankfully Graeae, Unlimited, DaDaFest, and all the other brilliant companies, initiatives, and individuals are good at all that.

Onwards!

Pete Rowe

Artistic Director, New Wolsey Theatre

Although I have been aware of and seen some of Graeae's work over a number of years, the relationship between the New Wolsey Theatre and Graeae started over ten years ago when myself and Sarah Holmes went to see Jenny's production of *Whiter than Snow* at the Lyric in Hammersmith. The show was witty, clever and funny treating its questions of pigeon-holing, demonisation of difference and collective resistance with a very light touch and including a winning central performance from Kiruna Stamell. We could see the show appealing to a mainstream audience in our four hundred seat main house space.

So began our conversations with Jenny which led to us booking and promoting the revival of *Whiter than Snow* in 2009, and also *Signs of a Star Shaped Diva* and *The Iron Man* for the IpArt Festival with Ipswich Borough Council. Most importantly Jenny invited me to co-direct a new play, Richard Cameron's *Flower Girls* which she had been developing and our two companies co-produced it in 2007. This was a vital learning curve for me— working for the first time with a company entirely composed of D/deaf and disabled performers, learning about, and exploring how to thread the various means of access—BSL, captioning, audio description—into the production.

Alongside my learning the organisation was learning too. Through the collaboration on the shows and some specific Disability Awareness sessions that Jenny and other staff from Graeae gave to our staff, the New Wolsey was improving its approach to D/deaf and disabled audience members. This included improved accessible marketing materials, pre-show touch tours, model and material displays and learning the best ways to communicate with D/deaf and disabled customers throughout their visit.

A turning point in this process was Jenny's production of *Reasons to be Cheerful* which we co-produced in 2010. This was a great idea for a show, written by Paul Sirett and incorporating a catalogue of much loved Ian Dury songs. Given our own reputation for popular, successful, actor-musician musicals, here was a real opportunity to attract a large mainstream main house audience. In discussions before the production we spoke about the need for Graeae to step outside the 'disability bubble' successfully playing to supporters, fans, D/deaf and disabled audiences, but with a general perception that this was issue-based work appropriate for a niche audience. This was a chance to blow apart that misconception and we felt well-placed, given our now shared history and close relationship to help the Company make that step. I remember Sarah Holmes, our chief executive, arguing forcefully that we should not put disability issues 'above the title' but should simply market the show as a new Ian Dury musical. The result was a fantastic production pulling in full houses and for the first time in our theatre, a sense that the Company was playing to a mainstream audience. You could feel it in the first minutes of the show as, in the soft start to the production, the audience encountered the wonderful motley crew onstage as they entered the auditorium.

At first some were taken aback but within minutes they were won over and by the end on their feet or waving their hands in the air. The show has been revived many times since and as I write is once again back in our theatre, a continuing proof of its raucous, ribald presence; a true reflection of Dury himself, and its continuing popular appeal.

It was with this successful history of collaboration between Jenny and myself as co-directors, and our two organisations as co-producers, that when I mentioned *The Threepenny Opera* and Jenny said it was a piece she'd always wanted to direct, I realised that it was a perfect project for us to collaborate on. If we could combine actor-musicians from my field with D/deaf and disabled performers from her extensive knowledge, we could create a truly extraordinary company of 'beggars' to deliver the piece, fuelled by a genuine outsider's anger, cynicism and gallows humour, delivering Kurt Weill's glittering score from onstage amongst their number, and representing humanity in all its wonderful diversity. So the plan was formed to recruit some other regional producing theatres to create a truly unique large scale production of Brecht's savagely satirical 'Opera for Beggars'.

After this, Graeae, the New Wolsey Theatre, Nottingham Playhouse, Birmingham Repertory Theatre and West Yorkshire Playhouse held a meeting to discuss the future for this form of work. The feeling around the table was 'we mustn't let it stop here'—the excitement about creating a diverse and inclusive piece of work for main house spaces and mainstream audiences in mid-scale theatres was infectious. Sheffield Theatres and Theatre Royal Stratford East come on board and Ramps on the Moon was born.

www.rampsonthemoon.co.uk

Jeni Draper

Sign Language Interpreter and Artistic Director, Fingersmiths

I first worked for Graeae at a time of great personal change. A long-term relationship had ended, I had no permanent home, and this was to be my first interpreting job. The big three stresses in life all in one go! I even faxed Graeae to say I couldn't do it because of the turmoil. The faxed reply told me in no uncertain terms I could quit but I WAS the right person for this job and not to worry, Graeae would look after me. I wish I had kept that fax as I would frame it and look at it whenever confidence fades.

This anecdote sums up my relationship with Graeae. My highlights illustrate how I have grown as an artist through working with an extraordinary group of people that I would not have had the privilege of meeting had it not been for their insistence and belief in me.

Working on Missing Piece 1 (Graeae's first actor training course) was my perfect job. I remember feeling pretty hopeless as an interpreter at the start of the project although I knew the subject inside out, having been to drama school and worked professionally as an actor for ten years. Sam Thorp, who turned out to be the best co-worker ever, mentored me through the interpreting process and the supportive management team kept an eye on my wellbeing. This, and the diverse group of D/deaf and disabled wannabe actors who blew my mind each day, meant going to work was a joy. Enduring friendships with both actors and support workers were made in that nine-month period. Those aspiring actors are now the go-to actors in the mainstream and Disability Arts scenes.

> *Into the Mystic* and *The Changeling* enabled me to combine my two passions: acting and interpreting. I loved interpreting from a character's perspective, interacting with the cast, and being a part of the action—not stuck on the side of the stage in a special light.

> My actor/interpreter roles changed scene by scene, requiring me to be a confidante, a spy, a jealous friend, an unwilling witness, and an onstage audio describer (thanks Jenny!). Jean St. Clair was brought in for both shows as a BSL linguistic consultant to support translation. This was necessary as the role of an onstage-integrated interpreter is rooted in theatre practice and that requires a corresponding theatrical language. Jean really opened my eyes to the wonders of creative sign language and influenced my BSL delivery from that first day onwards.

> We would look at the text and decide what it meant. If unsure, we asked the actors and Jenny what it meant to them. I would then sign the phrase and Jean would add the colour and theatre. The translation became visual and poetic, reflecting the language of *The Changeling* written in the seventeenth century. Realising that different texts require different styles of sign language delivery, in the same way that an actor uses different accents and delivery depending on the play, was a 'lightbulb' moment in my career as a theatre interpreter. Both Jean and Jenny also taught me practical considerations. Some linguistic choices

we make when interpreting in a community setting, such as a GP appointment, simply don't work in theatre. For example, fingerspelling a place or name is fine when the audience is three feet away but is pointless in a theatre where the audience are sitting further away. Additionally, I learnt to 'project' in BSL and use very clear hand shapes; the equivalent of projecting voice so the audience can hear the dialogue, only my audience needed to see the language. A few years later, Jean and I set up a theatre company, Fingersmiths, with Kaite O'Reilly (writer of *peeling*, another Graeae production which we had all worked on).

My role with Graeae has also included coordinating a team of thirteen interpreters for *The Vagina Monologues* at the Cochrane Theatre, London. This was the first time *The Vagina Monologues* had been done in the UK with an all D/deaf and disabled cast. I still felt I was a relatively new interpreter and now I was organising a team of my peers: ensuring they had scripts, rehearsal timings, and production details. I had no idea this early development of organisation skills would be so helpful later on ...

I have worked with Jenny in many countries but extensively in Japan and Bangladesh. As an interpreter, it is always fascinating to learn different sign languages and I always bond quickly with the D/deaf artists and with both spoken and sign interpreters. The joy of these processes is that Jenny finds a way for the team to communicate that doesn't rely on anyone's first language, thereby ensuring equality of communication is instilled from the start.

[A Series of Firsts + Jeni Draper]

Warm-up games using voice with gesture introduce everyone to the idea that people communicate in different ways, whether that is through spoken or signed languages. A game is played every day that builds as new rules are added, always with a corresponding gesture or sign that everyone can do; within a week the whole team are speaking Japanese and English words and signing JSL and BSL. Zip Zap Boing is now played in at least eight different countries that I can name! This process can then be adapted to the text or the play that is being developed in whichever country.

The role of all the interpreters reduces as the projects develop and the artists rely on each other to support their communication needs. This is part of Jenny's legacy—the participants take their learning and embed it in their own ongoing artistic practice.

I was with Jenny on a subway in Tokyo when she received the first text inviting her and Bradley Hemmings to interview for the job of co-artistic directors of the London 2012 Paralympic Games Opening Ceremony. After she had accepted the position, she appointed me lead interpreter and co-ordinator of the interpreter team for the professional cast.

I was there from that first interview moment until 29 August, the ceremony itself. Each day was a rollercoaster. I was challenged linguistically, emotionally, physically, and mentally as we entered into a new world of stadium-jargoned language to learn; processes to understand; names to remember; large meeting protocols to manage so that Jenny could access them as the only Deaf person in Ceremonies; relationships to negotiate;

interpreters to book; ATW (Access to Work) to sort out; D/deaf professional cast to check in with; Stephen Hawking to meet ... every day we would pinch ourselves to check it was real. I learnt so much. I feel incredibly lucky to have worked with Jenny so closely on this once in a lifetime occasion and I treasure the memories. Seeing the artists all over the front pages of every national daily newspaper the day after was extraordinary. I don't think that job can be topped.

Graeae spots potential and supportively develops it; assumes that anyone can do anything; bolsters self-confidence by encouraging individuals to be themselves; nurtures their creative skills on and off stage; and challenges their preconceptions of what they can do through hard work and teamwork.

The result is exceptional artists pushing boundaries in productions that have shaken up the mainstream theatre world, and us non-disabled allies finding our worldview broadened and artistic practice deepened because Graeae looks after ALL its family. Thank you for the fax!

Claire Saddleton

Relationship Manager, Arts Council England

You can't help but be touched by it. Changed by it. Made better by it. Frustrated by it. Empowered by it.

I joined Graeae as their first access officer at the same time that Jamie started as the ACE funded assistant director. A team of three—Jenny, Roger, and Annette—became a team of five. We worked out of an office at Interchange Studios (Belsize Park), had picnic lunches in the small and only meeting room, and went on the occasional Friday pub lunch up the road. I joined the company when *The Changeling* was just hitting the road and over the years I worked on (not in chronological order): two outings for *peeling*; *Blasted*; *Diary of an Action Man*; *Flower Girls*; *Signs of a Star Shaped Diva*; and the re-birth of the Missing Piece courses at London Metropolitan University.

I worked on new access developments that looked at both the artist and the audience perspective, such as the tactile set model box for the front of house area which could act as a mini-touch tour for visually impaired patrons. We created *SightLines* with the wonderful Tim Gebbels (aka Noodle), a DVD sharing techniques of creative access support for blind and partially sighted performers; devised creative captioning on *peeling* and *Signs of a Star Shaped Diva*, spending hours and hours pushing PowerPoint in directions it didn't want to go; and piloted the role of creative enabler, providing personal access support in the training or rehearsal room in a way that honoured artistic choices and was responsive to creative processes.

Where was I when I first met Graeae? Karen Spicer took me to see *Two*, Jenny's first production, and then I joined as an ex-actor who'd learnt Stage 2 BSL and some admin skills.

Where am I now? Relationship manager at Arts Council England, Theatre team.

What did I learn? Always ask, don't be afraid to ask, but remember that answers without context can be meaningless—how do I know what my access needs are going to be if I don't know what you're going to ask me to do?

What was the meatiest discussion? Creative access versus functional access.

What do I miss? Chaos and team spirit. Meetings with Jenny and Judith (prosecco with Jenny and Judith).

Who do I remember? Everyone, but I thank Graeae for introducing me to Alex, Noodle, and Sophie.

I saw first-hand the power of change that Graeae possessed, and still possesses, by its very existence but also, more importantly, by its creative bravado. I enjoy seeing the glorious ripple effects today. For example, the impact we had on Birmingham Repertory Theatre—the venue where we first opened *peeling*. You could see the change in people, from executives to ushers, technicians, and bar staff, as the company made the building their home.

[A Series of Firsts + Claire Saddleton]

Graeae is unique and if that's not reason enough to be Graeae then I don't know what is. It's much more fun being a part of something that swims against the tide and it certainly makes you more stubborn.

Caroline Parker

Actor

Any time with Graeae is amazing, and I have worked with the company on and off for many many years.

My first experience of Graeae was in the mid 1980s when Geof Armstrong was in charge—I was in the audience watching a production of *Frankenstein* with Hamish MacDonald playing the Doctor and Tim Barlow playing the monster, and Carolyn Lucas was the first wheelchair actress I had ever seen on a stage. It was not captioned or signed but seeing skilled D/deaf and disabled actors on stage for me was life changing.

I so wanted to work for this company. I was offered a part in *Working Hearts* by Noel Greig, but as luck would have it, it clashed with another job.

When Maggie Hampton was leading Graeae she asked me to step in to replace a stage manager when he had to pull out during a tour of Elspeth Morrison's play *The Cornflake Box* with Sara Beer and Hamish MacDonald.

After this I was on the board of Graeae chaired by Elspeth Morrison, ensuring they had the perspective of people treading those boards. (See what I did there?)

Finally I got a job ACTING for Graeae and I left the board. It was Ewan Marshall's *Ubu*, which was a groundbreaking production of pure anarchy!

All the roles I played were male, including a double act Heads and Tails. I played Heads standing up straight and Tails doubled over with a mask on my grand derrière. This show included sign interpreter Vikki Gee Dare, in costume amongst the actors on set, and at one point she had her head in a birdcage as you do! What a cast we had—Mandy Colleran, Jamie Beddard, Simon Startin, Sara Beer and Paula Garfield.

> I advised Ewan on integrating sign language interpreter Jacqui Beckford into *What The Butler Saw.*

> I trained with Graeae in the Boal Forum Theatre Technique and toured England and Northern Ireland working with disabled people in the community.

> When Jenny Sealey took over, she cast Garry Robson and me in *Two* by Jim Cartwright. This is normally a two-hander but in this production we had two speaking, myself and Garry Robson, and two signing. Vikki Gee Dare and Rob Chalk. People still talk about this production to this day.

> I was a mentor for actors on Missing Piece actor training.

> Along with actors Lisa Hammond and Sophie Partridge we were part of the team creating *peeling* which was then written by Kaite O'Reilly. My love of making soup was included in the script!

> I did *The Changeling* which entailed sitting on stage with a dressing gown and cold cream smeared all over my face. I did outdoor work with the others performing on sway poles! I never went up the poles, I'm far too fond of the ground to do that

but I was utilised as a storyteller in both *Against The Tide* and *The Garden*.

Graeae also produced *Signs of a Star Shaped Diva* by Nona Shepphard, directed by Jenny and Nona. I was in my element as Sue Graves, an undertaker with a sideline of signing songs of the great divas. I had some wonderful costumes and having the stage all to myself for two hours (with an interval!) was an incredible but tough challenge. Me on stage with those divas, with captions of the spoken text projected on PowerPoint and audio description supplied through headsets operating as a sound cue. *Signs of a Star Shaped Diva* toured nationally and internationally. Bring back Sue Graves please.

My time with Graeae has been important to my career, not only as a performer, but as a theatre-maker. I have evolved creatively and politically. I cannot imagine my future without Graeae. It is important not only to the history of theatre but to changing society's view of people D/deaf and disabled people.

Cherylee Houston

Actor

Ten Graeae Moments

1. ⠿ Wheeling into the bed on stage in the dark in Edinburgh, in *Diary of an Action Man*, there was a large splintering sound and my footplate got stuck in the bed, I couldn't move and Action Man (David Ellington) walked on stage in character and saved me in an Action Man manner.

2. ⠿ Karen Spicer (who played Mum and Spud) and myself used to sing Sounds of the Underground everyday before we went onstage in *Diary of An Action Man* to get ourselves giggly and energised. The song words were in my character magazine.

3. ⠿ Learning to sign more, in my first Graeae show *The Changeling*, I signed the lyrics to *A Whiter Shade of Pale*, which was the song my parents wanted to get married to, but you weren't allowed songs at the time.

4. ⠿ Back of the tour bus with Tim Gebbels (a blind actor playing Alsemero in *The Changeling*) was always great bus company, he had such a dry sense of humour. I remember him teasing David Toole for a long time because he left the lights on for Tim when they shared a room, resulting in David sleeping with the light on and Tim being totally unaware.

5 ⠿ Shopping with Karina Jones. Karina (Beatrice Joanna in *The Changeling*) got me in some very entertaining situations. I was once offered a job in shop whilst shopping with her, because of my powers of audio description. I can't tell you the name of the shop, but it wasn't one you'd expect us to be in.

6 ⠿ Rehearsing when 9/11 happened. We were all sent home early and I remember watching the television in the newsagents on Holloway Road and then sitting with David Toole in a very stunned silence.

7 ⠿ Jenny's pyjamas. Jenny had an amazing variety of pyjamas that she used to use as casual wear in rehearsal.

8 ⠿ Great friends made, so so so many great friends made.

9 ⠿ Nickie Miles-Wildin's lighthouse in an audition, one of the first of many of my friends I made was from the Graeae woman's audition. Nickie did this amazing piece about being a lighthouse, where she turned with a torch on her head. I think she had a torch, well even if she didn't she was that good I believed she had a light on her head.

10 ⠿ Working with Kathryn Hunter (a Graeae workshop exploring Bernada Alba), learning different Theatre de Complicité methods was incredibly exciting, the balancing the plate, the shoal of fish, all work underneath the story onstage, all very very clever.

[A Series of Firsts + Cherylee Houston]

Nadia Albina

Actor

Reasons to be Cheerful was my first encounter with Graeae. I had an ambivalent attitude towards a theatre company that was disabled-led while I was at drama school. That attitude was fed by own complex feelings about my disability and the fact that I didn't want to identify as such. In the six months leading up to being spat out into an unforgiving industry, and in the fall-out of graduating, the bubble and purity of drama school training was beginning to burst. Obviously, the drama school I attended had no infrastructure in place to deal with a disabled student, let alone prepare me for what discrimination lay ahead.

I'm glad that I had the journey I did; meeting Jenny and everyone in the Graeae family was of huge significance. The R&D and rehearsal period for *Reasons* that followed was a fabulous time. I had never been in a room that was so political. It was different to any rehearsal room in which I had ever been. It wasn't polite. It wasn't neat. It was messy, it was loud, and it was angry. Singing Ian Dury's lyrics brought everyone together. The feeling of passion was tangible and powerful.

I watched a company of people engage with each other during the rehearsal process, listen to each other, and make space for each other; in turn this made everyone grow. We rallied behind a script, a band, its leader, and his lyrics to stand up and be listened to. The show was an undeniable protest to the rest of the theatre community that Graeae and disabled artists were to be taken seriously.

Jenny's passion and that of the team that she surrounds herself with is infectious. The tenacity and fight to bring equality and awareness to society through the work that Graeae produces is astounding. It is a constant in everyone that walks through the doors of the building. The legacy that it has on the people who have been in and out of those rooms is tantamount. I have personally taken everything that I have learnt into conversations with directors, writers, and actors. Through being changed by Graeae, I have seen change being made through seemingly imperceptible interactions with other people.

> Seeing the impact of *Reasons* on the road was mind-blowing. The reactions from audience members was emotional. Not to mention the amount of laughter that was present in dressing rooms, pubs, and vans up and down the country. It was a raucous time.
>
> **I have nothing but gratitude for that time and opportunity. It feels like Jenny and Graeae have been a part of my most life-altering moments and for that I can say nothing but thank you.**

Jodi-Alissa Bickerton

Creative Learning Director, Graeae Theatre

Lying in my parents' backyard in a small town in Australia when I was eighteen, I found a four-leafed clover. I glued it into my *Collected Works of William Shakespeare* tome, given to me by my parents for my seventeenth birthday. Inside the tome, I wrote a letter to my future adult self. It detailed my dreams, ambitions, and fears about training at drama school, being an actor, a playwright, working in dark theatre studios, and then traveling the world to wherever else theatre happened (New York and London I thought then, but of course I soon learned this could be anywhere). I recall feeling sad though, reading the letter back to myself. Did I dare to think this could be possible? My future felt so uncertain as I lay there listening to Pearl Jam and Violent Femmes to numb the teenage fears—theatre was for the tall, slender, eloquent, and beautiful types. I was short, tubby, with a bunch of impairments that scored me exclusions from school athletics and long walks on the beach.

Fast forward ten years, after drama training, a couple of fringe shows (I thought my career had really taken off when our forty-seat theatre above a pub sold ten tickets), and dream-like experiences working in community arts and the disability sector. I set off with a backpack full of rice crackers, maps of Europe, the letter and the clover, and a confidence which had been instilled in me by my family, friends, and drama and university tutors who all said I could, I should, and I would.

And I have. My curiosity, stubbornness, and belief that theatre is for everyone have led me to where I am now, the Creative learning director at Graeae.

As I sit here in London, at Graeae's home, I am wondering what letters are disabled children and young people writing to themselves right now? I can only hope their expectations are high. I can only hope they know it's worth the tears, the rejections, the embarrassment, the bullying, and the misunderstandings. I can only hope they realise they are creative and they will always be enough, regardless of the fact that often society unfairly asks them to prove it.

I hope they too have teachers who believe in them and parents who don't balk when their child declares they want to train in theatre. I hope no one tells them not to be ambitious.

In 2017 in the UK, we are seeing drama, dance, and expressive arts taken out of the curriculum. The very place where we experience what it could be like to be free, take risks, be listened to, face our fears. Where now do these students go to feel safe, to be great, to grow their confidence, to belong, to be part of a community; to be told they can, they should, and they will?

It is September 2017 and the United Nations has just declared that the current Tory government led by Theresa May has violated the rights of disabled people under austerity measures.

[A Series of Firsts + Jodi-Alissa Bickerton]

I have many conversations with parents of members of our young company *The Rollettes* about the politics of survival. They are fighting so many battles to ensure their child has equal rights to a good education, healthcare, and proper access. It is so important that we support them to support the ambitions of their children.

I know the power of making, seeing, and breathing theatre, of participatory arts and its extraordinary ability to be a platform for social change. So if the government won't, I'd like to think the arts can create the future we want to see.

Teachers: you are under enormous pressure right now and yet you've never mattered more. Never underestimate the power of your encouraging words to a young person who has a dream. It will become their plan, then their success.

Parents: have high expectations of what our society, services, and industries should be providing for you and your children. Don't be fooled into thinking you are a bad parent for telling your child to hunger after art, happiness, and fulfillment— disabled or not.

Theatre: if I'd not found you, that four-leafed clover might now be just a blade of grass. But I still like to think I would have found my way here somehow.

Children, young people, everyone: write that letter to yourself. We are waiting for you here.

Judith Kilvington

Executive Director, Citizens Theatre

Ten Graeae Moments

I remember clearly my first experience of a Graeae show, *peeling*, and I knew then that working for this company was going to change my life. So ten of my Graeae moments are:

1. Creating a home for Graeae at Bradbury Studios and setting new standards in inclusive creative design.

2. Running Missing Piece 3, 4 and 5 and collaborating with drama schools on *Scene Change* and *Into the Scene* to ensure wider access to drama training for disabled actors— but mainly remembering firm friendships established amidst the endless saga of lifts breaking down on Missing Piece 3.

3. Sharing a moment of exhilaration with director Amit Sharma as *Prometheus Awakes* came to its dramatic conclusion, spectacularly and on time, at the Greenwich+Docklands International Festival in 2012, and crying out 'we did it' in joy and disbelief. For context I should add that in a year where Jenny was directing the London 2012 Paralympic Games Opening Ceremony we had anticipated having a relatively quiet year. That was until Amit (with input from GDIF artistic director, Bradley Hemmings) decided he wanted to direct an outdoor aerial show with Catalan company La Fura del Baus, who specialise in blurring the boundaries between audience and performer in mass outdoor theatrical events. So we are talking flying 75+ volunteers fifty feet in the air, suspended off cranes and nets, and operating a twenty-five-meter giant Prometheus puppet. La Fura dels Baus had never worked with D/deaf and disabled volunteers before. We had four days. Our first and final tech run was interrupted by high winds, and, leaving rehearsals at 10 pm on the night before the show for my friend's wedding, I really didn't know if we would have a show the next day. But we did. And it was awesome.

4 ⠼ Being part of a unique team at Graeae including staff, trustees and a wider circle of artists and supporters who were passionate about changing the theatrical landscape of the UK and beyond.

5 ⠼ Enjoying an extraordinary partnership with Jenny Sealey, knowing that the next innovation and transformation of the company was just round the corner, and then making it happen.

6 ⠼ Working with David Beidas (New Stages), Nichola Plummer (Artillery Architecture and Interior Design) and Matt Bray (Paragon Management) on the creation of Bradbury Studios. From the start, our Design Team fully embraced Graeae's values of inclusion and creativity, best illustrated by the moment Nichola came up with her idea for using the five windows in the arches of our façade (and

the door) to spell out the company's name in a range of different materials and textures. Each letter represented a moment in Graeae's history and its move to Bradbury Studios; and more, it announced Graeae's arrival in Hackney with verve and panache.

7 Watching with pure delight as the entire New Wolsey audience gave the first preview of *Reasons to be Cheerful* by Paul Sirett a standing ovation.

8 Being Joint CEO and part of the strategic leadership which moved Graeae from the margins to a central influence on theatre in the UK.

9 Feeling dismay as the government began to dismantle the support system which enables disabled people to work.

10 Proudly picking up the award for Diversity at the TMA/UK Theatre Awards with Jenny Sealey and then promptly dropping it and watching it break into pieces on the beautiful stone slabs of the Guildhall.

Roger Nelson

Freelance Projects Director and Interior Designer

Ten Graeae Moments

1. Realising that Jenny Sealey and I were going to have fun (and quite a lot of wine) along the way as we got to know each other.

2. Early on being able to create two significant new posts and make great appointments, in the form of Claire Saddleton and Judith Kilvington.

3. Seeing Patrick Baldwin's beautiful photo of Sophie Partridge in *peeling* and choosing it to promote the show.

4. Teaming up with Claire Hodgson at London Met university to re-launch the Missing Piece training programme.

5. Being accepted onto the Arts Council's capital programme in 2003—but then eventually realising it was going to be personally overwhelming.

6. Sharing the joy that *Diary of an Action Man* brought to young audiences.

7. Going to see *Reasons to be Cheerful* and feeling this was a quantum leap!

8. Walking into the Bradbury Studios for the first time to see Graeae with a permanent—and beautiful—home of its own.

9 Seeing the reviews shift from patronising to genuine critique as the work matured and the critics (largely) overcame their confusion!

10 Bursting with pride and amazement at the London 2012 Paralympic Games Opening Ceremony.

Jodi-Alissa Bickerton

Steve Moffitt

Liz Carr

Christopher Holt

Dr. Claire Hodgson

Amit Sharma

Training & Learning

Nickie Miles-Wildin

John Kelly

Rachel Bagshaw

Jodi-Alissa Bickerton

Creative & Learning Director, Graeae Theatre

Telling the Story—Classroom to Stage

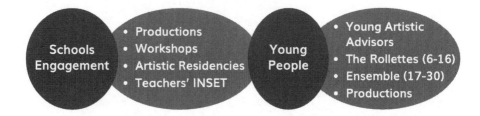

Schools Engagement
- Productions
- Workshops
- Artistic Residencies
- Teachers' INSET

Young People
- Young Artistic Advisors
- The Rollettes (6-16)
- Ensemble (17-30)
- Productions

This is more a factual journey of Graeae's Learning Department than anything else as there are not enough words to describe the emotional rollercoaster of working with young people, or the pride we feel in everything we have, and hopefully will go on to achieve. Graeae has never shirked its responsibility or commitment to this area of work and even when times have been financially tough, we have neither compromised nor neglected it.

Graeae made an application to the ACE *A4E* scheme in 1997 to run two five-month training courses in partnership with 'mainstream' drama schools and universities—one in London and the other in the north of England. A grant was awarded by ACE and the complex process of putting together the biggest ever professional training programme for D/deaf and disabled performers began (*Missing Piece Evaluation, 2009 Alan Dix*). Missing Piece ran until 2009. New generations of D/deaf and disabled artists emerged, centre stage on television and radio.

Graeae has a strong track record of working in education settings, supporting the next generation of artists and cultural leaders. These journeys for

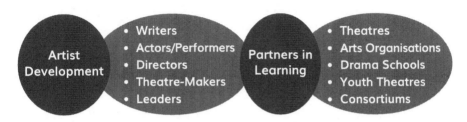

children and young people often begin by seeing a Graeae show, or in a large circle in a classroom at their first Graeae workshop.

Graeae artists and workshop leaders have led education projects for and alongside 8,000 children and young people in school settings over the past ten years (2010–2017). Across all Key Stages (KS1–6), and across the ever-changing curriculums (there have been many over the past ten years!), Graeae has continued to pave the way for inclusive, D/deaf and disabled-led theatre in education and workshop programmes.

***Whiter than Snow* education programme, 2009:**
'They spoke to us like we were adults, and not babies like most people do when they come to our school.'
—Participant

***Just Me Bell* tour and workshop programme, 2010:**
'I learned that people are different but they should be treated the same.'
—George Greens School

[Training & Learning + Jodi-Alissa Bickerton]

'Thank you for such an enjoyable, imaginative, and thought-provoking workshop. Students and staff were engaged throughout. Your facilitators were human dynamite! They worked with loads of energy and enthusiasm to inspire participants.'
—Maggie Tildesley, Acting Tutor and Outreach Manager, Full Body and The Voice (Mind The Gap workshop)

The Iron Man outreach programme, 2011:
'Our Deaf children enjoyed the experience of meeting D/deaf role models yesterday. They were extremely willing to participate and felt confident doing so because the adults leading were all using sign.'
—Shauna Semple-Sepiso, James Wolfe School, Greenwich

Urban Access, 2011 Graeae and East London theatre company Kazzum completed their first collaborative education project *Urban Access* in 2001. The project reached ten primary and secondary schools and colleges in London and 390 young people. The project, inspired by the Ted Hughes story and Graeae's 2011 outdoor summer production *The Iron Man*, was part of A New Direction's Olympic-themed programme, *Biggest Learning Opportunity on Earth*. This creative collaboration had a significant, positive impact on Graeae's outreach models and discussions continued between Graeae and Kazzum to build on this success, both in terms of the organisations' collaboration and sustaining these new relationships with the project's partner schools.

One highlight to emerge from *Urban Access* came from Brookfield House, a school in Waltham Forest. Up to eighteen disabled young people created large-scale puppets in the spirit of *The Iron Man* through the project, and performed a procession for the rest of their school on the final session. The concept of 'procession' performance and creating new, accessible ways for young disabled people to work with and lead large-scale puppets was the inspiration for a new Olympic and Paralympic-themed project. We identified schools to continue working with and devised *Day of Games*, a project that created a platform for D/deaf and disabled people to lead alongside young people in celebrating the Olympic and Paralympic values in an alternative and fully inclusive Olympic celebration.

Day of Games, 2012 The 2012 project *Day of Games* became one of Graeae's largest education programmes. The project was led by D/deaf and disabled artists and drew on Graeae's aesthetic in drama, puppetry, and marketing to explore social inclusion, diversity, and accessible performance. The project was broadened across schools through medal design competitions. The designs went on to influence tactile medals given to game winners on the *Day of Games* celebration day in July 2012.

British Council Pakistan's Arts-Abled programme, 2014–2016 Graeae began a pioneering theatre-makers training programme in Karachi, Pakistan for D/deaf and disabled young people between 2014 and 2016. It was delivered in partnership with the British Council, local theatre artists, schools, and Deaf Reach training centres.

Graeae's *The Iron Man* was used as a creative tool for encouraging new thinking, exploring universal themes, and encouraging a celebration around difference and disability. Training was delivered first to artists and teachers in an artistic residency incorporating disability awareness, Graeae's aesthetics of access, and puppet-making labs. Workshops then followed with young people to develop confidence and independence in expressing new ideas and theatre making approaches. What emerged was a re-imagined performance of *The Iron Man* as created by young people in their local city of Karachi. The performance featured a mid-scale Iron Man puppet made from truck art and local metal objects and materials, operated by young D/deaf puppeteers. *The Iron Man* in Karachi incorporated Pakistan Sign Language and Audio Description in Urdu, and a music ensemble with singing and sound effects designed and performed by two visually impaired students alongside professional musicians. Young people performed in front of a full house at NAPA's main theatre; it was the first time young D/deaf and disabled people had performed on the stage in NAPA's history.

Graeae worked across two years to develop training and community capacity building for greater access to theatre for D/deaf and blind young people. Young people today have continued their passion to perform and created their own D/deaf-led youth theatre in Karachi. We hope to return again soon to see how they are progressing.

Artistic Residencies, 2013–2017 We were invited to develop a dance project with Greenmead School in London in 2013. Delivered weekly across the term by Graeae directors, the aim was to enable artistic independence for disabled children in the creation of a new performance for their peers. We were invited back the following year to develop their annual production and decided to commit to this model of working to shape our education stream at Graeae. Opportunities for teachers to develop their creative practice and for young people to co-author their own stories are firmly embedded in the artistic delivery of these residencies. The model continues to be a success in building our engagement with schools.

Ensemble Schools Tour, 2016 Graeae's young ensemble culminated an intensive six months of drama training with a reimagined production of Mike Kenny's *Stepping Stones* in March, 2016, and also led post-show education workshops. The learning for our ensemble was immense, launching them out of their comfort zones and heading back to school to perform in front of young audiences.

***Reasons to be Cheerful* engagement programme, 2017** *The Reasons, The Rhyme, The Revolution* was a three-step education and community engagement opportunity to provide a social change platform for original protest songs created by people across the UK. Built in association with the *Reasons to be Cheerful* 2017 UK tour, our protest song hub houses a selection of material created as a result of song writing workshops and a country wide callout for protest songs (graeae.org/protest-song-hub). Over eighty songs and hundreds of participants took part.

A report from the Education Policy Institute (epi.org.uk/report/entries-arts-subjects, September, 2017) found that Key Stage 4 Arts Subject entry rates in 2016 were the lowest in the past decade, an impact of Ebacc. The understanding that drama and theatre studies in formal education can develop transferrable skills seems lost on our government. **As a theatre company who reaches out to children and young people and provides role models for the next generation of artists, we must continue to build relationships with schools to ensure young D/deaf and disabled people are not shut out of the arts.**

[Training & Learning + Jodi-Alissa Bickerton]

Steve Moffitt

CEO, A New Direction

Graeae—a twenty-five-year Relationship

I first experienced the work of Graeae when I moved to London in the early 1990s. I was at college with Ewan Marshall, former artistic director, and the first Graeae production I saw was *Ubu*. The visceral energy of the piece was seductive. It was crude, base, and hilarious. The show was the first time I had seen disabled actors in central roles. I had no idea sitting in the audience that night that the company was going to be part of my life for the next twenty-five years.

I have seen seventeen Graeae productions over the years and collaborated on numerous learning partnerships and projects. These projects have involved thousands of young people from a range of backgrounds with different needs and abilities, exploring opera, theatre, visual art and film. All this of work was disabled-led. Which seems obvious—Graeae is an organisation that places D/deaf and disabled actors, writers, directors, producers and artists centre stage promoting equality of access—but for many of the environments the work was (and to some extent still is) delivered in, this disabled-led approach did not feel obvious. Many of these projects and partnerships have changed my practice, my commitment and my approach to how and why I work with young disabled people.

Central to this is my relationship with Jenny Sealey. Ever since I met her, Jen has been a collaborator, a colleague, a partner, many times a teacher, and an extraordinary means of support. When she became artistic director of Graeae, I joined English National Opera.

When running the education team at a national opera company or any organisation receiving significant public subsidy, you are continually reminded of all the things you aren't doing, the young people you are not involving in your programme and the adults who are not experiencing what your organisation can offer. I was aware our work with disabled people was inconsistent and wanted this work to be strategic. Jen approached me with an idea of developing a project around *Mad Meg*, the Mike Kenny and Sam Paechter opera piece she directed for schools at Interplay. The success of the project was not just the simplicity and beauty of the piece, but also the fact that we had connected two schools, Frank Barnes (Deaf School) and Swiss Cottage (Special School). Ironically, they shared a playground but had never collaborated or worked together. The project not only challenged the schools to collaborate creatively, but more importantly, the disabled artistic team had a significant impact on the young people involved. I remember vividly the impact Jamie Beddard had working with two Year 5 students with cerebral palsy who by the time we reached the project sharing had rejected their walking frames to move independently and freely across the stage. The importance of adult disabled role models for disabled young people in SEND Schools (Special Educational Needs and Disability)

[Training & Learning + Steve Moffitt]

must never be underestimated. A minimum of one residency at a special school became integrated in the annual programme of the Baylis Programme (ENO's Outreach and Learning team).

Our next collaboration, *Sense of Opera* was an endeavour to develop an offering for the small cohort of 'hard core' regular D/deaf and blind audience members at ENO. It was not uncommon for questions to be raised within the organisation around the value of audio described and signed performances and I felt it was not only important to protect this aspect of the company's work but also explore whether the offering to D/deaf and blind audiences could grow. I was particularly interested in what kind of programme D/deaf and blind people audiences might be interested in engaging with and how they might help us shape this. Jen and I devised an annual programme of introductory talks, workshops and events that involved ENO musicians, directors, designers, singers and dancers that were fun, practical, intellectually stimulating and went deeper into exploring the sensory characteristics of the art form than the average pre-performance talk. Jen introduced many blind singers, D/deaf writers and musicians to co-lead the events and share their experience of opera. The programme was highly valued and popular particularly with many new D/deaf and blind patrons the partnership with Graeae attracted, and it ran for years. It was successful because the access needs of the individuals involved were integrated into the work and they had an input into shaping and constructing the programme.

Making access visible and celebrating the access needs of disabled people is integral to how Graeae has developed the aesthetics of access. This was initially driven by cuts to the production budget of *The Fall of the House of Usher* and Jen's sheer determination to integrate the access needs of the audience into the work. Exploring access creatively not only demonstrates Graeae's commitment to equality but is also a way of developing a new theatrical language, that is universal, beautiful and political—a perfect example of this for me was the cast speaking Sarah Kane's stage directions in Jen's critically acclaimed production of *Blasted*.

> I joined the board of Graeae in 2005. The company was at a point of transition and change. The trustees were questioning the model of leadership for the company—exploring management structures, financial controls and what long-term planning should be in place—and Jenny asked me for some support. Meetings were often tense and I went along initially as a friendly face to smile across the room. It was a tricky and a difficult time for Jen; a new staffing structure and decision-making systems were introduced alongside an overhaul of the leadership model. Out of this a clarity and new sense of purpose emerged—Jen was given a platform to articulate her long-term vision and a partnership between Jen and Judith Kilvington emerged as artistic director and chief exec—the pair were insufferable!

> The company were based at London Voluntary Sector Council building on Holloway Road. I don't mean to be rude but it was not the most inspiring of offices for a theatre company and various plans for finding a home for the company had largely disintegrated.

[Training & Learning + Steve Moffitt]

A joint lottery bid with Ovalhouse and a partnership commitment to create a physical space within London Metropolitan University had fallen apart. Graeae's profile was on the ascendance, the work of the company was expanding, with a new associate took on writing and directing so new partnerships were developing all over the country. It was obvious to the board that the company needed an accessible space to make new work and a home which embodied its values and a message to the world that Graeae was not only here to stay but meant business. The company moved to its new home in Bradbury Studios and I remember the last thing I pushed for on the board was the development costs from reserves for the now legendary *Reasons to be Cheerful*.

> To avoid a conflict of interest, I left the board in 2010—not really because I wanted to, but at A New Direction we had worked out a way of adapting the relatively restrictive Creative Partnership Enquiry Schools model into a vehicle that could connect schools new to creative and cultural activity to the Olympic and Paralympic moment in 2012. We designed a programme that approached 2012 as a learning opportunity and I invited Graeae to be part of it. The Graeae Big Loop programme was called Urban Access and involved a partnership with ten schools exploring themes and ideas from *The Iron Man* production. The thing that was different for the company was the scale of programme as each school project was different and individually driven by the needs and interests of each school. Through Big Loop, I established an ongoing working relationship with Jodi-Alissa Bickerton, creative learning director, and helped reboot and rethink Graeae's learning offer to a programme that addressed the needs of the people involved.

I so wanted Jenny to direct the 2012 London Paralympic Games Opening Ceremony. It not only had to be her 'gig' but it was important that she take a leading role for Graeae to showcase and create a platform for the actors, signers, artists, talent and ideas that Graeae that supported for the last fifteen years. I was incredibly proud in the Olympic Stadium on 29 August 2012— great disabled artists and great art from the UK were visible to the world. It was a moment of optimism, joy and change in perception—I felt it was so important I took my whole team. I had seen the work of so many of the performers involved— not just artists from Graeae, musicians from Heart 'n' Soul, Tony Heaton's sculpture of the four nations on the Olympic podium, Denise Leigh who I had worked with on the Channel 4 Operatunity competition at ENO. It was an amazing evening.

But that night in 2012 feels like a long time ago now ... the euphoria is over and there is still a serious job to be done. What has changed for disabled artists since this moment? In truth very little. Through an incredible relationship with British Council, Jen has worked all over the world to share Graeae's ethos, ideas and approach— but there is still so much work to be done here at home. Yes, Amit Sharma's and Jack Thorne's *The Solid Life of Sugar Water* was shown at the temporary theatre outside the National Theatre— but is this enough? Why not the main stage and why has it taken thirty years for this to happen?

Yes my last twenty-five years have been informed by the work of Graeae and I know this will continue because there is still more to be done. Whether sending a group of fifteen-year-olds to Vancouver to tell the story of the Winter Paralympics through social media or taking a group of young disabled

[Training & Learning + Steve Moffitt]

people to speak at the World Creativity Summit in Oklahoma or more recently helping create a network of forty SEND schools across London—there is so much more to be done. No matter what progress has been made in the last thirty years the achievements of Graeae are overshadowed by inequalities disabled artists and young disabled people are still confronted with. The job is not over yet. Cuts to the Independent Living Fund, Access to Work, cuts to schools, the visibility and access to arts and culture of young disabled people is as bad as it ever was and access needs to be broader and better for children and young people with Special Educational Needs and Disabilities.

> Yet again, we are in difficult times—but one thing is for sure; Graeae will be at the centre of the fight for change, with passion, dignity and refusal to give up on the fight for equality, if anyone can make the voice of disabled theatre practitioners heard loud and clear, it is Jenny and Graeae. And I will be proud to be there in the room offering my support, smiling across the table.

Liz Carr

Actor

Ten Graeae Moments

1. In 1992, I wrote to Graeae and the then artistic director Ewan Marshall asking if there might be any opportunities to train/learn. I was at Nottingham Uni at the time studying law but was aware of Graeae. I still have a rough version of the letter. He never got back to me ...

2. The first Graeae show I remember seeing was *Sympathy for the Devil* and it blew my mind. Debs Williams was stunning in it and to see what seemed to be a professional show with disabled actors spurred me on. That would be the early 90s—probably before I wrote to Ewan!

3. It would be ten years before I finally did get to work and train with Graeae when in 2003, I was part of Missing Piece 3. Auditioning with a piece from *Mother Courage* was my first experience of the workshop style approach to auditions. I got a place, lived in student digs again and thought I'd stay for the training but would leave before the end of year show, which was to be *Mother Courage*. That was until I was offered the role of Mother Courage and the challenge was too great to pass up.

[Training & Learning + Liz Carr]

4 We teched for *Mother Courage* at Riverside Studios and one of our first dress rehearsals coincided with Beyoncé filming at one of the other studios at the time of *Crazy in Love*.

5 One of my favourite moments on that tour was when we were at the main space at the Albany Deptford and one of the cast fell off the front of the stage. He was fine but it was funny.

6 I worked as the Graeae admin assistant for six months in 2004/5 when I first moved down to London. I needed a job to make the move easier and so applied. My previous life experiences all meant I was fairly qualified and got the job. I had a lot of fun, got to go to some Missing Piece classes and ended up leaving when as a result of attending the classes, I was offered a part in Molière's *George Dandin*.

7 In *George Dandin*, I played Madame de Twitville and wore a massive brocade cloak that covered my power wheelchair and was tied under the neck. One night, I think we were at Stratford, I was waiting in the wings and when I tried to move forward I realised that my cloak was caught in one of my wheels and every time I tried to move forward, it tightened around my neck. I couldn't release myself and couldn't move and my cue was coming up. Thankfully, it was Sophie Partridge, our maid in the play, who released me and saved the day.

8 ⠓ I have not always been successful at Graeae auditions—I wanted to be in *peeling* but wasn't successful, but I did get roles in both *Flower Girls* and *The House of Bernarda Alba* but wasn't able to accept for various reasons.

9 ⠊ The Graeae I was most involved with was when it was on Holloway Road and working with London Met University. I miss it being there. I love it having its own spaces in its current location and I've benefited personally from them but I kind of wish it was a bit more rough and ready and a little less stylish.

10 ⠚ One of my favourite involvements with Graeae in recent years has been with their Write to Play scheme when I've been employed as an actor for read throughs. The opportunity to work with lots of different writers and directors and in some amazing venues (Royal Court, Soho Theatre, National Theatre Studio) is something I have really enjoyed and has made me realise how much I like to be involved in the development of new theatre pieces.

Christopher Holt

Voice Coach and Director

Ten Graeae Moments

1. I work for Graeae because working for Graeae is a treat, a thrill, an excitement, and a threat.

2. I feel it's the best of my work so it demands the best of me. I need to be my best and be open to learning and growing—not being all-knowing.

3. I have to be humble, be grand, be bold, and be sensitive. Be collegiate—a working ensemble will surely produce the best results.

4. I work for Graeae because it is work that I love, because it is so deeply human. We strive for art. Sometimes we succeed, often we fail. But, even in our failure, we spread the joy of art: its attempt.

5. I have learnt to grab my opportunities, to embrace my role, to respond to impossible demands, to take care of my fellow artists as they take care of me.

6. I have learnt to trust my work and to insist on excellence, never to compromise, always to reach for more innovative solutions.

7 ⠿

I have been challenged and been found wanting but I have been supported to return and conquer. I never thought I would be doing the work I do for the company ... I never dreamed it. I have a dream job.

8 ⠾

I work with voices, but the voice is the portal to the soul. The centre of the theatrical artist is their vocal expression. I work with that. Sometimes there is lots to do. Sometimes only tweaks. I put my heart into uncovering potential, stabilizing stamina, discovering unknown talent, producing spectacular results.

There are many issues when working with different bodies and abilities. Some exist around posture. Some around strength. Sometimes we struggle to find any voice at all because the person has never been in a place where using their voice has been expected. Many D/deaf artists are hampered by their own fear and lack of confidence. There is work for the body and the muscles but also psychological issues that need to be addressed. Is my voice worth listening to? Do I make a beautiful or useful sound? I try to approach these issues with a robust, emphatic YES. Just because you are a wheelchair user it does not mean you should not have the posture that any singer or actor would have. A D/deaf actor needs the breath and the posture and the skills and the knowledge of voice and its workings, the same way a hearing actor would. And because you make sounds and not words it doesn't mean that we can't

[Training & Learning + Christopher Holt]

work with the sounds and make them emotional and haunting, joyous and free. All these things are possible if everyone is approached with the proper method. I try in my practice to work with the differences I experience with positivity and joy. I approach each individual as that: a unique artist who is brave enough to trust me to help them grow and learn what I have to teach about voice. I have done this for ten years now and I feel as though I am just at the beginning. I learn more the more I do and I am very much looking forward to the next project.

9 I work with voices. I listen to actors. I take guidance from directors. I use my own intuition and knowledge and passion and experience. I learn. I teach. I love. And we make art.

10 The reason for Graeae is simple: it is for theatre's sake that this company exists. To deliver and provoke art that questions the mainstream, the WASP, the heteronormative, the humdrum. We are the outsiders and the queers and we have power. We have power to change the world: we make art to shock and change the world and we do it one show at a time.

Dr. Claire Hodgson

CEO, Diverse City

Between 2003 and 2007 Graeae ran its training course, Missing Piece, at London Metropolitan University. I was the course leader of the Performing Arts degree at the time and those years were transformative for the students who took part, the staff who taught on the course, and for the university itself. I remember Graeae in this period as subversive, brilliant, and efficient. Graeae should be fully acknowledged for training a generation of disabled performers who have gone on to transform theatre, film, and television.

It comes back as a flood of happy memories. Jamie Beddard, a long-time friend of mine, had mentioned to me that Graeae was looking for an education partner to deliver a training course and suggested we all meet. I had some ability to make this course happen as a senior lecturer and course leader. Now at a distance, I can't remember any official meetings at the university, no smart suits and agendas, although there must have been a few of those. Instead, I remember afternoons in pubs drinking wine with Jenny Sealey, Sophie Partridge, Judith Kilvington, and others. It was fantastic to see the work Graeae was doing and form friendships with the people working there. Judith was highly organised and set up the structures we needed. Jenny charmed and won over the performing arts department.

The university itself was often unhelpful and unwelcoming. An incompetent bureaucratic web couldn't see the value of what was being offered by Graeae. But the inefficiency was to our advantage and, because one hand didn't know what the other was doing, before they knew it we had a course, people auditioned, and an accredited qualification. The university itself may not have helped, but there were many people working there who were strong and capable allies: Owen Smith, Lucy Richardson, Jane Turner, and others that supported us to get the company and course into the institution.

> I remember a professor saying it was a lovely idea but we should wait until the university was fully prepared to accept disabled people as otherwise, 'we will have lots of people in wheelchairs waiting outside lifts. There isn't really the capacity'. He had a long discussion with me about how the lifts would break down and there would be annoyed students (actually this was a premonition!). This argument is often presented as a block when fighting to achieve equality: 'we would do it but there are not enough resources right now'. The answer of course is that access to education is a fundamental human right and so resources need to be reallocated. I met resistance from those who managed me. However, I learned early on in my academic career never to let a 'no' get in the way of making things happen. I got the consent necessary whilst the professor was on leave.

> And so, the course began. Bursting with talent. The first year of students included Liz Carr, who has gone on to have an amazing television and theatre career. The course was taught by some of the very best in the industry, including Barb Jungr

and Philip Osment. For the non-disabled students on the degree course, it was life changing. They met many talented disabled artists and collaborated on performances. It ultimately meant that more disabled people have undertaken the degree in subsequent years. Having Graeae in the building meant that all the work was much more closely tied to the industry itself. There were amazing productions for students to see and it put true diversity at the centre of the department.

It wasn't without real hitches. The university systems often let the Missing Piece students down. I remember how the students got the institution to mend its ways through direct action. There had been a long-standing problem for wheelchair users and those with mobility impairments in the halls of residence. The two lifts often broke down and the contractor would then take over twenty-four hours to come out and fix them. One evening, when the lift had broken down yet again, the students booked themselves into the Hilton Islington hotel and sent the University the bill. The university got the lifts serviced rather quickly, changed the contractors, and got a company in who would fix lifts on an immediate call out. Job done. Hats off to the students but of course it should never have been necessary.

The artistic work of Graeae during this period was extraordinary. I remember sitting in floods of tears watching Martin Sherman's Bent directed by Jenny. It was astounding and profoundly moving theatre. The play talks about the holocaust and sexuality. Jenny had made it speak also of race and disability, adding a sharp analysis of the intersection of oppression. It gave the Missing

[Training & Learning + Dr. Claire Hodgson]

Piece students something to aspire to and raised the creative game for everyone involved. Placing a company in a university really works. It gave an enormous return to everyone involved for a period of time. I still have contact with some of the Missing Piece students and I know it was a pivotal moment for them. I saw people truly becoming themselves and launching themselves as artists. Importantly, many Missing Piece students have gone on to be not only performers, but makers and creators of work.

> My own artistic work over the last twelve years would not be possible without the training Graeae has provided for disabled artists in the UK. I made an Olympic Opening Ceremony with Alex Bulmer, Dave Toole, and Jamie Beddard. All of these artists have been nurtured and developed by Graeae. As the joint artistic director of Extraordinary Bodies (the UK's integrated circus company), I employ many disabled artists who were given their first experience of aerial work by Graeae. Many artists we collaborate with undertook one of the Missing Piece programmes. What Graeae has done consistently well is to unearth talent. All the disabled artists we work with were in some sense 'found' by Graeae. Every Graeae show is always a revelation in terms of new talent. Talent that the rest of us in the industry will then hire. I can't think of another performance company that has shown such a long-term commitment to talent development. This has of course been out of necessity, as the rest of the sector hasn't made their training open and accessible to disabled people.

Graeae decided that the universities and dance/drama colleges must take on the work themselves in the end. There would be no need for Missing Piece if the universities and conservatoires across the UK truly opened their doors to disabled people. I can see movement, but it is slow. The approach is often too passive, waiting for individuals to apply. There needs to be more collaboration with youth arts so that there is a stream of disabled applicants rather than a trickle. Every institution should have strong partnerships with 'feeder' special schools and integrated youth theatres. The arts are still not suggested to disabled young people as a career option. Graeae made a dent in the universe and all training institutions must now aim for 20% of their cohorts to be disabled. This would then match society where around 20% of the population is disabled.

The university itself missed a great opportunity. Graeae's long-term home was to be built in the University's old boiler house. It would have been a unique venue and an opportunity to build an astounding creative community. The university couldn't see the real value of what was on offer and didn't come up with a lease that would work, although the home Graeae did get is beautiful and very fit for purpose.

In the ten years or so since Missing Piece ended, day-to-day living has become much harder for disabled people. There has been a systematic violation of their human rights by a government that has little interest in equality. However, because of Graeae's work, the mainstream theatre world has woken up to the importance of casting disabled artists.

[Training & Learning + Dr. Claire Hodgson]

I recently sat in a meeting at the National Theatre where artistic director Rufus Norris was asking Jamie Beddard, Liz Carr, Alex Bulmer, and others what he should be doing to increase representation. We are not there yet but the main houses are now involved in the fight for equality.

Jamie, Liz, and Alex are activists—finding a place for themselves as artists with no role models in sight. Mandy Colleran, Mat Fraser, Penny Pepper, and Sophie Partridge are trailblazers—building a road in front of them because one does not exist.

I have been privileged to be an ally of the disability movement. I have learnt about resilience, activism, and the long haul. The people I have had the honour of working alongside have changed how disabled people are seen in society. I also learnt from them how to be subversive and effective. And for that I am very grateful.

Amit Sharma

Associate Director, Graeae Theatre and Royal Exchange Theatre, Manchester (secondment)

I arrived at my acting audition for the Missing Piece course. I was young, nervous and undecided about whether I should stay at uni. One of the audition pieces we had to present was a Shakespeare (I did Puck's 'My Mistress with a monster is in love' speech) without ever having done Shakespeare before. I'd covered a tennis ball with some foil so that it looked like a crystal ball, which I thought was right clever!

I then started to very badly blurt out some prose and to my surprise one of the panel members leaned in and I thought 'I'm doing alright here!' After the interview process I was offered a place and was delighted. We were a right motley bunch and without realising, it I'd made the best decision of my life. I started to learn sign language as I was hanging out with Jason Taylor, a BSL user. The course was varied and I was learning loads. One thing I hadn't quite anticipated was how full on the course would be and I started to struggle with the commute and the early starts which are always difficult for a teenager ... After a kick up the backside I didn't look back. I sat in a rehearsal room probably annoying the hell out of Philip Osment by questioning his directing choices for *Woyzeck*—not to undermine but through a curious mind. I still use the actioning work I did with Philip to this very day. *Woyzeck* is a very masculine play and in a sea of men, the only woman character

Sophie Partridge was a class above. She played Marie with such subtlety and elegance and we had Samantha Thorp signing for Marie and some of the boys. Jason was Woyzeck, so he signed his character (and some of our characters too) and we all took turns to voice over him! This sounds like chaos but it really did work and made us work hard too!

Missing Piece was invaluable to me. It gave me tools to work in an industry that I'm still in. It broadened my networks and I made some amazing relationships and friends from it. Seventeen years on the lack of opportunity for D/deaf and disabled people to train as actors, designers, directors is woeful. Missing Piece was meant to tackle that. As an industry it seems that we're missing the point again and again.

My first proper touring job with Graeae was *Into the Mystic* by Peter Wolf. The acting company hired a car and we toured up and down the country with *The Lord of the Rings* playing through the speakers. To me it sounded boring and a world away from what I grew up with so I listened to R'n'B and hip hop through my headphones. The biggest lesson I learnt was generosity. I remember forgetting a critical prop towards the latter part of the play—on press night! I was sure it was in my pocket and sure enough it wasn't there. We improvised around it and Jenny was incredible. She could have gone ballistic at me but was calm and firm in letting me know not to let that happen again. The production gave me the opportunity to fully appreciate the Graeae family. It's a big and incredibly supportive bunch.

One of my favourite plays ever is *Diary of an Action Man* by Mike Kenny. The brilliant team of me, David Ellington, Cherylee Houston and Karen Spicer had such fun in making this hard hitting, beautifully dynamic play about boys and their fathers, boys and their mums and divorce. We opened as the UK government had decided to go into Iraq, so suddenly the make believe soldier that was Dad had extra resonance about the role of war and heroes. Ian Scott's (our LX designer) son came and saw the show in his Spiderman outfit and was transfixed. By the end of the show he was rapidly signing 'September 7th 2003. Time what? 1500 hours'. This was a recurring motif throughout the play as it was told though Ezra's (my character) diary like a way of storytelling. Jenny and I still text each other whenever we're about to board a plane or a train with another *Diary of an Action Man* saying 'On the train. Made it!'

I remember with utter bewilderment when Jenny had asked me to become associate director during a tech rehearsal of *The Iron Man* (another bleeding classic Graeae production). It was for eight months whilst Jen was on secondment to direct the London 2012 Paralympic Games Opening Ceremony. It was meant to be a quiet year. Yeah? Hell No! GDIF commissioned a new production and we worked with the Barcelona-based company La Fura dels Baus, (they did the Opening Ceremony for the Barcelona Olympics in 1992) to make *Prometheus Awakes*. It was the first large scale outdoor production artistically led by D/deaf and disabled artists. IT WAS MEGA! Over seventy volunteers, a twenty-four-foot roaming illuminated puppet, people flying through the air at over fifty metres using large scale cranes. We used the Queen's House in Greenwich as our screen for our massive projections. Having just managed to tech the show, a huge storm arrived to completely wreck our dress rehearsal. It was always new territory for us but this was particularly new for La Fura as they had never worked with disabled people. We didn't know quite how long the show was but we had a forty-five-minute curfew and were told that if we went a second over we would receive a fine of thousands of pounds! With that in mind and concerns about the weather—the whole opening was butt-clenching. Nathan Curry, GDIF producer, had a wind-o-meter in one hand and a stopwatch in the other so I could focus on calling the show with stage management.

Five thousand people rocked and roared with us. It was sensational. I'll never forget Simon Sturgess' (our production manager) look of sheer bemusement at the fact that we had pulled it off!

One of the most awe-inspiring moments was concocted in a meeting discussing the show. The connection between Prometheus and the First Human was critical to the story and we discussed at length how best to represent this. The La Fura team spoke in Catalan intensely for five minutes. When finished, Pera (the other director) said 'We've got an idea but we don't want to tell you because if we do you'll want to do it and we're not sure that we can. It's best not to say anything'. I nodded my head but wasn't going to give up. After the meeting finished we went for a drink. After a respectable amount of alcohol I asked Pera 'Go on tell me. What's the idea?' He smiled, raised his eyebrows and said 'We want to have the First Human be born in mid air, around fifteen metres in the air, with water splashing all over the audience. Then we'll get the twenty-four-foot puppet to kneel and lift out his hands and we'll guide the two cranes so that the First Human will fly through the air and land into Prometheus hand'. My eyes widened. 'I want that!' He roared with laughter and exclaimed 'See why I didn't want to tell you?' But we did it and it was breathtaking and the audience roared and clapped liked they'd never done before.

Jack Thorne is a genius. That much we all know. *The Solid Life of Sugar Water* landed on my desk within the first week of me being associate director. Carissa, the literary manager said 'You have to read this'. I did and I had to do it. It took us three years, but was worth the wait. I auditioned some brilliant actors, but had a real gut instinct about Arthur and Genevieve. Arthur's audition was a bit more straightforward as he was in the country. Genevieve was a little trickier as she was away in Cambodia on holiday so we did a Skype audition. A lot of the material is sexually explicit but good old Gen was causing heads to turn in the Internet café!!!

The set was a bird's eye view of a bedroom cleverly designed by Lily Arnold with Ian Scott's sophisticated yet simple lighting and a subtle but emotionally charged soundscape from Lewis Gibson. We opened in Edinburgh and then went on to be Graeae's first show ever at the National Theatre. This was beyond our wildest dreams and the experience was delightful and the National couldn't have been more welcoming. It seems surreal to even write those words, as if they aren't real. Here was this boy from a council estate having his play on at one of the world's leading theatres. Wow! It's humbling and I have immense pride thinking about all the people connected to the show.

[Training & Learning + Amit Sharma]

I'm incredibly lucky that Graeae arrived in my life when they did. The ride so far has been amazing. I've been all over the world and all over the UK working, laughing, loving my job.

And now, being associate artistic director at the Royal Exchange Theatre in Manchester is testament to the support and belief that Jenny and Graeae had in me all those years ago. It wouldn't have happened without them. I'm eternally grateful.

Nickie Miles-Wildin

Associate Director, Royal Exchange Theatre, Manchester

As I sit in my temporary office at the National Theatre listening to the show relay of *Mosquitoes*, I am reminded of how I got here. I'm currently the staff director on Rufus Norris' production of *Mosquitoes* and I feel so proud. I would never have thought that I would be here when, two years ago, I made the decision to move into directing. One of the first disabled staff directors the National Theatre has ever had. Working with a brilliant award-winning creative team, fantastic crew, and truly talented cast including Olivia Williams, Olivia Colman, and Paul Hilton. I have to pinch myself to check that I'm not dreaming.

These opportunities keep happening in my life and I feel so lucky to be part of them. But as a friend reminded me, I have worked bloody hard to get here. As D/deaf and disabled people, we work doubly hard to get anywhere mostly because it takes us longer to get anywhere due to lack of access and lack of opportunities. Take those while you can.

The biggest opportunity I had, which completely kicked my career into action, was sending a letter (this was before email was the norm) to a theatre company I had heard about from Kaite O'Reilly, a temporary lecturer of mine during my first year at university. The theatre company was called Graeae. I sent them a letter and information about a show I was taking up to the Edinburgh Festival Fringe in 1998. It was called *3ft Off the Ground*.

A one-woman show written and performed by myself. Jenny Sealey came to experience the show and asked me to attend an audition a few weeks later in London as they wanted to meet more D/deaf and disabled women. WOW! I jumped at the opportunity. My brother drove me to the audition. I was nervous—what if I couldn't do all the drama exercises we were given? This had been the norm for me at university until I had challenged my peers on their choice of warm ups. I had nothing to worry about with Graeae. It was the first time in my life that I didn't have to apologise for needing to sit down, to challenge anyone over an exercise, take it easy, or go at a slower pace. This was so liberating! To be in a space with lots of D/deaf and disabled women with various impairments of various ages and backgrounds. This was the family in which I wanted to be a part. And that's where my journey with Graeae began, at that audition in September, 1998.

I remained in contact with Jenny from then on and, after a couple of years being a stage manager at the Nuffield Theatre in Southampton, I made the move into acting and that was when my relationship with Graeae grew. It blossomed and, fifteen years since applying for their training course Missing Piece 3, I have worked extensively as an actor, workshop facilitator, and assistant director. Shows have included *The Trouble with Richard*, a school-based forum theatre show written and directed by Jamie Beddard, and *Flower Girls* by Richard Cameron, which is a beautiful story about the disabled women of John Grooms care home who made paper flowers for the rich but, during the Second World War, made rivets! There was also *The Rhinestone Rollers*, a wheelchair line dancing troupe; our *Swan Lake* choreographed by Marc Brew is like no other version! Of course, if I hadn't met Jenny I would not have played Miranda in the London 2012 Paralympic Games Opening Ceremony. I would never have flown through the Olympic stadium.

Graeae is family. It's support. It's people who get it and make work happen. And with that come challenges; you meet actors, writers, and other directors who do not understand the importance of creative access. I was the assistant director to Jenny in 2015 on *Blood Wedding*, a Graeae co-production with Dundee Repertory Theatre and Derby Theatre. Here, we met resistance from some of the actors regarding the integration of sign language, live audio description, captions, and even their views of D/deaf and disabled actors. We were faced with the attitude that, as theatre-makers, our work is not as high quality as our non-disabled peers and with this comes a lack of respect for what we are creating. Diplomacy is the key but we should never make our work feel of lesser value. It is extremely valuable to evoke change in theatre and indeed the world in which we live. Working as assistant director on *The House of Bernarda Alba* was also not without its challenges: balancing the rehearsal room with a mix of seasoned actors and first timers, and negotiating a show in the round. All valuable experience for doing *Mosquitoes*, which is also in the round.

From my time with Graeae, I continue to make work that is creatively accessible because that work is widely needed in the arts world. We have to challenge mainstream theatre as individual artists and get our voices heard. Graeae and the people I have met through that network, including working with Kaite O'Reilly on her production of *peeling* many years after meeting her at university, have given me the confidence to voice my opinion and to make work. Without that confidence, I would not be sat here about to go and give notes to well-known actors at the National Theatre. Graeae is a professional, accessible platform that has enabled me to grow alongside it. I am not sure where I would be without Graeae. I'm not even sure that I would be working in theatre. I would have given up by now. But instead, I'm off to be resident assistant director at the Royal Exchange Theatre for eighteen months from October, 2017.

> **Thank you Graeae for giving me the confidence, the strength, the understanding, and the voice to allow me to create and make the thing I love: theatre.**

John Kelly

Musician, Actor and Disability Activist

Ten Graeae Moments

My moments—not in order:

1. First time I read about Graeae as a young person and finding out we existed in theatre.

2. Hearing rumours that Graeae were talking about doing an Ian Dury related project and getting a little buzz about feeling oh gawd I'd love to do that, never thinking I would. Even whilst doing it the first night I kept thinking someone 'proper' will be doing this and I'm just covering until that happens ...

3. Playing with Rockinpaddy (bunch of very talented musicians) at a drama course Jen and Pete Lawson were running at Orpheus Centre (a residential arts based course set up by Richard Stilgoe) and then Jen asked if I'd like to come for a day as part of the script R&D for *Reasons to be Cheerful*.

4. As part of my learning and development, Graeae sent me on a Continuing Professional Development vocal course. I felt totally out of my depth with all the vocal gymnasts around me, but I got to sing a love song with Sophie Partridge (the song was called *Ten Minutes Ago*); it was beautiful to do.

[Training & Learning + John Kelly]

5 ⠨⠴

In the run up to the 2012 Paralympics, I worked with Graeae as part of a huge team working with a large number of schools both for disabled, mixed and non-disabled pupils, called The Day of Games project. The idea was to work with each school for a term to develop a theatre-based inclusive game that would be played at a day of games by all the schools involved, of course including an Opening Ceremony. It was hugely ambitious, almost impossible. The day felt like one huge mountain that we were only halfway up, however the team were the A team of practitioners, the students were amazing and it was such fun, that the ambition, challenges and impossibleness of it all were so easily overcome. We just got on, trusted in the process and each other, did it and it was wonderful.

6 ⠨⠦

My first taxi drive to Graeae to do the first day of *Reasons to be Cheerful* R&D, I remember going home and saying to the driver (Barry), just for tonight I'm living the dream, I've been singing, not just singing but singing one of my hero's collection of biggest songs, with a bunch of top musicians and actors and me ... and I've been paid for it!

7 ⠨⠒

Working in Tuke School is a really good example of why Graeae's Schools programme is so important. Reaching to children to ensure they experience inclusive creativity and have their own ideas pushed to the maximum to a place where students find new skills, confidence and belief in their own talents. The students at Tuke were not the students who usually did performing arts and were all experiencing challenges within the curriculum in one way or another. Again as part of a team we spent two terms working with the students and staff, raising expectations that they would create a stunning piece of theatre to be shared with the rest of the school. Every lesson spent, we learnt something about ourselves and each other; we created a simple and beautiful piece. The reason for this was each student shone, had 'a moment' as Jen would say, but each of those moments the students were true to themselves, they were shining centre stage totally in control of what they were performing. Giving choice and control whilst pushing expectations further is a hard skill to learn to facilitate, and the students at Tuke really helped me to learn something of how to do that. It was also very easy because we had fun and laughs from the word go, it was wild, creative beyond imagination and you couldn't do anything but go with the flow; it was exciting and challenging.

Every time I'm invited in on a little/massive secret, i.e. the paras Opening Ceremony/ recording *Spasticus*/writing a new song with Chaz and Derek from The Blockheads *If It Can't Be Right Then It Must Be Wrong*/all sorts ... I keep thinking, these amazing people who I look very much up to and respect/admire are asking me for my thoughts/input, it gets a bit mind blowing and scary, but so exciting and as a practitioner so creatively challenging to always try and pull something good out of the bag.

[Training & Learning + John Kelly]

9 ⠼ Reaction of the audience at the New Wolsey the first night we did *Reasons* in Ipswich. They all stood up at the end and we were all blown away by this.

10 ⠼ The day I overcooked it because I was desperate to deliver well for Graeae and didn't have the PA support worked out too well. I thought fuck it, I've got to try ... I struggled through in the morning and Dan McGowan (who was doing general admin for Graeae as well as part of *Reasons*) was around. We made friends and we muddled through but at the end of day I was so angry I had put myself in a position of relying on someone I hadn't known because I was so desperate to do the work. Dan was so unphased by it all and non-bothered, such a lovely supportive colleague to be with. Silly I know but I learnt a lot about the importance of access not from the traditional view but how access is critical to delivering above and beyond, to perform to my best. Access is an important part of the aesthetic, it's a critical part of how I perform and can perform to my ultimate and maximum self, to be able to give everything I have in each song I sing.

11.

Eleven ... sshh I know. But I didn't say anything about the songs that changed our lives Playlab, or rockin' Trafalgar Square, or that big gig we did at the paras, or EANA bike meet or Ronnie Scotts or Brazil or Mexico or Germany or Air Studios, Reframing The Myth, doing the conga to the Dolphin from Hackney Empire with Judith (joint CEO) ... it goes on.

xxx

Rachel Bagshaw

Theatre-Maker and Director

I first encountered Graeae as a student, when I saw *The Changeling*. The production took my breath away creatively but I did not identify with it; at the time I had recently been injured but certainly did not consider myself disabled. A few years later I met Jenny. By this time I was a wheelchair user; having just finished training at drama school, I felt completely at sea in the mainstream theatre world but didn't know how else to develop my career. Jenny invited me to do a little bit of work for Graeae, which turned into assistant directing on *Flower Girls*.

I went from not understanding my place in the world, to having a whole new network and team of people who understood completely what it was like to be me. Graeae offered me the time and space to develop not just my creative skills but also the confidence and ability to communicate effectively what I need in order to be able to make the best work I can make.

Once I had experienced this, I wanted to be able to work with Graeae to create opportunities for others to feel like this too, and running the company's Training and Learning programme was the perfect place to do this. I felt really privileged to be able to work with the Graeae team to develop projects that engaged with such a wide audience. It was not always easy. I couldn't always grasp why things seemed to take so long. We knew what we wanted to happen and yet the rest of the industry always seemed to be so far behind! The reality is that change is always going to take time.

I've taken the core Graeae principles into my own work as a freelance director. My recent show, *The Shape of the Pain*, used captioning and audio description. With the skills I learnt from Jenny as the bedrock, the creative team and I were able to push this into something which became as much a part of the aesthetic as the performer and the design. Audiences didn't notice the access as tools but rather as integral to the show.

The defining moment for me of seeing how much Graeae's change has affected the world was sitting at home with my newborn son watching the Paralympics Ceremony. When I had started working for Graeae several years previously, I could not imagine that I would see those same artists on such a huge stage, directed by the person who had opened those doors for me. It felt as though the world was being given a glimpse into my own life. **Graeae's work is about exactly that—it's not just about representation in training or on our stages. But that representation creates work which reflects the disabled person's lived experience, something that I took from my own encounters with Graeae which will always inform the way I live and work.**

[Training & Learning + Rachel Bagshaw]

Jenny Sealey
Milton Lopes

David Ellington
Kellan Frankland

**Plays
Beginning
with B**

Kathryn Hunter
Alison Halstead

Jenny Sealey

CEO/Artistic Director, Graeae Theatre

Plays Beginning with B

Bent, Blasted, Blood Wedding, and *The House of Bernarda Alba* all benefited from the trials, tribulations, and learning from *Two*, *Usher*, and *peeling*.

● **Bent by Martin Sherman (2004)** This all-male cast, diverse in impairment, ethnicity, and sexuality, took on similar dual casting to that of *Two*. All the main characters had two actors playing them, one disabled and one Deaf so that each character had voice and BSL. The character of Max was played by Milton Lopes (voice) and David Ellington (BSL); Rudi was played by Neil Fox (BSL) and Mark Smith (voice); and Donal Toolan (voice) and Mark Smith (BSL) together took on the role of Horst. Some of the actors took on multiple roles: Neil played the Nazi Officer, providing voice and SSE (Sign Supported English); and our cellist Desmond became Wolf, using SSE while Milton provided voice over in Portuguese to give our blind audience a sense of another actor in the space.

The questions Wolf asked were always repeated in Max's answer in order to give enough spoken word information for blind and visually impaired audiences to access the scene. Desmond and Milton also narrated stage directions and set each scene. This style reinforced the horror of what happened to gay men during the Holocaust as well as to D/deaf and disabled people, who were some of the first to be sent to the camps.

● **_Blasted_ by Sarah Kane (2006)** This play was a gift. I remember watching Alex Bulmer doing a voice class with our Missing Piece Trainees using Kane's _Blasted_. Alex experimented with voicing Kane's directions (given in closed brackets in the text) to function as audio descriptive lines. I had thought on my first reading of the play that this was Kane's intention but Alex explained that Kane meant they functioned within the rhythm of the text as action.

I got permission from Simon Kane and Mel Kenyon (Sarah Kane's agent) to play with this style and also to use the stage directions vocally to enhance the audio accessibility; and I got Alex on board as assistant director!

We cast Gerard McDermott (a visually impaired actor) as Ian, who becomes blind in the play; Jenny Ellison as Cate, a gorgeous slip of a girl with a gait like a new-born foal; and David Toole as the Soldier.

Each actor took on the action described in closed brackets, which were attached to their lines in the text. Each stage direction was given careful consideration—which character should own it and why? Cate led the first few pages because it was she who was fascinated by Ian and scared of the gun. Ian took over later as a way to prey on Cate's naivety. The extraordinary discussions enabled the heart of the play to beat with a different intensity.

Jo Paul and I collaborated in the design, which included a steep upward curve that Jenny could not physically walk up because of her mobility. This was deliberate, it enhanced her vulnerability and gave the character of Ian control of the set. However, at the end of the play, Ian finds himself stuck in the cage of the bedframe as Cate crawls to the edge of the stage, swings her legs over and looks out, sucking her thumb. The whole stage was now hers.

This was another play where the dynamic of the lead couple would be fractured if there was a live signer on stage. Instead, we projected film footage above the stage. Neil Fox (Deaf), dressed in the same clothes as Ian, signed for Ian during Act One. Cate becomes the main protagonist in Act Two so Adele Walker, dressed the same way as Cate, replaced Neil in the projection and signed for Cate. Daryl Jackson (Deaf), dressed in the same costume as the Soldier, signed Act Three as the Soldier until his death whereupon Adele returned with Cate, signing until the end.

The style of the projected film blended signing with action described but not portrayed on the stage. For example, Neil smoked and drank as Ian talked about doing it; Daryl ate sausage and bacon as the soldier talked about eating it. This is better described through extracts from my rehearsal script:

Extract One

VIDEO: *Stage directions now scroll up over image of singer dressed identically to Ian. He is reading a newspaper. Track ends with singer and Ian looking at each other establishing a connection between the screen and the stage.*

IAN   They enter.

CATE   Cate is amazed at the classiness of the room.

IAN   Ian comes in, throws a small pile of newspapers on the bed, goes straight to the mini-bar and pours himself a large gin. He looks briefly out of the window at the street, then turns back to the room.

            VIDEO: *Singer holds up and examines a gun, then signs as Ian speaks.*

IAN   I've shat in better places than this. He gulps down the gin.

           VIDEO: *Singer drinks gin and looks at his gun as Cate's spoken stage directions scroll up.*

CATE   Ian goes into the bathroom and we hear him run the water. He comes back in with only a towel around his waist and a revolver in his hand. He checks it is loaded and puts it under his pillow.

           <u>**Extract Two**</u>

           VIDEO: *Soldier on screen signs and sniffs knickers when stage soldier does it.*

SOLDIER   She in there?

IAN   Who?

SOLDIER   I can smell the sex. He begins to search the room. You a journalist?

IAN   I ...

SOLDIER   Passport.

IAN   What for?

SOLDIER   Looks at him.

IAN   In the jacket.

IAN   The Soldier searches a chest of drawers. He finds a pair of Cate's knickers and holds them up.

SOLDIER   Hers?

IAN   Doesn't answer.

SOLDIER   Or yours. He closes his eyes and rubs them gently over his face, smelling with pleasure.

[Plays Beginning with B + Jenny Sealey]

Extract Three

VIDEO: *Signer mirrors Ian but it is clear she is watching him, as is Cate. When Cate laughs, so does the signer.*

IAN	Takes the gun and puts it in his mouth. He takes it out again. Don't stand behind me.
	He puts the gun back in his mouth. He pulls the trigger. The gun clicks, empty. He shoots again. And again and again and again. He takes the gun out of his mouth.
IAN	Fuck.
CATE	Fate, see. You're not meant to do it. God ...
IAN	The cunt. He throws the gun away in despair.
CATE	Rocks the baby and looks down at it. Oh no.
IAN	What.
CATE	It's dead.
IAN	Lucky bastard.
CATE	Bursts out laughing, unnaturally, hysterically, uncontrollably. She laughs and laughs and laughs and laughs and laughs.

We worked with filmmakers David McCormick and Benedict Johnson from Snake Oil Productions who created a Kane-esque style of voyeurism and claustrophobia. From an audience perspective, there was always someone looking at you. Added to this were the spoken stage directions and personal actions, which meant you could not escape from the horrors of Kane's world.

Alex worked on the soundscape with sound designer Gregg Fisher. As a blind person, Alex wanted the visuals to be matched with a score that underpinned the same voyeurism and brutality, the explosion and the aftermath. Gregg created an array of beautifully abstract but emotionally real sounds that had delicate touches interlaced throughout, such as the sound of the migration of geese (which I could never quite detect but, as he said, this was for Alex, not me!).

I sincerely believe Sarah Kane would have loved this production because every single word she wrote was spoken or signed or captioned. There was no escape because it forced people to take on the importance of what she was saying.

● **Blood Wedding by Lorca, adapted by David Ireland (2015)** This co-production with Dundee Repertory Theatre began with an actor saying, 'Lorca did not write *Blood Wedding* for people like you [D/deaf and disabled people] to be in it!' In response, James Brinning (artistic director, Dundee Rep) and Jemima Levick (associate director, Dundee Rep) said, 'well, we are doing Lorca with Jenny!'

David Ireland brought the script up to date by using the cast members' impairments as an intrinsic part of the drama, so there were no elephants in the room—the characters said what the audiences were thinking. The Mother of the Groom was played by E.J. Raymond, a BSL user who also used her Deaf voice. A blind audience struggled to understand her voice and sighted audience could sort of understand it because they had visual reference as back up. The script developed to allow a real family dynamic to emerge; the Groom was frustrated at his mother so he repeated what she said as part of his annoyance. This habit allowed a blind audience to know what she had said. Both characters signed but in the 'shorthand' way in which families sign to each other. The relationship between the two was further challenged when they met the Bride's family. The Mother would not use her voice in public and expected her son to interpret and voice over everything, which he did although not accurately. In turn, the Mother would enact the 'Deaf thing' of being brutally direct in expressing her thoughts about his choice of bride: 'she got no legs' and

MOTHER   (BSL) My son is a fine man.

GROOM   I am a fine man, she agrees.

MOTHER   (BSL) Never been with a woman.

GROOM   Mum?

MOTHER   (BSL) What? You haven't? Have you?

GROOM   She says that she's raised me to treat women with respect.

FATHER   Yes, I can see that.

GROOM   (BSL) He can see that.

MOTHER   (BSL) Is his daughter a virgin?

GROOM   Mum.

MOTHER   Ask.

GROOM   She'd like to know more about Lisa.

Having a Deaf Mother added an additional layer to the distress she felt that her son was leaving. He was her primary means of communication, exacerbating her isolation and his guilt. Her neighbour Eileen had learnt basic signs which was some solace for both mother and son. In our production, the Mother 'booked' an interpreter for the wedding and party. This amplified an overall signing ethos for the production: family sign, neighbour sign/gesture, and moments of BSL between interpreter and Mother when she knew she was being voiced over.

Everything was captioned by the cast operating the laptop on stage to keep clarity for D/deaf audiences. This fitted well with the design concept which was simply a large picture frame and a few pieces of naturalistic furniture. We also had huge light boxed letters with the initials of the two couples L (Leo), V (Vicky) and E (Edward), O (Olivia) which rearranged spelt LOVE. The photographic set image ran through the play, evoking the notion that they were all in it together. Everyone played their part in the death of the Groom and Leo. This also created a rationale for exposing the captioning on stage and was also the rationale behind everyone sharing the audio description.

Different cast members described scenes which were emotionally appropriate for them to describe. Microphones were rigged at the side of the picture frame to enable actors to practise timing the lines between action and text. The original plan was that the actors would sit near the laptop table and give 'in the ear' audio description for blind audiences but it was quickly obvious that live description, on stage through the mic, raised the stakes emotionally and theatrically.

I do rather love this review because it endorses our commitment to the wider context of diversity.

> **Watching this version of Blood Wedding I was struck by the realisation that Graeae are pretty much *the* blueprint for what I wish Mainstream British Theatre was like. At the same time, the company offers more British national and regional voices than you hear over a whole season at the National. I look forward to the day when this level of textual and visual interrogation of a piece, and this extent of diversity-of-casting, comes as standard in British theatre.**

[Plays Beginning with B + Jenny Sealey]

—Andrew Haydon on Graeae's production of *Blood Wedding*, *Postcards from the Gods* blog entry, 22 April, 2015

For further reading on the process go to Rebecca Sweeny's paper at www.graeae.org.

● **The House of Bernarda Alba by Lorca, translated by Jo Clifford (2017)** I had wanted to direct this play since I became artistic director at Graeae. It took nineteen years to finally do it and it was more than worth the wait. But I would give anything to do it again to get it right, especially for a blind audience. It was my first time creating an accessible play in the incredible theatre in the round space at Royal Exchange Theatre, Manchester. I was fortunate to work with a creative team who knew the theatre extremely well. They held my hand as I struggled to understand that the space itself is a character which informs everything.

I had always wanted the set to be seven individual chairs, one for each of the main characters. Designer Liz Ascroft took this instruction, along with my penchant to use stage directions within a narrative, and created a claustrophobic design consisting of the seven bespoke chairs arranged in a circle, each in a line with one of the seven doors of the theatre. Each chair was placed either facing or turned away from Bernarda's chair. Adela's chair faced away whereas Martirio's (whose name means two-faced) had a corner/double chair facing Amelia but, if she shifted, could be in her mother's line of sight. Magdalena's chair had her name embroidered on the seat, a tactile reference to her being visually impaired. The word DOOR was painted onto the floor by each exit. Lorca's words describing other aspects of the setting were written onto boards and hung between the second and third tiers of seating. Seven TV screens providing captions were mounted along the seven sides of the first tier. The idea was that wherever you sat you could see a screen.

The only other piece of furniture on the set was a table which had the word TABLE written on it and was set at the top of Act Two. Above the table hung seven pieces of cloth signifying the materials the girls had to embroider. These pieces of cloth were also part of the only trick we used, which was for the suicide of Adela. Bernarda and her daughters were sat in their chairs and Adela's chair (with no one near it) flung backwards, toppling with a crash at the same time as the cloth above the chair dropped with real force. Liz gave me this moment through the design process. I knew my ending before I knew my start!

As always, I cast the best people for the right parts. Therefore, Bernarda's eldest and youngest daughters both happened to be Deaf BSL users who sometimes used their voices. The play had many facets of communication because here was a family of Deaf, visually, and physically impaired girls with their maids. When they were altogether, we played with the shorthand of authentic family signing.

One of the servants was also played by a Deaf actor. Through the rehearsal process it became apparent she was Bernarda's main servant, providing all the communication between Bernarda and her Deaf daughters as and when Bernarda demanded it. Sometimes she was sent away when Bernarda wanted privacy to sign with her girls. The choice to sign or not to sign was all part of Bernarda's control. In her last speech, she could not speak, shocked at the death of her daughter, so she signed only, laying bare her vulnerability and pain.

The action had to be audio described in a similar familial fashion. The main audio descriptive narrative was written by our translator Jo Clifford as the visual language of the play

[Plays Beginning with B + Jenny Sealey]

developed. I had originally intended Granny and/or a maid to sit in a stage area close to the blind and visually impaired audience members and describe what happened.

My mistake was not trying this out prior to rehearsals; it quickly became clear that this did not work as convention. What could have worked instead was to have the actor describe their own actions:

BERNARDA *You whore.* She raises her stick intending to strike her daughter's face.

My initial approach did not sit well with Jo, nor with any of the actors. In hindsight, I perhaps should have stuck with my guts and pushed my idea further. Our blind audio description consultant Mandy Redvers-Rowe worked with Jo to explore the right language to be written within the text but this was so seamlessly embedded into the dialogue that it did not read as a visual language signifier.

On realising the potential ambiguity of our audio description strategy, we found other ways to give additional information to audience members. Adela wore bangles so a blind audience would know she was signing. Amelia would always voice over for her because Magdalena needed this access too. We had a life-sized model of the seven chairs displayed in the great hall of the Exchange. A beautiful pre-show recorded audio description commentary by the cast and designer accompanied the model.

This was designed as a gateway for audiences to own the visual narrative of the play. However, if blind audiences were not directed to explore this pre-show installation, they would find themselves at a significant disadvantage during the show and this did happen more than once so we had some understandably irate blind audience members.

One blind woman did not want to listen to the audio description.

She said she came to the theatre to escape being blind and ultimately did not like D/deaf and disabled people on stage as they reminded her of her own impairment.

The captioning screens for D/deaf people who do not sign worked but if you were a D/deaf, non-signer with a visual impairment, then the screens were too far away to read and people said they would have preferred a hand-held iPad with the text so they could control the font size.

Finding the perfect balance between creative experimentation and equal access for all audiences is a constant challenge. It is always such a blow when we fail or if attempted solutions do not work as planned. *The House of Bernarda Alba* demonstrated that we still have a long way to go before we create a perfectly accessible, artistically brilliant show.

I would give anything to remount this production knowing what I now know. I want the opportunity to get it right. It is such a shame the Young Vic was producing *Yerma* and felt another Lorca did not fit into their programming. I know in my heart of hearts we will do it again, somewhere, sometime.

For further reading on the process go to Colette Conroy's paper *Watching Graeae's Bernada Alba* at www.graeae.org.

[Plays Beginning with B + Jenny Sealey]

Milton Lopes

Actor

Ten Graeae Moments

1. Meeting Jenny in Glasgow after a performance of *San Diego*. I never thought, after that meeting, I would be working with her regularly for fourteen years.

2. Playing Max in *Bent*. My first time in a lot of things:
- Playing a lead character.
- Sharing a character with another actor.
- Living in London; first job working in London.
- Speaking in BSL.
- Working with D/deaf actors and a Deaf director.
- Working with other disabled actors.
- Learning how to be an activist and an artist after befriending Donal Toolan, who played Horst.
- Getting my sign language name.

3. Playing the role of Macheath in *The Threepenny Opera* in one of the biggest D/deaf, disabled and non-disabled ensemble on a main stage.

4. Spending a month in Rio de Janeiro, learning and teaching circus to D/deaf and disabled people.

5 � The amount of times I pissed the night away with Graeae cast, crew, and company members.

6 ⠆ Doing outdoor shows in the rain, thirty-degree heat, windy weather—you name it.

7 ⠶ Friendships that will last forever and a day.

8 ⠦ Learning sign language on my second English speaking show.

9 ⠲ Playing Zip Zap Boing as a warm up game in every production since 2004.

10 ⠼⠚ The 'never give up' spirit.

[Plays Beginning with B + Milton Lopes]

David Ellington

Actor, Circus Artist and Film-Maker

Ten Graeae Moments

1. ⠿

Diary of an Action Man by Mike Kenny: a lovely collaboration with Unicorn Theatre. My first acting job playing imaginary and real Dad. My favorite character was Spud who was dressed in a huge anorak like they do in the *South Park* cartoon series. This was to hide the fact that Spud was played by Karen Spicer who was also playing Mum. Spud signing and communicating was surreal and very funny.

2. ⠿

Diary of an Action Man: real Dad had a great scene arguing with Mum. Both of us rowed in BSL and our children, Ezra and Louise, had to voice over for us. D/deaf kids always said that was their favorite scene.

3. ⠿

Bent by Martin Sherman: I loved the message about respecting human value, no matter who you are!

4. ⠿

Bent: playing Max and sharing the character with Milton Lopes. There was no interval, which helped portray the relentlessness and suffering.

5. ⠿

Wheels on Broadway with *The Rhinestone Rollers*, Graeae's powerchair dance troupe: I loved how sexy and naughty we were. We started dressed as nuns signing songs from *The Sound of Music* and then stripping to our hot, kinky, red Pretty Polly fishnet tights and infamous high white boots and blonde wig. It blew audience's minds!

6 ⠿ Being an associate artist and part of thought-provoking campaigning but finding it frustrating to change people's perceptions of us.

7 ⠿ Associate artist: I was very privileged to be involved in influencing others who were isolated, had low self-esteem, were unable to own being D/deaf or disabled, and did not have pride in who they were. We opened the 'freedom and independence' door for people, so that they could pave the way to their right path, career, and achievements.

8 ⠿ Moving to Graeae's new building at just the right time: it is a place that feels like home for professionals, non-professionals, CEOs, artists, writers, technicians, and visitors from all over the world.

9 ⠿ Being a sway pole artist: showing the world at the London 2012 Paralympic Games Opening Ceremony that we, D/deaf and disabled, can achieve anything and if you ignore us, you will see us marching for our rights.

10 ⠿ I love being part of a movement as D/deaf and disabled people with the clear message that we are part of society, in work and social life. Together we can fight against inequality and elitism!

[Plays Beginning with B + David Ellington]

Kellan Frankland

Actor

I walked into my audition for Graeae thinking that I knew what it was going to be like. I realise, looking back, that this was incredibly naïve. It was my first introduction to Graeae in any capacity and I had presumed it would be exactly like any other audition. Short answer: it wasn't. Long answer: ok so, when I arrived, I was very nervous but for most of the audition I forgot it was an audition. It was so much fun. Instead of stern, expressionless faces, I believed we all had the support of everyone in the room. What was more surprising was that we did a workshop which was so enjoyable that by the time you had to do your monologue you felt positive about the experience.

The audition was for the Graeae Ensemble programme, offering a six-month training course for six D/deaf and disabled artists. We had tutors from drama schools, theatre companies, and universities to train us in different genres of theatre. It was a learning curve for both us (the participants) and the tutors as they got to understand us and our different needs. Some tutors were surprised that making the lessons accessible for everyone didn't stop them giving the lessons that they would normally teach. It was really refreshing.

We put on a children's play, *Stepping Stones* by Mike Kenny and directed by Jenny Sealey, to complete the course. This was a useful experience; it was my first involvement in creating a fully accessible show. This was complex because of the different methods the six of us used to communicate (BSL/visually, audibly, and using eye gaze technology). We had to find a way to be confident that we were understanding each other as well as making sure the audience could fully relate to the characters and the story we were telling, regardless of our variety of communication methods. Our solution was to have other actors give voice overs and act as interpreters for certain characters; we also programmed Dave's eye gaze with audio description. We worked closely as a team so no one was stuck doing something that they found physically difficult, such as when changing the set. *Stepping Stones* was a useful way to get used to Jenny's style of directing (a lot of time just 'going for it' and seeing where we ended up), which I liked, and getting some idea of the hours that go into making a professional show. It was helpful to have that prior knowledge when I was cast as Martirio in Graeae's production of *The House of Bernarda Alba* and then be pushed further as an actor than I ever had before.

> The closeness between the cast and crew on *The House of Bernarda Alba* took me by surprise. We were a family being torn apart in the play and it was exactly the same off stage! No, I'm joking. It couldn't have been further from the play. We looked out for each other. I learned from watching my fellow cast members during rehearsal and strived to match their energy in the performances. The whole experience cemented my belief that Graeae is a family. They have a real care and understanding of everyone because they are more than a theatre company. They are constantly aware of, and evaluating, individual needs. Graeae is a family and one in which I'm very happy to be a part.

Within the same timeframe that other productions rehearse a full show, we also had discussions on how to incorporate sign language and audio description in a creative and accessible way for both actors and audiences into our play, as well as learning what is needed to make this happen. The major thing I learnt during my time in the Ensemble and with *The House of Bernarda Alba* is that accessibility shouldn't be an afterthought. It is a necessity. It's still surprising that it took me, as a disabled person, nineteen years to fully realise this fact.

I didn't really know any other disabled people before Graeae, so being part of the company has been a helpful way for me to meet other people with whom I can relate. I've been able to talk about my disability more since joining Graeae, ask for help more, and basically be proud to be a disabled woman. Not only have my eyes been opened to accessibility but, because of my involvement with Graeae, it now really matters to my family and they try to include access in the different areas of theatre that they do, which I think is really sweet.

I feel that Graeae is the leading force in integrated theatre because many other theatres are too scared to take the risk of dealing with accessibility out of fear of getting it wrong. It should be known that *The House of Bernarda Alba* wasn't perfect in terms of accessibility because it is difficult to get right and there's no simple answer to how it is done.

But every show Graeae does, works on how they can improve. Therefore, there is no excuse for other theatre companies not trying to make their shows accessible.

> It won't be 100% straightaway. It will be challenging, but everyone should work towards the goal of fully integrated theatre.

Kathryn Hunter

Actor and Director

Working with Graeae on *The House of Bernarda Alba* was a revelation. It was a dream that had been over ten years coming when Jenny asked me to play Bernarda. I immediately said yes.

There was the strongest sense of community on entering the rehearsal room. There was excitement and enthusiasm and (as I discovered daily) care, patience, trust, diligence, and joy in creativity over and above that which one usually encounters.

The most striking aspect was encountering a new language: BSL. It was like entering a country I had heard of but now I was going to live there for a couple of months. I was going to soak up the language and its people and try to learn it and communicate with it. Gradually, I began to discover the beauty of BSL which has a very different structure to spoken English, with tremendous poetic potential. It was fascinating to watch Jo Clifford also discover this and re-write her adaptation accordingly. Lorca's poetic language and BSL made very good bedfellows!

There were wonderful inventions. Philippa (playing Amelia) voiced over for Deaf sister Adela (Hermie) but, in the last act, all the speaking daughters spoke for Adela. This was creative licence but spot-on; all the daughters wish to seize Bernarda's stick and break it, though in the original only Adela expresses this desire. By speaking chorally, the daughters in our version became united against their mother; the choral speaking and choral signing gave a dimension of Greek tragedy to the situation that felt both natural and very powerful.

> I discovered through working on *The House of Bernarda Alba* with Graeae that silence is a many-layered country. It became clearer than ever that the spoken word and speech, which has such supremacy in most societies, is only one part of communication. The origin of communication is silence. It's an urge that lives deep in the gut. In BSL, it appears first in the eyes then in the hands and the upper body and face. I was fascinated to see how differently it was used by each person. The read-through was extraordinary, with long silent passages where people signed. Silence—often deemed to be a time when nothing happens— became a country full of atmospheres and events.
>
> We learnt the sign names for each other and gave our characters sign names. This was enormous fun and very useful. I learnt that silence has rhythm and texture. Jenny would watch a scene then comment on whether it was slow or lifeless: she was always right. She could feel the absence of rhythm. On the other hand, I learnt that speed is not always efficient. When Alison and I spoke our dialogue too fast, it left no time for EJ to sign; the languages became garbled. It required a different kind of listening. Listening to the silence of the signs. This was challenging but exhilarating because it required you to communicate with your hearing partner but to have a 'third ear' open to your silent partner who was signing for you and

[Plays Beginning with B + Kathryn Hunter]

the D/deaf audience. It felt that the added ripples of communication made for a richer experience for D/deaf and hearing audiences alike.

EJ, who was playing Bernarda's maid, was signing for Bernarda and we began to enjoy a special relationship over time. If Bernarda was in a bad mood, I would throw her a furious look as she signed, or order her to sign for my Deaf daughters. At other times, we would enjoy a joke together, like sighing with relief that Poncia (the housekeeper) had finally got the message to go away, then a look of exasperation when she returned to continue her endless warnings! We enjoyed this enormously, as did the audience.

I had my doubts about doing a play where women seem to oppress women when Jenny first proposed *The House of Bernarda Alba*. But the themes of *Bernarda Alba* became more vivid doing the show with Graeae. Bernarda locking up her daughters appeared as an act of protection, which many of the disabled actors recognised from their own parents' actions. Bernarda's fear of what people would say also appeared in a different light. Many actors shared experiences of isolation and exclusion and discrimination. Taxi drivers and bus drivers refusing to stop for actors using wheelchairs, rude and condescending comments coming from the so-called 'able-bodied', as if it was their right to do so. It felt that Bernarda was justified on one level, wanting to protect her daughters from these assaults on their dignity.

Jenny and I identified immediately after the read-through which scenes should be signed by Jude (actor/signer). Jenny had a strong feeling from personal experience that, like many speaking mothers with Deaf daughters, Bernarda would punish her daughters by not signing. Then later, when she wants to come closer to her daughter Angustias, she makes a point of signing in order to move closer to her world.

> It was a joy to do this scene with Nadia. Nadia and Jude were such brilliant teachers—and very patient also—that learning BSL was a joy. These scenes were initially captioned but, in the end, Jenny decided it should play uncaptioned. Hearing audiences often picked out this scene as one of their favourites, albeit 'untranslated'. I believe this was because they saw a different kind of communication, which read as mother and daughter sharing as they had not done until that moment and did not need words. In fact, the silence spoke far more eloquently.
>
> The young actress playing Martirio was brilliant. Lorca says that in one scene the mother strikes her daughter. We pondered how to do this— any physical contact was out of the question with Kellan's delicate back. What we found was that the constraint opened a far more potent language: I raised my stick and threatened to hit my daughter. The terror she expressed was much more frightening than any literal physical violence.
>
> Finally, to the last scene. This is where the youngest daughter Adela, believing her lover Pepe to be dead, hangs herself in despair. Bernarda commands her daughters to be silent (Bernarda's first word is SILENCE and her last word, SILENCE).

[Plays Beginning with B + Kathryn Hunter]

She instructs that her daughter be let down, dressed in white, as a virgin. She forbids weeping in public. 'Save your tears for when you are alone. We will all drown in a sea of mourning. Silence,' she repeats. 'Silence, I said silence.'

> Jenny and I agreed that, as the funeral bells rang, I would speak Bernarda's last words then sign them. The bells would signal to the non-sighted audience that the play was not finished yet. Action was always incorporated into the text so that non-sighted audiences could picture what was happening; Jenny felt wearing headsets was alienating from the theatrical experience. Frankie Armstrong and other blind practitioners were also feeding in their responses as to clarity throughout the rehearsal process. Access was always a priority during the process which made rehearsals very intense and demanding but hugely rewarding.

> Working with Graeae has changed my perception of what communication is and can be. It has changed my perception of what silence is. I have a very strong memory of each night as I signed the last word of the play 'SILENCE': the silence widened and deepened and spread beyond, into, and around the audience at the Royal Exchange Theatre, above and beyond into the city, beyond Manchester, a widening, deepening, largely unknown country ... still to be explored.

> In my next production, Untouchable, I had the pleasure to again work with Nadia and again, many of the cast members learnt BSL for the show. Once again, I saw actors and audiences enriched by the experience of what was a new language to many.

Working with Graeae, I met actors that are so gifted yet often excluded from the so-called mainstream. It strikes me that any kind of exclusion only makes us poorer—inclusion makes us richer by far.

> **I am extremely grateful to Jenny and Graeae for my experiences on *The House of Bernarda Alba* which I believe has changed my perspective of theatre and its possibilities.**

Alison Halstead

Actor

I have now worked with Graeae four times within my professional career. It is Graeae that gave me the opportunity to play two of the meatiest roles of my career. Full, satisfying, challenging roles. Sensual and sexual. Flawed and fierce and powerful. Lots of language. So much stage time. I am an actor who constantly plays, listening and following my instincts. And within the Graeae rehearsal process, I have tons of room to go, go, and go.

Not all of the rehearsal process works for me. When we are asked to play games, I'd rather be working on the real text. When we are drawing pictures of our faces or peering into a mirror, I'd kill to be on my feet and looking at a scene. However, I honour the space and commit to all that's asked of me to the best of my ability.

There is such humanity within a Graeae production. Gorgeous and diverse and challenging and awesome. I am a member of a richly represented company when working with them.

Because I only work with D/deaf actors when working with Graeae, I have to re-learn what's required to honour actors who are not me, a hearing performer. The tentative, delicate, and sometimes testy beginnings of discovering what's needed to tell the story in the best way with a specific group of people—just like any company of artists.

An actor took off her prosthesis on stage in the last production in which I performed. A short-statured actor, heavily relying on two canes, walked into the space. Witnessing something that I rarely see ... the stump, the different gait ... I was honored. It takes guts to let oneself be seen in such a public arena. I got to see the beauty in their vulnerability and fragility. I challenge myself to be as vulnerable and exposed as possible in my art. Working with Graeae affords me the opportunity to continue that exploration. On stage, risking and revealing. Living fully in myself, offering my difference, being fully human.

Graeae not only asks their artists to risk, but also their audiences. Asks those watching to sit with any discomfort because they might be seeing or hearing something new/different/rare. And then to trust.

Graeae makes work for all—accessible. By hiring non-disabled, D/deaf actors and performers and artists, the story being told is for everyone. And actors and audiences alike can know that they are being seen, represented, and reflected. Honoured for who they are. Human beings.

[Plays Beginning with B + Alison Halstead]

Jenny Sealey
Sofie Layton
Lewis Gibson

Jez Scarratt
Grant Mouldey
Willie Elliott

**Outdoor
Work**

Dr. Tina Carter
Dawn Langley
Jenny Sealey

Jenny Sealey

CEO/Artistic Director, Graeae Theatre

People Beginning with B

If plays like *Bent* and *Blasted*, and countries like Brazil and Bangladesh, have had an impact on Graeae, then it is the man Bradley Hemmings who has had the most profound impact on the company. As artistic director of the Greenwich+Docklands International Festival, London's leading outdoor performing arts festival, Bradley is a genius at fostering artistic collaborations as well as supporting and challenging artists to take new risks.

Bradley inspired us to be brave enough to step out from the safety of the black box theatre and into the outdoor arena. He was intrigued by how the intricate weavings of Graeae's access-focused process could be presented in the outdoor setting where visual storytelling, soundscape, and a sparsity of spoken language are foundational. This curiosity combined with thoughts about audience seating and backup plans for weather conditions, were all part of his territory and our overall baptism of fire. Our earliest commission from him was also to be our first ever collaboration with Strange Fruit, an Australian sway pole company who use four metre long bendy poles topped with perches for actors to balance on (strapped in of course) and swirl and swish in the sky. The show, *The Medal Ceremony*, was born out of the news that London had won the bid to host the Olympic and Paralympic Games in 2012. It had three sway pole performers, three Deaf Graeae actors, and a soundscape which featured recordings of *Small Town Boy*, *Young Gifted and Black*, and a cover version of *Feeling Good* sung by Karli Perkins from Heart n Soul. It was show of physical and signed prowess and had a certain charm, though little did we know this foray into the world of medals and ceremonies would have a different reality further down the line.

When D/deaf and disabled artists watching the show asked whether they could be a pole performer, Strange Fruit were initially sceptical. I react strongly when people assume we cannot do something before we have been given the opportunity to try! So, we quickly secured funding to set up a circus training initiative with National Centre for Circus Arts (then Circus Space). The main rationale we gave at the time was that we needed to start training artists in preparation for 2012.

Tina Carter (AirHeadz) and Lindsey Butcher (Gravity and Levity) led the training. Their brief was to not only to introduce aerial skills to D/deaf and disabled people but also to educate Circus Space tutors on inclusive practice and adaptive methodology. The training included silks, hoops, static trapeze, rope, and intense body conditioning work. It was with an attitude that everything is possible and through mutual support that we created a space of shared exploration. We adapted conventional ways of training to make the various pieces of circus kit work for the diversity of bodies in the room. Sway pole training came next, led by Strange Fruit artistic director Sue Broadway and founder member Grant Mouldey. It was a brutal process but all twelve artists successfully climbed the poles.

The training initiative included a new audio description strand for people interested in this area of work. The course was run by Alex Bulmer and Willie Elliott and focused on developing the language of circus performance. Each participant was assigned the task of describing the short final solo performances by the aerial trainees.

Bradley commissioned three more sway pole productions from Graeae and with great insight suggested new sites as inspiration for the productions. The first, *Against the Tide*, was devised by the company and set against the backdrop of the Thames river in Greenwich. The show told the story of a land without water and was our first production exploring the impact of climate change.

●   *Against the Tide* An engaging band of pirate-like individuals living in the desert lamented the loss of water and, with it, memory. They played games and told stories, sung and signed. The text was lyrical and compact, and each image was a gift: a bird was a man pulling a carriage of copper wings; a ship's sail became the wedding veil of a bride marrying a seaman; a washing line of clothes was packed away and sent to sea as love and family are lost. Excerpt from review:

'The rhythm of the swaying poles, mounted by both Strange Fruit performers and the Graeae cast, found its analogue in the rhythm of waves, the rhythm of speech/signing, and the loss of memory and its return. It was an incredibly beautiful visual piece; on the Friday I saw the performance it was an extraordinary day—the sky was blue and the clouds white, the hot and cold colours of the costumes vibrant and clear, the men and women atop their poles in positions of grace. I caught a little of it again the next day in the evening, having spent an hour of the afternoon hiding in Greenwich Market from an intense thunderstorm, water pouring in from outside and up from the overflowed drains. When the character Flo recounted her birth during a huge storm the crowd thought it was funny but there was a little extra electricity, too, from the close memory of the violence of nature. When I left that performance midway through, it seemed to be headed somewhere sadder and darker.

Running the length of human emotion and experience—and with music from orchestral strings to Dolly Parton—*Against the Tide* was a terrific success. It was a big adventurous step forward from where Strange Fruit had been the last time I had seen them, performing *The Field* at Greenwich+Docklands International Festival in 2007. The show was a great example of two companies combining their different skills in a way that concealed the join.'

www.sideshow-circusmagazine.com/index.php/reviews/
22-strange-fruit-a-graeae-against-the-tide

● **The Garden** *The Garden* by Alex Bulmer was set in the deconsecrated graveyard of St Alfege Church in Greenwich. A site visit with a detailed audio guide for Alex gave us time to explore the clashing world of the ancient tombstones and the story of life still there: the young couple eating their sandwiches, an old person drinking Special Brew, the condoms, needles, and flowers popping their petals through cracks in the gravestone. Alex wrote a parable about The Keepers of the Garden—a band of people who collect the stories of those who have passed but died in limbo and need their stories to be told before they can rest. The show was performed not only in St Alfege Church but also at the Southbank Centre, London in 2012 and Rio de Janeiro in 2016 with a mixed UK and Brazilian cast, creative team, and crew.

Willie Elliott's audio description notes for *The Garden*, performed outside the Royal Festival Hall, September 2012

'Welcome to this audio described performance of *The Garden* by Alex Bulmer, a co-production between Graeae Theatre Company and Strange

Fruit which is presented in a combination of English and British Sign Language. It has been directed by Jenny Sealey and Grant Mouldey. The performance lasts for approximately twenty-five minutes and the live audio description will be given by Willie Elliott.

Strange Fruit, from Australia, create innovative street theatre using sway poles. These five-metre-high flexible carbon fibre poles stand on huge weighted tripods. The performers haul themselves up hand over hand to the top and stand on footrests with their legs strapped in around the thigh. Just leaning forward or back sways the pole in any direction and when they release their feet, they can lie horizontally forward or backward.

A tribe of shamanistic storytellers, the Keepers, while still honouring the storytellers of the past, seek out stories from new sources to be shared and planted in their garden. They transform into characters from the new stories, including flowers, birds, and fish. The Keepers wear different coloured floor length duster coats of the type first worn by Victorian ladies in motor cars, with a large floral patchwork pocket and matching high collar. The coats are black or different shades of blue and grey and flow to the ground giving the keepers an ethereal quality when they move. They almost glide, heads held high, which belies the strength required in ascending the poles with apparently little effort. To aid movement and climbing, the front corners of their coats can be folded back like the petals of a flower and buttoned, revealing a triangle of silk lining in a complimentary colour. At the tops of the poles they dive and soar back and forth with their coat tails beating, like a flock of unearthly birds.

Three new storytellers share their tales: a young man, Gibson, has short hair and wears blue and white striped flannelette pyjamas; a Japanese woman, Lavinia, in a white organza wedding dress with a pattern of delicate leaves; and an olive skinned man, Rui, with grey cotton trousers, a brown jacket, and a black fedora hat. Once their stories have been shared, they are presented with a coat of their own. Their titles are written on the back in a sweeping script, Keeper of Time; Keeper of Dreams, Names, and History; Keeper of Hope, Learning and Possibility.

There is a cast of seven, four women and three men, and all bar one work on the sway poles at various points throughout the piece.

The Garden is a magical space for the imagination. Everything is brightly coloured and much larger than life, miniaturising the performers to the size of small animals or insects as they climb the stems of flowers, or creep over the edges of the lawn. *The Garden* is fifteen metres across by ten deep.

In the middle is a raised stage four and a half metres wide by four metres deep. It's overhung with a grassy green cloth imprinted with pink, black, and white flowers, making it look like a lawn. The lawn rises from chest height at the front to head height at the back, where it's accessed via an unseen ladder.

A sway pole stands at each of the four corners. The poles at the rear are around a metre higher than those at the front. Affixed to the top of each pole is a huge flower head a meter in diameter making them look like giant colourful plants. In the back-left and near-right poles are white petalled daisies fringed with pink. Each has a yellow ball of pollen in the middle, sparkling with tiny mirrors. The daisy at the back has a sapling attached to the bottom of it and a metre-long blade of grass is attached to the one at the front.

The back-right pole has a yellow dandelion with finger like petals shooting outward and the front-left pole has a dandelion flower that has gone to seed; now a white feathery ball.

[Outdoor Work + Jenny Sealey]

There are two Victorian metal framed double beds, painted black, incongruously set a metre from the stage on either side. A black metal tree sprouts from the head of each bed with luggage labels attached to the branches that flutter in the breeze. On the right, an earthy brown satchel hangs in the branches beside two coats awaiting new owners. Another coat hangs in the tree on the left. In place of a mattress each bed has a solid wooden floor covered with matching grass green sheets. On the right, three musicians, also wearing black coats, sit on the bed in chairs. There is a man who plays cello, a woman who plays trombone and saxophones and a male trumpeter. To the right of the bed, surrounded by drums, gongs, and cymbals is another man, The Keeper of Song, who sings into a microphone and plays violin as well as a couple of home-made instruments. These are two wood blocks, one with dowels sticking up that he strikes with a beater and one with the chimes from inside a grandfather clock, creating eerie bell-like sounds when he strokes them with the violin bow. Three large bell jars hang on a stand and, when tapped with a beater, ring out a deep bell-like boom.

All around the space, old fruit boxes have been planted with brightly coloured flowers, transforming the grey concrete of the South Bank centre into a world of green with splashes of yellow, pink and white.

A group of musicians wearing long coats take their places and begin to play.'

●   **The Limbless Knight** The third sway pole commission came after 2012 when we not only had a cohort of twenty trained sway pole performers to cast from and the war veterans from the training introduced us to other disabled veterans who were interested in working with Graeae.

Performance artist Mark Storor and Sofie Layton and I led on an intensive R&D period with six men, two of whom had previously worked on the 2012 games and four new men. The core component of the project was a sculpture made of slate that contained written statements from the men, 'it is better to come back dead than disabled', 'it was not your fault', 'my life book is burnt but it can be rewritten'. I asked the veterans to write a narrative of their wartime experiences as if telling a fairy tale to a small child. When Bradley Hemmings asked me to create a response to the centenary anniversary of Stravinsky's *The Right of Spring*, Steve Gill's story of *The Limbless Knight* became the title and lead narrative of our new piece.

The theme of sacrifice within Stravinsky's most famous work could not have been more poignant at a time when D/deaf and disabled people were being held up as a sacrificial lamb by the government who were and (at the time of writing) continue to cut away benefits and the right to live independently. Cards were handed out to the audience who were encouraged to give their answer to the question, 'what does it mean to be alive?'

The Limbless Knight devised text and William Elliot's audio description (AD).

Extract One

AD: *From all around the space, men and women step into the performance area beneath the tower.*

They stand posed and upright dressed in monochrome, uniform greys and blues, spread evenly throughout the space.

A soldier steps forward with the sign language interpreter.

Two other soldiers sit on the right of the tower.

The soldier at the mic hands a card to an audience member who reads from it.

[Outdoor Work + Jenny Sealey]

VOICES My Name is Amit. These are the words we wanted when we are children.

My name is Sophie. Article 12. We wanted them to have the right to have their say and to have their views taken seriously.

My name is Vikki. Article 23. We wanted disabled children to have the right to live a full and decent life with dignity and independence and to play an active part in the community.

My Name is Angie Article 27. We wanted the right to a standard of living that meets their physical, social and mental needs.

My Name is Liz. Article 28. We wanted the right to an education.

My Name is Grant. Article 41. We wanted the right to relax and play.

My Name is Lewis. That was our past. What was our future?.

AD: *They go and sit on the left of the tower, as the others move in their own space.*

The Queen rises to the very top of the tower to address us.

Extract Two

QUEEN Once upon a time in a world that was equal there was a glorious Knight and his beautiful Queen. The Knight had had his limbs severed to save his Queen and country. But in time it was she who would need to save him because she had been deemed too costly a burden.

A costly burden.

She had been deemed a costly burden.

And so for him she was prepared to die.

AD: *The blood red hem of a giant version of the Queen's dress is lowered, curtaining the tower, symbolising a leap to her death.*

Her subjects demonstrate from far below, calling for her to make the ultimate sacrifice.

The dress falls.

Two soldiers step forward.

They fold the dress, like the folding of a flag at a military funeral.

They went with songs to the battle, they were young.

Straight of limb, true of eyes, steady and aglow.

They were staunch to the end against odds uncounted,

They fell with their faces to the foe.

They shall not grow old, as we that are left grow old.

Age shall not weary them as the years condemn.

At the going down of the sun and in the morning,

We will remember them.

They place the dress into a metal case.

Mik Scarlet @MikScarlet21 Jun
@graeae @GDIF #LimblessKnight – Amazing. Like being hit by a brick wrapped in a beautiful velvet cushion.

[Outdoor Work + Jenny Sealey]

● **The Iron Man** In between sway pole productions, I went to Bradley with one of my favourite books, *The Iron Man* by Ted Hughes and convinced him that a family show was needed at Greenwich+Docklands International Festival. The story is, at heart, a disability fable about difference, acceptance, and forgiveness. Hogarth is a young boy who does not judge; he befriends the Iron Man and helps him to belong. A Deaf actor played Hogarth and a beautiful authentic communication between Hogarth and the Iron Man emerged. They made sounds, signed, and gestured to each other, their desire to understand each other cemented in the truth they were both sidelined by society.

Paul Sirett adapted the book, ensuring that all the audio description was embedded within the text but, where more detailed audio description was needed, Mr. Chapman (the scrapyard owner) would have his own private conversation with blind audiences.

This was a story that would need a bloody great big puppet that was ...

HOGARTH Taller than a double-decker bus.

CHAPMAN With a head like a giant bucket-thing.

ANDREA   Eyes like car headlights.

CHAPMAN One of his arms is a massive spanner.

FRAN   Half his body is all corrugated and rusty.

CHAPMAN One leg is made from shiny steel.

ANDREA   And on the other side is a huge wheel.

CHAPMAN 5 metres tall!

ANDREA 5.1 metres tall ...

FRAN 16 feet and 2 inches tall.

ALL The Iron Man!

The Iron Man puppet was designed by Sofie Layton and built by Mike Pattison and Tony Mason from power chair components so a wheelchair user could operate it. David Toole was the first actor to operate it with Milton Lopes manoeuvring his arms. David could transfer from chair to other areas of the set, walking around on his arms. When we revived the show we cast Thom Jackson, who does not transfer, so a total redesign was necessary to ensure Thom had access in and around the playing space.

The Iron Man puppet being taller than a double decker bus presented unique challenges but designing a Space Bat to be 'bigger than Australia' was something else entirely. We made the decision to make a giant head with one giant wing, which were each placed far apart to attempt to indicate the scale. A second puppet in the shape of a flying glove puppet, landed on a yellow balloon to create the illusion of the Space Bat draped over the sun. This experimentation in scale almost worked. Amit Sharma, directing the revival, had the simple but inspired idea of only being able to hear the Space Bat speak or fly so we could play with scales of volume and distance. The sound level was portrayed for a D/deaf audience by the physical reactions of the other characters and by Jude Mahon's signing.

The Iron Man is a much-treasured part of our repertory and we continue to use its narrative to frame issues about disability when training teachers, and people working in the private sector. We have plans for the Iron Man himself to return in 2021, starring in a new work in development, *The Iron Woman*.

[Outdoor Work + Jenny Sealey]

● In 2012 our associate director Amit Sharma decided to go even bigger with the production of **Prometheus Awakes.**

Audiences felt the earth move and the sky explode as an eight metre high Prometheus rose from the ground and created fire and humanity in defiance of the god Zeus. Created in collaboration with Catalan masters of visual magnificence, *La Fura dels Baus*, *Prometheus Awakes* inspired audiences with extraordinary stagecraft, giant puppets, mass choreography and special effects. Disabled and non-disabled performers recruited from London boroughs and local towns took to the air in this thrilling piece of outdoor theatre both as part of the main cast and as volunteers for an audience of thousands. *Prometheus Awakes* was Graeae's first experiment with volunteers, cranes, human nets, and projection onto buildings.

'There are no limitations here, just glorious liberation.'
—Lyn Gardner, *The Guardian*

'This is street theatre at its best: epic, emotive and full of surprises.'
—Jake Orr, *A Younger Theatre*

'Not only did [the audio description] signpost relevant information but it was delivered in a poetical style.'
—Colin Hambrook, *Disability Arts Online*

'A visual feast executed by a daring, creative and enthusiastic cast.'
—Catherine Usher, *The Stage*

● Our next venture is **This is Not for You** by Mike Kenny. It is a *14-18 Now* commission with additional funding from the Gulbenkian Foundation and BLESMA (British Limbless Ex Service Men Association).

The title is taken from the experience of a veteran who was wheeling towards The Cenotaph on Remembrance Day when someone shouted, 'this is not for you, it is for the dead'. The production is in memory of the two million veterans who came back disabled from WW1 and the many more veterans disabled in the many wars since then. It is a memorial for the living.

Disabled veterans and professional performers will premier *This is Not for You* at Greenwich+Docklands International Festival in June/July, 2018.

> This is for the ones
> Who did return
> Who though forgotten
> Could not forget
> Whose presence
> Was an absence
> Surrounded by silence
> Their war inside.
> And this is for the world
> To which they came
> All changed
> Nothing the same.

[Outdoor Work + Jenny Sealey]

Integrating accessibility into open-air performance can be challenging but, ultimately, outdoor theatre is a glorious equalizer. It serves to democratise the art form because it is free and open. More than in any other type of space, creating outdoor theatre for all people must, by its nature, be accessible. Thank you Bradley Hemmings for giving Graeae a plethora of new platforms for our work and for being there for us.

Sofie Layton

Designer

Working as a designer for Graeae's outdoor, site-specific productions has been a privilege. I remember Jenny Sealey and I first meeting one snowy January in my living room to discuss *Against the Tide*. We had this extraordinary rollercoaster conversation that conjured up a narrative and took me on a journey into the beautiful world of sign language, movement, and physical uniqueness.

This was the first of what became a series of amazing conversations that has so far lead me to design five collaborative, outdoor, site-sensitive shows where any preconceptions of what might restrict a disabled performer within set design, puppetry, and costume design were constantly challenged and became integral to the design process.

Visually, the body became a canvas for sign language. I was made aware through discussion with Jenny that over patterned and striped fabrics would make it difficult for the audience to read the performers' gestures and that the length and cut of the sleeves should enhance a signed movement, not become a distraction. *Against the Tide* was set originally against the River Thames with an open backdrop of river and sky. Here, using bright, bold, block colours would make the performers stand out against the open skies.

The collaboration with Strange Fruit, which required planning for sway poles, became another design exploration drawing on years of experimentation with puppetry and object manipulation. The sway poles became masts of a ship before being transformed into supports for a washing line. Each performer brought their own unique physicality to the sway pole which, in turn, meant that the design had to evolve to accommodate these nuances.

> These design explorations were developed further in the setting of *The Garden*, originally set in the deconsecrated churchyard of St Alfege Church, London, among gravestones and with a backdrop of lush green trees. The set was a giant raked bed that transformed from a symbolic flowerbed with pre-set giant flowers that could be animated, into a four-poster marital bed with canopy and later stripped back to a bare ticking mattress. One of the stories was of a boy played by Daryl Beeton. While most performers stood on platforms on top of the poles, Daryl would swing around his pole, sometimes even appearing to fly off it. In *The Garden*, the boy hides under a giant dandelion flower head—Daryl's performance brought tension and a feeling of danger to the role. This re-focusing of the way the flowers were animated by the performers became a part of the choreographic movement and story development.
>
> We re-staged *The Garden* at the Southbank Centre, London in 2012 as part of the Cultural Olympiad. The backdrop was now concrete and the green landscape had to be re-envisioned. We grew a garden of herbs and flowers in earth-filled fruit boxes with strange plants under glass cloches and bell jars on tables. This gave a different dynamic to

the piece. It was now a garden of inhabitants and vegetation that were literally growing through the concrete cracks in city, redefining site-sensitive performance.

The piece evolved again in 2016 when we were invited by the British Council to take *The Garden* to Rio de Janeiro as part of the Paralympic Games in Brazil. I am a very hands-on designer; the aesthetic of a piece is conceived, loosely sketched, and then brought to life with a team of artists and makers who literally seed, draw, sew, print, and grow the elements of the show. So, the prospect of re-creating the staging a third time for new performers with different disabilities and physicalities, for whom we needed to adapt the existing costume designs, was challenging.

In addition, we needed to have the set and props re-built in Rio de Janeiro as the original set was too heavy to ship. This all added to the challenge of making it work on a shoestring budget. To add to this further, I broke my heel ten days before I was due to fly out and could only move on crutches or using a wheelchair. I am not sure I would have had the courage to attempt this journey and the workload had it not been for the support of Graeae. My access needs were met and humbly, as an honorary temporarily disabled member of the team, I set off for Rio (teased ruthlessly by the company members).

The challenge of working with the Brazilian team of makers who translated the designs in their own ways was interesting and, even though I had sent scaled drawings, I discovered on arrival some things were slightly lost in translation. However,

[Outdoor Work + Sofie Layton]

we were working with an amazing Brazilian producer and her wonderful team of designer-makers alongside a team of students, which made me feel very supported. They took me to flower markets at 5 am to buy flowers, fruit boxes, and soil with which to transform the newly opened Praça Mauá (the old slave trading port) into our new 'garden' performance space. The new set worked well after a steep learning curve for the prop makers, who had not understood that a flower made of steel wire would look beautiful on the set but was impossible to animate on top of a sway pole, particularly if you were visually impaired. The dandelion also changed form from a giant sway pole flower to an extraordinary hat worn by Stephen Bunce, who brought a humour and wonder to the role of the boy as he removed both of his prosthetic legs and filled them with soil and flowers.

Our first show was at 10 am, set to coincide with the Paralympic Games opening events. The show had an extraordinary audience of nearly 1,000 people, even at this early hour. People of all ages had gathered in the square and they embraced the piece with respect, empathy, and humour. An old woman in tears talked about the transformative nature of the performance and how important it was for the people of Rio to experience another worlds and realities.

Creating designs that work with the uniqueness and physical differences of the performer has been central to design development with Graeae; probably the most challenging and thrilling was developing The Iron Man originally written by Ted Hughes. I was tasked with conceiving a set, costume, and puppetry design that allowed this amazing story to be told by a company of disabled performers in an outdoor street theatre setting.

Having worked on a lot of outdoor theatre, I knew that the large Iron Man puppet would have to be at least five meters tall (bigger than a double-decker bus) to make any sort of impact outdoors. This in itself became a technical challenge as weight, wind, and the ability to tour this giant figure were essential to the remit of the project.

> *The Iron Man* was conceptually designed to be created from found objects: oil cans, aluminium conduit, and mesh; different metallic surfaces moving parts that were asymmetrical. A rebuilt figure assembled with a wheel for a leg. Working with engineer Mike Patterson, puppet-maker Tony Mason, and performers with different disabilities, we did a lot of object manipulation to help inform the design's functionality and the quality of the puppets. A single leg of the Iron Man appears in the show, looking for its body; its movement comes from the rotation of the wheelchair's wheel. Tony also created a giant moving hand that crawled along the ground like a giant crab. The hand's movement was developed to be used specifically by Alison, who is of small stature and beautifully manipulated the hand puppet, playing it like an organ grinder. Two versions of the Iron Man puppet were finally created which explored the scale of the Iron Man (particularly important in relation to the Space Bat Angel Dragon). A sixty-centimetre Bunraku (a traditional Japanese style of puppet) operated by two performers opened the show, then the deconstructed body parts came to life before revealing the giant five-meter high mechanical puppet. The giant Iron Man raised up from behind the set and was literally bigger than

[Outdoor Work + Sofie Layton]

a double-decker bus. Mike created the mechanism from motorised wheelchair parts and the puppet's movements were controlled by two performers: David Toole and Milton Lopes.

I have a practice as an artist in addition to my work as a designer with Graeae. Over the past five years, I have begun to explore the role of the artist within the medical landscape. I began a conversation with Jenny in 2013 which emerged out of *Bedside Manner*, a residency at Guy's and St Thomas' hospital where I worked with parents of sick children. The piece explored the parental space of nurture and care in a hospital setting. It also opened up a plethora of questions about the invisible and visible nature of disability and disease; the reality that some children and some people's lives are not as long as others. How do we, as parents, celebrate those precious— though shortened lives. I was awarded funding by ACE and the Blavatnik Family Foundation in 2014 for a project which explored these stories. *Rest* was an R&D project that explored end of life and was developed with Graeae and SLOW, a charity working with bereaved parents. Jenny and I worked with the bereaved mothers through workshops; we explored ways of remembering and created screen printed images of our children that created a universal legacy for those whose lives do not follow a classically prescribed trajectory.

How do we treat the end of life; the medical, ethical, and emotional issues associated with palliative care? Stories differently lived; memories of those who are not physically, but are emotionally, present. I am looking forward to continuing to collaborate with Jenny on Rest and to continue the journey of how Graeae makes you see things differently.

[Outdoor Work + Sofie Layton]

Lewis Gibson
Composer and Theatre-Maker

I have written the music and designed the sound for a good number of Graeae shows since around the start of this millennia. There always seems to be a collaboration of some sort boiling away and I very much consider myself a cub of the great, warm, kind and determinedly tenacious beast that is the Graeae family.

Making work with the same people over a number of years can lead to a deep understanding of each other, shortcuts to a shared language, a symbiosis of visions and of course the most fantastic implosions. As each project ends, its ideas, like leaves, are blown around and it then falls to the ground, making mulch for the next one, then becoming foundation earth, then a seam far below. Eventually, as these seams are piled on top of one another over time, you might be lucky enough for some of the thoughts, experiences and friendships to be compressed into tiny rough diamonds. Here are mine:

Because Graeae's work is always constructed with accessibility in its DNA, sound is given space and consideration on a par with the visual messaging. This is surprisingly rare in conventional theatre. A key component of my role involves trying to tell the story with sound, to help locate the movement of people and things, to represent what is happening visually without repeating it. One should always avoid putting a hat on a hat. I have attached portable speakers to performers, and put car stereos in giant puppets so the soundtrack literally tracks their movements, made and played new instruments constructed from the same elements of the set (glass cloches, metal poles) so you hear what is being seen, developed whole musical scores around character motifs and always tried to allow space for the text and silence and to keep it all as simple as possible. My sign name is 'simple'. As Jenny is Deaf, she has had to learn to trust my sonic instincts and I have had to learn to be aware of all things aural for her. This has really honed my listening skills, and I pay much more attention to actors' rhythms and timbres than I would have done otherwise. The collaboration is much richer and interwoven because of this. Trust is a true fundament of the Graeae process.

For all of their politically correct rhetoric, artists are usually terrible listeners. Creative meetings can be a chaotic cacophony of voices all racing towards an idea. This can be thrilling, but there is often collateral damage. Quieter voices are trampled on, key thoughts devoured without acknowledgement. Graeae meetings are different. Because usually everything is being translated in or out of BSL, you have to wait till someone has finished and then the translation to be completed before you can respond. This can take some getting used to, but it has the advantage of making you actually listen to whole thoughts, and to consider them properly. I have seen the most incredible ideas grow from the smallest of seed notions because of this process. During our exploits in Brazil, the translation game became a fantastic ritual of its own. English would be spoken, then translated into BSL, Brazilian Portuguese and LIBRA (Brazilian sign language),

[Outdoor Work + Lewis Gibson]

then reversed in response etc etc. It was in itself a testament to making access and communication a two way street. The loud and the boorish have always occupied too much of our attention and it certainly seems to be the case in our current political landscape. Theatre can shine a light on more delicate and diverse ideas, and so it should.

> I have met many extraordinary individuals through my times with Graeae and made some really cracking theatre. Memories that persist include my time with Amit making a version of *The Iron Man* in Albania with local D/deaf and disabled artists and spending days with a blind drummer who, despite having a kit that was falling apart and very little experience managed to learn a full on score and give an awesome performance to a massive outdoor crowd in Tirana. Another is when I met a brilliant young man in Rio whilst running a workshop. I was using rubbed wine glasses filled with water to create a sonic texture and he played them with his toes. It was just a delightful image.
>
> Sometimes, after spending days and weeks within the company of Graeae artists, I find that the outside world can seem strange and bland. I miss the expression of hands communicating in the air, I miss the particular sound of D/deaf voices, I miss the diversity of body shapes and sizes (I have even imagined meromelia that is not there). But most of all I miss the laughter, the love, and the determination to make good shit happen.
>
> **Thank you Graeae.**

Jez Scarratt

Actor

I go back to 2012, when I entered The Gin Stills at Three Mills Studios, London. There were a few people, all strangers to me, going about the business of putting people in a harness and winching them up some fifteen feet. They then gave instructions on how to somersault forwards and backwards. Some found it easier than others. I loved it and, as I stepped out of the body harness, said to myself, 'well that felt good, almost like I'd done it before'. We had to do a series of other ground-based exercises to demonstrate core strength and then that was my audition done. I had given it my best chance.

And I made it. There I was, a fifty-three-year-old below the knee amputee, a former Royal Marine and endurance cyclist being trained to be a performer in the London 2012 Paralympic Games Opening Ceremony (POC).

The six-week boot camp in a bespoke tent at Circus Space was brutal but, having been a Royal Marine for fifteen years, I understood and liked the discipline of being pushed and told what I had to do. I enjoyed being supportive to the younger lads who were not as comfortable with their prosthetics as I am with mine.

A blonde woman and a tall gent watched as we were training hard. They were smiling and looking up quizzically at us lot sweating away, talking to our guru Tina Carter who led the training. They were Jenny Sealey and Bradley Hemmings— the ceremony directors.

After the training ended, we had to specialise in either aerial or sway pole—a four-foot bendy pole that requires strong arms and, in my case, a strong leg to climb. Stephen Bunce, who is a double amputee, had to rely on his arms only!

By August 2012 I was a very competent user of this amazing piece of equipment. I started to develop an understanding of choreography and performance technique and learnt how to shift physically and emotionally between the different elements of the narrative—soft and graceful for *Bird Girl* and totally punk for *Spasticus Autisticus*.

Being a part of this amazing POC was just superb, an experience I will never forget, a one-off occasion where I met many lifelong friends. It was also my introduction to Jenny who has since inspired and pushed me onwards in my life, allowing me to be here today still working with Graeae!

An idea grew from a spark to a raging flame in 2013 that involved myself and other disabled veterans talking about the experience of coming back from action disabled. This was the first time for all of us that we had really opened up about this topic and from those discussions emerged *The Limbless Knight*—a story asking what it's like being alive AND disabled. I was extremely happy to be back on my sway pole!

I was part of the Graeae team working with Rio de Janeiro circus company Crescer e Viver in 2014, sharing our learning from 2012 with people new to circus. My solo was on the hoop, which was out of my comfort zone as it is tough on your arms and hands (with the sway pole you only have to manage one climb, after that your arms are free). We premiered *Belonging* at the Roundhouse circus festival, then performed in Rio. We also had the honour to open the circus festival in São Paulo.

2016 arrives, the year of Brazil Olympic and Paralympic Games. I find myself in Rio, back on the sway pole, performing a revival of *The Garden* as part of Rio's Cultural Olympiad. We were astounded by the emotional responses of the Brazilian audiences and it was an extraordinary sight, seeing 1,000 people all making the sign for turtle!

I appreciate that I'll never be a big player in the life of cinema, theatre, or performance. But one thing I can assure you, I now love what I do. It is hard work for me, it does not come naturally. But as time goes by, I'm gradually feeling more comfortable in my skin and, with each show, I am becoming a better performer.

So thank you, Jenny Sealey.

[Outdoor Work + Jez Scarratt]

Grant Mouldey

Associate Director, Strange Fruit

Sway Pole Work with Graeae

We started to work with a diverse group at Circus Space. Gradually understanding how differently each practitioner could access and then control the sway pole. It is always difficult for people to approach the sway pole apparatus. The work is subtle and requires a lot of trust in order to make the learning work, to enable the counter-intuitive ways a sway pole rider has to work and to be relaxed while flying through the air. The D/deaf practitioners took very quickly to the poles—Daryl Jackson and David Ellington almost instantly making the work their own. This ease with the apparatus was incredibly valuable as we started to include BSL in the work, extending sign gesture and form into the framework of a dance.

We worked hard to find a way for Daryl Beeton to be able to control the apparatus. The structure of the harness requires leg strength which made it difficult for Daryl, despite his agility and body strength. After several failed prototypes, we found a way for Daryl to control the pole with just one wrist in a hand-loop for his security while sitting near the top. His agility and dynamism were finally able to work. There were plenty of tears in the room when Daryl finally made the apparatus work. As the poles rely heavily on timing to make patterning work we discovered that, given the distribution of his weight on the poles, he was able to work in double-time against the other practitioners who were riding the sway poles in harnesses. This was a great piece of freedom for us as we made more work. By ensuring we could free the practitioner's work on the apparatus, we discovered differences in rhythm and timings that were new to the work and made the patterning and choreography so much more intense and dynamic.

A woman called Ali was the first visually impaired person to ride a sway pole. She described the immense freedom of space: how negotiating space on the ground requires encountering boundaries for blind people but the experience of flying through the air, knowing you would never come across any obstacle (except perhaps another sway pole rider), was an incredible spatial freedom. Amelia Cavallo and Jonny Whitwell also spoke of this sense of freedom in space and it was evident in the way they worked the pole during rehearsals for the London 2012 Paralympic Games Opening Ceremony (POC). Both Amelia and Jonny are musicians and understood the rhythm of the work. They heard the positions of neighbouring poles in space and led the choreography with everyone else looking to them for cues. Both started working without safety harnesses very quickly. They won every argument regarding their safety because they knew with absolute certainty the pathway into the harness by feel. It all translated into a real fearlessness with the apparatus. Jonny was able to circle at such speed that he could feel the 200kg apparatus base begin to move. We used Jonny's super-speed circles in creating several sequences; so intense was this speed that several poles disintegrated their outer coating and had to be replaced.

[Outdoor Work + Grant Mouldey]

There were challenges with the amputees in the group: how do they get into the harness? Each performer had the task of climbing the pole and then finding a way into the harness with their prosthetics, depending on the nature of their amputation. This was quite straightforward for Jez Scarratt and Joe Bell, but still not without some physically extraordinary moments as we slowly 'mapped' the way in and out of the harness, taking into consideration the prosthetic.

Sean was intending to perform with his full-leg chrome prosthetic. But we could not find a way for Sean to climb with this prosthetic intact. After many attempts, we had the idea to cable-tie Sean's chrome leg onto the pole and have him climb into the harness with the prosthetic already attached to it. He succeeded in climbing and attaching his leg straightaway. His chrome leg, proudly sitting atop the pole and waiting for its owner, was a magnificent sight and one we showed to advantage again when we got to work with Sean in *The Limbless Knight*. Sean, like many of the 2012 legacy group, had very minimal performance training and took a while to relax into the work enough to make substantial progress. We started to see a marked development in Sean's pole and performance skills after several weeks. Unfortunately, he was asked by the 2012 Organising Committee at that moment to leave the project. Not only was the entire team gutted to lose such a valuable member of the ensemble but morale across the team dropped as we realised that this opportunity was still controlled by those who had little sensitivity to the hard work and commitment of the legacy group. Sean, who had been making such wonderful progress, was out in the cold. We vowed that we would find the space to work with him again once the 2012 project was over.

With Stephen Bunce, we only discovered that both his prosthetics would require some kind of stability after he found his way into the harness. In the early stages of the work, Stephen was not secure in the harness. His double prosthetic could 'flip outwards' at any moment as it wasn't designed for the kinds of outward forces needed to control the pole. Stephen's ascent up the pole and into the harness is still something that defies the imagination. Once we worked out that he was essentially 'floating' in the harness without any secure force from his feet on the perch, we were able to find ways to ensure his complete safety. Stephen's eventual comfort at floating on the poles meant that during the performance (and also later projects) he was able to take off both his prosthetics and show the dynamic of a double amputee—stumps and all—flying through the air on a sway pole.

Even after the amputees had worked out safe ways of getting in and out of the apparatus, we still had to find ways to keep them safe while in the harness. As we had seen with Stephen, the horizontal forces acting on the bodies flying through the air could only be alleviated by applying pressure with both feet. If we had a situation in the case of the amputees where these horizontal forces meant they could not secure themselves, we would have a real problem. All of the amputees mutinied against being in the elaborate safety harness (attached

[Outdoor Work + Grant Mouldey]

by a belt to a ceiling-fixed safety rope). I found them all one morning up their poles at the other end of the room from where the safety harnesses were set up! They told me in no uncertain terms that they no longer required the safety harnesses. They were encumbered by this extra gear and we should really free up the safety harnesses for the wheelchair users who really required them. We compromised by attaching a belt loop to the pole from their waists so that, in the event that they lost their footing, we could ensure our sway pole riders would at least stay attached to the pole.

> Jonny Dawson and Samantha Bullock are both paraplegics and required a seat atop the apparatus to fully work the pole. The technicians worked tirelessly to provide solutions that enabled the performers. Jonny's seat differed from Samantha's to account for the best distribution of their weight in order to effectively ride the poles. In order to come off the safety harness altogether they had to climb the pole, get into the seat, and strap themselves in. Jonny got in very quickly and safely; as a result, he was able to contribute to the creation of the work straightaway. Samantha took longer to find security in her ascent to her chair, and joined the group as an independent sway pole rider. However, Jonny's speed in taking to the pole revealed a terrible by-product: in his haste to climb the pole and work with the group, Jonny had been injuring himself. He did not realise this was happening and so did not notify us. We only discovered the extent of his injuries in the week before the POC. Jonny had come all this way to ride a sway pole in the ceremony and now he was barred from climbing!

The entire group felt the loss that would occur from not having Jonny in the show. We argued and worked very hard to find a way to include Jonny. We finally persuaded the Organising Committee to use the fly system above the arena to lift Jonny, attached to his pole and already strapped to his seat. In the end, all the sway pole riders were present for the show.

Then we had issues with costume! We finally had everyone working successfully through the dance sequences: suddenly there were folds of fabric to negotiate on the climb, bringing different challenges for the performers. By this stage, we needed everyone working together as the sequences had been built to encompass every performer's specific dynamic on the poles; but the effectiveness of the ensemble owning their costume and working it out was a testimony of their understanding of becoming performers.

The POC provided an extraordinary platform for the group. The initial concept for the poles was to find a way to make the actor most visible in space.

We had a whole population visible in space—the most diverse population of people, riding through the air, making a spectacular addition to the show.

[Outdoor Work + Grant Mouldey]

Willie Elliott

Actor and Audio Describer

For me there has always been more than one reason to be Graeae. It has been the starting point for many careers within and beyond the company and I include my own journey in that fraternity.

As an actor, one is always looking to keep busy and earn a crust whilst waiting for the next job to appear. I worked a lot in small-scale touring, which is a tight-knit community and everyone knows each other, or knows of each other.

I first became aware of Graeae, when I was in an actor's co-operative agency. Caroline Parker was also a member and she got a job in a tour of *Ubu* with the company. Therefore, as her agent, I went along to see it. It is strange to think that I have become friends with many of that cast who, at the time, were complete strangers.

I had met Jenny Sealey whilst on tour in Nottingham, just before she took over as artistic director, so we were aware of each other. As time moved on and we met more often, we came to know each other well.

In a period where there was little acting work around, I got a call asking if I would be available to do some driving for the company, so I jumped at the opportunity, little thinking that it would be start of a new adventure.

Graeae were doing a series of workshops in Northern Ireland. I was thrown into the deep end, touring with a group of people I did not know and discovering, on the hoof, the various needs of disabled performers. There was another long tour about a year after that, which went to Scotland and back.

At this time, I had been performing in pantomime every Christmas, in various parts of the country. One evening I was having a drink with Jen, when she asked me where I was working next. I told her that it was not happening that year. Things seemed to have dried up. She was shocked and asked, 'What are you going to do?' I do not know what made me say it aloud, but I said 'I'm going to come and work for you!' Jenny immediately perked up and said, 'Don't joke about that! There's a job coming up and I wondered if you'd be interested. For the next tour, we want the access person to be able to audio describe every performance on the tour. We'd get you trained.'

Audio description is a way of accessing the arts for blind and visually impaired people. Typically, an audience member will come to the theatre and put on a set of headphones. A describer will sit in another part of the theatre with a microphone and a script and fill in the visual information in a production that someone might miss, because of their sight impairment. Audio description is also used in television and cinema, live events, museums and galleries, as well as architectural tours, such as the annual Open House event.

So, in 2001, I was sent to VocalEyes, the UK's leading audio description company, who happened to be

[Outdoor Work + Willie Elliott]

doing a rare training course for front of house managers at the Theatre Royal in Bath. Over a period of three weekends, we began with simple description exercises of people and photographs, building up to theatre sets and eventually a live performance. The theatre was in the middle of a run of a play at the time and we were given access to it, in order to allow us practical experience. Of course, any training course only scratches the surface of the subject and experience comes from actually doing the job.

And so it was that my journey began with Graeae's production of *The Changeling*. While we were on the road, I dropped VocalEyes a line and asked them to keep me in mind. With my actor's head on, I thought that it would be nice thing to fall back on when I was not working. What I wasn't prepared for was the transformation that was about to take place.

Suddenly, as an audio describer, I was working far more than I ever did as an actor. However, the skills I had learned in three years of actor training came to the fore, here, in a combination that I had not expected. I realised that I had found a niche that I had a real affinity with and took to it like a duck to water. Work has taken me to places that I would never have gone to, otherwise. On two occasions, I travelled to Adelaide, in South Australia to teach new describers and to work at the international festival, there. On the second occasion, I was able to use two of my previous students as co-describers and they have continued to work in the field in Adelaide and beyond.

Lots of research with blind and visually impaired people has led to a particular and well-proven way of working. Nevertheless, always challenging the norms has been a driving force behind Graeae's work. They have been at the forefront of integrating British Sign Language into all of their productions, and so it has been with audio description, continually experimenting with different forms. In their 2007 production of Sarah Kane's *Blasted*, the script's stage directions were used as audio during the piece for all the audience to hear.

In their outdoor production of *The Limbless Knight* in 2013, a movement sequence was accompanied, not by direct description, but with text the actors had written about their own journeys and in *Reasons to be Cheerful* another tack. The describer was present onstage for all of the time, as a character, even though most of the audience didn't hear what he was saying.

In 2012, Jenny co-directed the London Paralympic Games Opening Ceremony and insisted that I was one of the describers. It was a completely unknown quantity at this time. Channel 4 television were responsible for the broadcast and had made the remarkable decision that, for the first time, they would have a dedicated channel for audio description. And so they opened More4, to run alongside the usual commentary on the main channel. It was certainly a night to remember. My colleague, Hannah Brownlie and I had been given access to all of the rehearsals and creative meetings, which helped to immerse us in the event and it was this depth of involvement that really saved our bacon.

[Outdoor Work + Willie Elliott]

The athletes' parade lasted about an hour longer than scheduled and for both of us it was a marathon in itself to keep the flow going. But, the live production was even more of a surprise. The dress rehearsal took place the night before and all seemed well. Hannah and I were ready. However, overnight changes were made to the script and the information never got to us. So, during the live broadcast, the show had sections that were different from our very carefully crafted scripts. It was a real lesson in on-the-hoof description for someone who has never done it in a live television broadcast before.

That night is still the highlight of a continuing career, which brings new challenges with every show that I work on, from street theatre at Greenwich+Docklands Festival, to regular performances at the National Theatre and the Royal Opera House, or describing contemporary dance in London and abroad. I often think about the work I do and continually smile when I realise how lucky I am to be doing it.

It is amazing to look back at my past with Graeae and know that, after all this time, I still have a working relationship with the company. Even as I write, I am working with a member of the team, who wants to learn more about audio description, as part of her job. I hope it's a relationship that will continue far into the future with an organisation that produces groundbreaking work and the director who introduced me to a new career and a new way of life.

Dr. Tina Carter

Aerial Tutor and Choreographer/Academic

Accessible Aerial—A Reflection

In spring 2009, Graeae ran their first intensive aerial workshop for D/deaf and disabled people. I was invited to lead on this at Circus Space, now the National Centre for Circus Arts, in London, as I had a developing practice devising and teaching accessible aerial. The limited availability of accessible aerial training at that time was aimed at children or, offered in participatory and social settings, rather than as artistic professional development. Graeae's ambitions to explore and develop accessible circus, focusing primarily on aerial and sway pole, was professionally ambitious from the start. It stemmed from artistic director, Jenny Sealey, who told me in an interview in 2011.

'It was at Liberty Festival [in 2008] and I was watching the audience, watching, and I saw a Deaf woman sign to her friend, 'why are there no Deaf up there [on the sway poles]?' And I thought, absolutely, why are there no Deaf people up there?'

Graeae worked in partnership with Australian sway pole experts, Strange Fruit, on *The Medal Ceremony* to which this comment referred and the seed was sown to find ways of involving Graeae's own artists in the circus elements. Additionally, the aims of the programme were clearly directed towards 2012 and the return of the Paralympics to the UK.

'The programme will develop a range of new skills for D/deaf and disabled performers in London (and the UK) and is part of a long-term initiative to increase employability within the ever-expanding circus and street arts arena and other cultural events requiring (accessible) spectacle. The new skills' bank will enable a wider diversity of people to be able to respond to subsequent 2012 tenders.' (Graeae funding application)

> Whilst the ambition was evident, serious professional training in circus skills requires dedication over years and with limited resources—time, space, suitable trainers—the week-long programme would only ever offer an initiation to the craft. Despite one unfortunate incident where a participant fell a short distance to the safety-mat, most participants clearly demonstrated significant aptitude and interest in the new skills. Furthermore, all involved learned important lessons that were shared in an internal report after the accident. The most pertinent for future work related to clarity of information for participants and trainers, before and during the sessions; this was unsurprisingly, especially important for D/deaf participants, as suspending upside down, communicating between teacher and signer, plus the use of touch proved confusing at times. It was noted that 'a shorter training session over a longer period is a better model than an intensive five-day course of seven-hour sessions', as this can minimise fatigue and injury through musculoskeletal stress on the body. Finally, whilst Graeae do not generally require information on 'participants' medical conditions, due to the physical nature of the work' it was thought potentially useful to 'set up one-to-one sessions with participant and trainer at the beginning of sessions to discuss an individual's physicality'.

These and other recommendations influenced the later extensive training programme that successfully led to over forty D/deaf and disabled performers suspending and swaying in the London 2012 Paralympic Games Opening Ceremony (POC), and introduced conventional circus tutors to alternative methods of inclusive aerial practice.

I write extensively about the POC in my PhD thesis, ultimately offering my view on 'how diverse disabled aerialists have challenged and sustained aesthetic and methodological conventions of aerial'. In my view, the engagement of D/deaf and disabled people in aerial opens an art form to a wider population (as participants and audience members), thus facilitating the exploration of new stories and movement vocabularies. It also forces trainers of the disciplines to re-evaluate what they are teaching, how they are doing it and indeed why. The Paralympics offered participants and teachers alike the opportunity to throw away the rule book and start afresh—which was admittedly challenging for some. Nevertheless, when the trainees present radically diverse life-experiences, physiologies and professional arts practice, the beginning is already markedly different from many other professional performing arts training programmes. The author, Lois Keith, certainly provoked me to seriously analyse my practice after attending her enlightening Disability Confidence Training day prior to the Paralympic training programme. Her suggestion that we consider the task and its purpose rather than simply prescribe an activity or action resonated with me as a theatre devisor; in warm-ups, for example, it made more accessible sense to ask people to 'raise their heart rates'—and offer diverse ways of doing this—than run on the spot, as some would not be able to stand let alone run. I was excited by this adventure, but I noted in my journal that there was a lot of anxiety.

> 'In the packed library at Circus Space, to my surprise, many present were nervous of the project we were about to begin. All except Keith were, (at least visibly), non-disabled with many admitting they had little experience of working with, or indeed knowing, any disabled people. Not only were there concerns over general practicalities (accessing the various spaces, offering assistance, communicating with D/deaf people via interpreters and understanding the complexity of the various personal assistants that might be present), there was also significant concern over language: what can you say? And how should you say it?'

Not only did the trainers have to face their insecurities around access for disabled participants, (from appropriate language to devising and safely sharing complex aerial vocabulary), but the D/deaf and disabled trainees had anxieties and concerns that raised further questions for all of us. For example, we had to find appropriate ways of sharing information with D/deaf aerialists once they were out of reach; we devised protocols of having them look to us before undertaking a manoeuvre, in case we needed to give them additional information or indeed stop them before they released to do a drop. We also minimised speech when demonstrating new aerial actions, so they did not have to look between two people, the trainer and the signer. For amputees, there were other concerns. Those wearing prostheses, questioned whether or not to wear their 'legs' in the air, and if they had different styles of 'leg', which ones would be most appropriate. Questions related to the type of aerial they were engaging in, the choreography, the aesthetic and safety for the audience and their fellow participants—would the legs come off mid-air? It also proffered the question of identity. Most of the bi-lateral amputees chose to wear different 'legs' in the air, but they were keen for those to be visible as they did not want to pass as non-disabled; most of the uni-lateral amputees chose to work without theirs.

The very process of declaring, showing and then removing 'legs' in the space was a major personal undertaking for some who had not previously been in such an environment with other D/deaf and disabled people. One artist, B-, later shared that he had never taken his legs off in front of anyone other than family, even hiring a swimming pool to swim with his son rather than share a pool with strangers and exposing his amputations. Years on, he is a proud man who is happy to share the badge of disability with his fellow amputees. I remember at the start of the process everyone was very polite, even shy of bearing witness to people handling their legs, but by the end of the intensive time together there was much more openness and plenty of laughter. One moment lingers, as bi-lateral amputee P- failed to complete a full salto in the vertical rope, ending up suspended by his prostheses; he was low to the mat and in no immediate danger, so I called to Mark Morreau— 'Quick grab the camera!' Looking up in pain-free bewilderment, P- enquired how to release himself.

[Outdoor Work + Dr. Tina Carter]

Untangling his legs from the rope was exhausting him, so he decided to remove his legs from the prosthetic extensions, leaving them both hanging on the rope for us all to admire.

> Lindsey Butcher and I were probably the most experienced accessible aerial teachers in the Paralympic team, but even we had not experienced the breadth of diversity in one space, nor worked in such intensity that ultimately led to a performance of global importance. I was fortunate to join the LOCOG creative team after the rehearsals, working alongside Phil Hayes and Alex Poulter and was eventually asked to choreograph the aerial scenes. This was the biggest moment in my aerial career and, whilst I felt capable, the vastness of the organisation meant that decisions I could usually make instantaneously—when working on my own productions, or with Graeae—required extensive consideration by committee. This resulted in significant challenges for me and the participants. Choreography was unable to be fixed and rehearsed; appropriate equipment arrived too late for real comfort and purposeful rehearsal, and personal exhaustion sometimes meant I made the wrong decisions.

(From my private diary)

> 'I made another faux pas today, only this time it was a really bad one ...

L– 'Can you lower the trapeze for me Tina?'

TC 'Can't you use it at that height, as you have been doing?'

I was hectically running around the space trying to manage all the artists, and constantly lowering and raising the trapeze bars added time and broke the fluidity of the rehearsal.

L–   'M – has to lift me on and off each time.'

TC   'If that's what you've been doing all along isn't that okay?'

L–   'I don't want to be constantly picked up and carried by people!'

Thankfully, most of the time, the teams worked well together and with me, however, for some of the small statured artists the rehearsals proved especially challenging. Their smaller equipment failed to arrive on time forcing them to struggle with the larger apparatus, and as they witnessed their aerial colleagues, develop their skills and hone the choreographies, they felt abandoned.

Throughout the process that started with an intensive aerial workshop in 2009 and culminated in the POC on 29 August 2012 there were extraordinary moments that are, in 2017, still contributing to the development of accessible aerial globally. The National Centre for Circus Arts is now taking proactive steps to engage all their trainers in accessible and integrated practice. Through them, I have started to deliver Accessible Aerial Teacher Training in Japan, in preparation for the Paralympics in 2020. Performers from the ceremony are creating and touring their own work and new companies like Extraordinary Bodies have

[Outdoor Work + Dr. Tina Carter]

emerged to build on those endeavours. Graeae contributed to the development of accessible aerial in Rio prior to their Olympic Games in 2016, and of course continues to explore ways of using aerial and circus within its performances. I have the privilege of continuing to work with them as together we explore new ways of working accessibly in the air.

> 'Above all, the aerialists have transformed my view of what is possible—if we allow ourselves to look for it. It's by no means easy. There has been plenty of frustration; fear; pain; panic; moaning and complaining; and more frustration. But because there was also so much humour; so much love and support; determination; stubbornness and yet again more humour—oh and an army of physios as well—it became what it was. A lifetime achievement all round.' (Private journal. Last entry 2012)

> www.airhedz.co.uk

Dawn Langley

Independent Researcher and Consultant

Looking Up at the Stars

Graeae has long been known for its approach to challenging preconceptions, breaking down barriers and putting D/deaf and disabled artists centre stage. During my seven years as chair of Graeae I saw this delivered on so many levels, from the world stage of the London 2012 Paralympic Games Opening Ceremony (POC) to the outdoor antics of Iron Man, from small local school groups to the Edinburgh Festival.

In many ways the POC, for me, summed up much of Graeae's approach; it was undoubtedly thought provoking, often witty, sometimes mischievous but at all times uncompromising in its commitment to exploring the depths of the human condition. In 2010, I started in the role of chair and I am acutely aware that the capacity of the organisation to step onto this world wide stage was very hard won.

I think if there is one observation I would make about how Graeae has come to occupy its current position within the theatre sector in the UK, it has been a story of growing confidence. This may sound simplistic but it required us all to take some tricky decisions and to be willing to step forward and live our values in spite of the possible backlash or criticisms that might follow. This needed us to build strong bonds as a board and team and to not be frightened of having difficult conversations internally and externally. It also required the company to get out there and shout about what it was doing, to engage with those who might not share the same worldview but find ways of building a dialogue. It also sometimes meant taking a risk and just doing something to see what would happen.

> Throughout my time as chair (2010-2017), and beyond the aesthetics of access has been at the core of all Graeae does, by which I mean an artistic approach that recognises the full sensory impact and potential of theatre and storytelling.

> I have been privileged to sit among audiences and attend events where I have witnessed people being utterly absorbed thanks to multiple communication channels and recognition that we all need different points of connection.

> Being part of this organisational culture caused me to pause and think about how I could contribute as chair. One approach I took was to be more visual in the way I shared my observations with the board and team. I hope this helped me communicate more effectively; it certainly had a personal impact in terms of being a reflective chair and ensuring I contributed personally to our commitment to inclusivity.

> Graeae continues to work with some extraordinary D/deaf and disabled performers and creative practitioners, and while things are changing, for many the company still offers opportunities that are sadly not as widely available as we would like. This is not something Graeae can achieve alone, and working in partnership has to be the way forward. New initiatives have come online in the

wider sector that are trying to effect change but from my perspective we are still some way off there being a full recognition of the richness of diverse approaches and the challenges (including the costs) of full access.

Although, if I learnt anything during my time at Graeae it is that some of the solutions to these challenges can be quite simple, for example around our board table we had at least four different types of chair available in recognition that those who used chairs might have different needs. My favourite was the chair shown in 'Essence' as it was the one that seemed to be most comfortable for my height and joints.

I was fortunate to experience some real high points throughout my time with the company but I have to say these experiences were often bitter sweet. After the real highs of the POC, the wide ranging changes and uncertainty around benefits and the Access to Work scheme left our staff and D/deaf and disabled people feeling vulnerable, confused and more marginalised rather than less. The debates are complex and the rhetoric impassioned on all sides. If anything I am pleased to say it strengthened Graeae's resolve in creating theatre that is wedded to accessibility. **I would like to thank all those D/deaf and disabled people, including the Company's amazing team, who continue to work to deliver Graeae's extraordinary vision given this context. The need for change continues.**

An in-depth study of the London 2012 Paralympic Games Opening Ceremony, *The Eyes of the World or Out of the Shadows*, can be found at www.graeae.org.

[Outdoor Work + Dawn Langley]

Jenny Sealey
CEO/Artistic Director, Graeae Theatre

Unlimited and Beyond*

I have a rather wonderful piece of art, which is a small rectangular box. The exterior is white and the interior sides and back covered in aqua sequiny blue sandpaper-like material. The fourth side is glass. Just behind the glass is a tiny, tiny dark haired figurine of a girl wearing a red swimsuit and with red armbands. On the back blue wall is a plaque, which says 'The world is scary place but I have my armbands'. She became and still is my talisman/girl!

Flash back to 2005 when London won the bid to host the Olympic and Paralympic Games and the conflicting feelings of the joy of the challenge, excitement, apprehension and the very British mentality of 'oh we will fuck it up'. If ever we needed armbands it was now!

The arts world was a buzz with possibilities of a global stage and D/deaf and disabled artists also realised that here was an opportunity to match artistic excellence with sporting excellence. Our way into the Cultural Olympiad was through Unlimited—an ACE funding stream to fuel, support and present the ambition of D/deaf and disabled artists. Unlimited was designed to embrace diversity in the broadest sense and to encourage collaborations but the key criteria was that we led the art and the decision-making process.

*Originally commissioned for the *Unlimited Anthology 2012*

I was appointed artistic advisor to Unlimited and worked closely with the team who were developing it. As always diving into uncharted waters the learning curve was steep and somewhat stressful because it was so important to get it right and we had to try and pre-empt and sort out the teething problems in the what's and how's of it all. BUT sitting surrounded by a hundred applications from the first round I was aware this was a moment in the history of disability arts.

The sheer diversity of applications, the depth and breadth of artistic genre, of engagement, the articulation of artistic processes, the choices of site specific spaces and the stories waiting to be told, felt like we had unearthed not only some new communities of artists but a new scale of ambition from the more established artists. The scope of possibility felt extraordinary and knowing how competitive and complex the decision making process was going to be was fantastic in itself.

The journey of disability arts towards excellence and our right to be in the public domain shouted loud and clear from each application and I allowed myself a moment of reflection to back in the 80s when we were just starting out. Then there was little room for difference or indeed any acknowledgement of difference and no real platforms to celebrate difference but I so remember setting up London Disability Arts Forum with a group of like-minded mavericks and working behind the scenes at The Workhouse gigs profiling Heart n Soul, Wonder Barbara, Jag Plah, Alan Sutherland, Elspeth Morrison with Tragic but Brave, Pink Fingers and others. Oh yes, we had a flourishing disability arts scene but we remained underground using only each other as role models and critics, but like all ghettoized, disenfranchised artists we built our own networks, supporting each other in artistic endeavour, always pushing the boundaries of expectation. In our independence we formed a body of extraordinary work encompassing a diversity of genres and styles.

> The fight for acceptance in the wider world gave us the drive, ambition and skill to parade their differences against a construct of set standards. As the community grew in numbers so did our vitality and energy until we were ready to dare place ourselves at centre stage and be unashamedly who we are.

> Our excellence is rooted in the ability to own who we are and to work with what we have. We establish our own sense of 'normal' into the work thus making it extraordinary. We also have a strict code of ethics, personal and political awareness of access and the need to ensure our work can be accessed by a diverse audience. No other community has displayed that enduring commitment to profoundly understanding equality and rights as both a performer/artist and as an audience.

> Back amongst the applications I realized that the visibility and scope of the work would challenge perceptions of disability through creativity and emotional engagement and lead to the de-ghettoization of us once and for all.

> The worrying blot on the landscape was however, that the actual pool of skilled artists to partake in Unlimited was still painfully small which is

why many artists were named across several applications. Training and lack of opportunity to training initiatives became my stuck record mantra in and around Unlimited.

It was crucial that we had the numbers of people and the skills necessary for all the work. The arts are a precarious and exposing profession presenting a relentless environment of opinion and judgement. We had to find ways to empower ourselves to match expectation and take responsibility.

When London got the bid, Graeae, aware of the skills gap in circus skills, and wanting to be responsive to the needs of the ceremony directors, started training in aerial skills. We had to be in a position to say 'here—we have some extremely skilled people' so that there was no excuse not to use D/deaf and disabled artists.

Our first foray was funded by ACE Cultural skills funds and we focused on sway pole training and silks. We also set up an audio description initiative specific to outdoor work. The subsequent CPD funding (Esmée Fairbairn and others) only allowed us to train a small pool of D/deaf and disabled people on sway poles, rope, hoop and silk work in partnership with Circus Space. When our CPD funding ended Circus Space then picked up and Graeae sourced the access costs. The working relationship with Circus Space (now National Centre for Circus Arts) was and still is one of the most rewarding collaborations to date. We shared the learning, the ambition and determination to make something happen. They understood the need to present a wealth of talent to the ceremony shows so we were united in our mission to have the Cultural Olympiad and stadium as our playing fields, showcasing our Deaf, disabled and non-disabled talent.

Graeae was thrilled to receive Unlimited funding in the first round because it gave us space and time to hone the sway pole skills further. It gave us a new artistic challenge to develop a language between ground-based performers and the sway pole performers and as always with Graeae a chance to explore new aesthetics of accessible narrative.

Our production—*The Garden*, a parable which drew inspiration from the tombstones and the on going life around the churchyard of St Alfege Church in Greenwich. It presented a troupe of nomadic story-keepers (the Keeper of Dreams, Keeper of History, Keeper of Song, Keeper of Names) who shared three stories of love, innocence and hope. For a brief moment in time, the Keepers open their garden-ritual—a ceremony of renewal, transformation and harmony. The beautifully composed music was designed to fill the sky as the artists swayed on four-metre-high sway poles creating stories in the air.

The production was extremely well received by a diverse audience and it was wonderful to be given the opportunity to premier the work Greenwich+Docklands International Festival. However, the show needed to run the test of relocation to see if it was a transportable commodity.

As *The Garden* was happening, the other nine Unlimited commissions had also started their productions across England (Graeae, Candoco Dance Company and *Irresistible* by Mind The Gap, *Bipolar Ringmaster* by Stumble), Wales (*In Water I'm Weightless* by Kaite O' Reilly, *Turning Points* by Chris Tally Evans), Scotland (*Snails and Ketchup* by Ramesh Meyyappan, *Ugly Spirit* by Fittings, *Private Dancer* by Janice Parker) and Northern Ireland (*The Screaming Silence of the Wind* by Maurice Orr).

The work, encompassed soundscapes, visual art, digital and audio—visual experiences, story telling, songs, music, installations, circus skills, physical theatre, dance and choreography, taking us to barren landscapes or taking over theatre spaces. We were there across the country. Unlimited had truly started and we had over fifty companies/individuals waiting in the wings to apply for the second round of commissions which was linking with British Council to become Unlimited International. We had the opportunity to seed bed new work, develop new talent through Unlimited Talent and start showcasing work in preparation to have a solid presence.

The handing over of artistic power to disabled people spoke volumes about our changing role and status within the sector. The Unlimited festival was part of the cultural programme running alongside the games which meant that we were going to be part of the world's largest celebration of arts and culture led by D/deaf and disabled people. We were setting the artistic agenda, championing accessibility and creating work like we have never created before. There was no time to be smug or dream about it all as we had a commitment to ensure the quality of Unlimited surpassed all expectations and left a lasting legacy way beyond 2012.

[Outdoor Work + Jenny Sealey]

As artistic advisor I was in talks with Martin Green, the director of ceremonies, about how Unlimited commissions could be integrated into the torch relays and opening and closing ceremonies. Of course, me being me I was shamelessly trying to find out who they were going to appoint as artistic director of the London 2012 Paralympic Games Opening Ceremony (POC)!

In 2010 it was back to business as usual at Graeae. I was opening the Ian Dury inspired musical *Reasons to be Cheerful* by Paul Sirett at New Wolsey Theatre and Theatre Royal Stratford East and reclaiming his infamous song 'Spasticus Autisticus'. We were then touring regional festivals with Sirett's adaptation of Ted Hughes' *The Iron Man*, developing skills in large scale puppetry. I got wind that a non-disabled-led company would be leading the POC. The company had an extraordinary reputation, but for me having been in and around the applications of Unlimited One and Two and us being in artistic control on a scale like never before, I felt our sector was being cheated. I strongly believed that the ceremony had to be D/deaf and disabled-led to be able to bridge the world of art and sport. The experience of what it is to be D/deaf and disabled would manifest its way into a creative narrative about what it is to be human. Anyway—I told Martin Green my view.

Months and months later in early February 2011, I was on the tube in Tokyo when I got a text from Martin saying that Ceremonies would like to consider Bradley Hemmings (artistic director Greenwich+Docklands International Festival) and me as joint artistic directors for POC! The first team had pulled out.

After six interesting, creative, brutal and challenging interviews over four months, we were finally appointed on 24 June 2011. We had just fourteen months (actually it was a lot less because eight months were part-time) to pull off the biggest show of our lives.

That is when I bought the artwork and knew that we would need armbands.

In our first five weeks in post we had to come up with a narrative and artistic framework to be presented to government, the International Olympic Committee and International Paralympic Committee. They had to approve it before we could go onto the next stage and appoint our creative team.

We had to work at the speed of light. It was terrifying, exhilarating, daunting. In our day jobs creativity tends to fit in and around the management of our organisations, administration, fundraising etc but for five whole weeks all we had to think about was art. It was truly liberating.

Through the interview process we had identified key elements/ethics/politics and personnel to underpin our narrative.

Our wish list included Stephen Hawking who is arguably the most famous disabled person in the world, Ian Dury's disability anthem *Spasticus Autisticus*, 'I am What I Am'—because we are what we are and a quote from Miranda in *The Tempest*.

[Outdoor Work + Jenny Sealey]

O wonder!
How many goodly creatures are there here!
How beauteous mankind is!
O brave new world that has such people in't!

Miranda looks without judging and we also wanted to feature Staff Benda Bilili disabled street band from The Congo whose name means look beyond appearance.

The whole notion of not judging, looking beyond appearance and transforming perception underpins Graeae and GDIF and naturally formed the foundation of our Ceremony.

It was crucial that the entire production team and creative team bought our philosophy physically, emotionally and practically and were prepared to come on a huge journey of discovery.

One of my favourite jobs is putting creative teams together and casting. We got together D/deaf and disabled dance captains, filmmakers, disabled-led companies and individual artists but our process was gloriously (!) hampered by Unlimited!!! So many of the artists we wanted to bring on board were way too busy working in their Unlimited production! ARGH!

So I went back to my stuck record re the dire need for training. ACE saved the day by funding the largest circus training for D/deaf and disabled people in the history of time. Our forty-four D/deaf and disabled people (artists, ex-Paralympics, ex-service men) trained in a beautiful bespoke tent by the side of Circus Space. The Circus Space tutors put them through the most rigorous regime. The first sharing four weeks in was truly awesome. For most people this was the first time they had ever performed in public. So much had been achieved in so little time and seeing these guys who had their legs blown off in war creating the most beautiful static trapeze work with skill and elegance is etched in my memory forever.

We were aware that for some people there is a huge emotional agenda attached to where they are in the process of understanding of their new physicality in line with when and how they became disabled. It is a lot to consider but the energy of humour, support and grit held them together.

The narrative continued to be informed by the skills being developed and as we honed in on detail, the elements of the story with the design, choreography and music started to really inhabit our playing field and challenge the scope of what was possible.

I wrote to my board saying my diary and note book were incomprehensible with notes on timings of sections in nanoseconds, notes on resolution of pixels, timing of wind, weather charts, more timings, casting notes, spreadsheet after spreadsheet with casting costume changes, timings again, protocol, MOD information, protocol updates, audio description, Channel 4 clearance for songs, ditching lyrics, harness notes, LED, programme, media guide crib notes, pyros, radials, aerial trolleys, storyboarding, mass choreography charts and more bloody spreadsheets. I also wrote about how wonderful it was to work with Bradley who sometimes scared me with his huge brain and

[Outdoor Work + Jenny Sealey]

knowledge and how lucky I was to have a tight team of sign language interpreters led by Jeni Draper who I have worked with closely over twelve years.

Introducing the story to our 3,500 volunteers was an emotional experience. A sea of expectant faces wanting to know what 'the original Jen and Brad' (this is how we introduced ourselves) had up their sleeve. We needed them to want to be part of the story and to fully realise that their involvement was integral to placing the Universal Declaration of Human Rights on a global stage and that they were a crucial part of a theatrical landscape changing perception of human diversity and artistic collaboration.

We were able to start the introductions with a Stephen Hawking quote:

'Look up at the stars and not down at your feet ... try to make sense of what you see ... be curious'.

This underpinned the gravitas and the playfulness we wanted to encompass. Placing Spasticus Autisticus with our volunteers was another extraordinary moment. There were concerns from the top about doing this song and we were warned that some volunteers would walk. After I had finished explaining the song was a triumphant disability anthem based on solidarity and about anyone who has been disempowered, disenfranchised or ridiculed, the 400 volunteers cheered, voicing their passion to own and reclaim this song. I can still feel the goose pimples, the feeling of utter joy and the knowledge that a certain Mr Ian Dury was beaming down thoroughly delighted.

Graeae's 2012 year started with a national tour of *Reasons to be Cheerful*. The last tour date was the final day of Unlimited and the end of the Paralympic Games so Spasticus was there at the beginning, the middle and the end!

Amit Sharma, Graeae's associate then went onto direct *Prometheus Awakes*, a co production with Greenwich+Docklands International Festival and La Fura Dels Baus. A twenty-five-foot puppet led the narrative, extraordinary graphics of thunder, cracks and flowers hit the walls of Queen Ann's House and our D/deaf and disabled professional dancers, many of whom went onto to be in other Unlimited shows, scaled the puppet and flew on harnesses suspended from a crane. The D/deaf disabled and non-disabled Volunteers took to the sky in a human net which prompted Lyn Gardner to write:

'There are no limitations here, just glorious liberation'.

It was an awesome start to the festival profiling a real diversity of people and again all part of claiming 2012 as a year to be seen and heard in as many artistic ways as possible.

I gave a speech at the launch of GDIF voicing my pride of Amit and Nathan Curry who was a young producer bought in to cover for Bradley's time with me on 'sports day'. 2012 was also a year of handing the reins over to others and supporting new emerging talent. And from that moment we hurtled into the scariest two months of my life but what was wonderful was taking time to read about,

[Outdoor Work + Jenny Sealey]

see and be inspired by Unlimited shows. Caroline Bowditch was in the midst of *Leaving Limbo Land*, Marc Brew was with Evelyn Glennie developing *Fusional Fragments*, Jez Colbourne was on the Ilkley Moor, Rachel Gadsden was in South Africa as were David Toole and Lucy Hind and Diverse City were in Brazil. There was something comforting knowing that a whole other body of work was being created. Out there was a multitude of artists charging the air with ambition, theatricality, risk and determination.

Fast forward to 29 August 2012. Having gone round to say thanks to 3,500 volunteers who were high on adrenalin and so unbelievably excited, we took our seats by the control box, my heart thudding, sweat streaming down my back and my teeth being ground within an inch of themselves!!

The moment Mat Fraser took to the stage with Heart 'n' Soul and Lizzie Emeh leading Loud and Proud to 65,000 people was a moment I will never forget, then Bim Ajadi and Ted Evans' film, the Aerobility fly over and the light slowly enveloping Professor Hawking on our protocol stage. And then the tears came.

It was without doubt the most surreal evening of my life, watching everything that Bradley and I had so carefully put together unfold before us witnessed by an enthralled audience and a global massive. A cast that included David Toole, Nickie Miles-Wildin, Denise Leigh, Deepa Shastri, John Kelly, Garry Robson, Stephen Collins, Nadia Albina, Laura Jones, Mark Smith, Sophie Partridge, James Rose, Mik Scarlet, forty-four sway poles/aerial performers, the D/deaf and disabled volunteers—we were there in our masses with

Spasticus and a forty-foot inflatable copy of Marc Quinn's statue of Alison Lapper—an iconic defiant image of femininity, motherhood and disability was a seminal moment in our history and onwards to Lizzie Emeh taking centre stage with Caroline Parker and Beverly Knight leading the entire cast and audience singing 'I Am What I Am'. I knew what I was at that point— a total emotionally wasted wreck!

But the very next day I was flung into the heart of *Unlimited Presents* at Southbank Centre and talked on a panel about creating work with D/deaf audiences. Bobby Baker's exhibition was up, Diverse City's *Breathe* installation was up and running, *Ugly Spirit* was being performed, Sue Austin was on the big screen, Heart 'n' Soul's Dean Rodney Singers' production had taken over the blue level, Ramesh Meyyappan was swinging from ropes in preparation for *Skewered Snails*, Clare Cunningham was in rehearsal with Candoco as was Marc Brew, Paul Cummings' English Garden had been planted in all its glory above QEH and my poles were being set up at Circus Space ready for *The Garden* rehearsals.

Grant Mouldey, the sway pole choreographer, and I found it hard giving instructions without a 'god mic' and now that we were now communicating with a cast of nine rather than a 1009!! But how lovely it was to be back in my comfort zone working on something I knew intimately and enjoying the challenge setting the show in an urban space right outside the QEH.

[Outdoor Work + Jenny Sealey]

Being part of *Unlimited Presents* was just brilliant, a feeling of belonging and that we had finally arrived. The wonderful diversity of people in and around the Southbank Centre felt that at last here was a true representation of society! I loved going from watching *Breathe* to Rachel Gadsden's exhibition to Candoco's double bill choreographed by Marc Brew and Clare Cunningham –the first disabled choreographers in the company's twenty-five-year history. It was a mind-blowing evening of skill, precision, hedonism, anarchy and brilliance and then Clare's own piece *Menage a Trois* is etched in my memory as is Mind The Gap's Jez Colbourne's haunting voice singing '*Thinking of home*'.

I was very proud of the Graeae team as they supported the development of access materials for other companies involved who wanted to make their work more accessible, they worked on the marketing and installed access structures sharing their expertise and in a way by default became silent producers to ensure that the vision and ethos of the festival underpinned everything and everyone.

What we proved is that we are superbly creative souls, we can hold our own in a festival and that we are a force to be reckoned with. It is crucial that this is not just a one-off.

There is a fear that with cuts across the arts and to benefits that we may once again be relegated to the sidelines. **I think we are braver now than we have ever been and we will face that fear to make sure we stay centre stage. We have an obligation to pave the world with possibility and opportunity for the next generation.**

We have to remember that the arts are a human right. And we must remember to always wear armbands.

> This article is in the foreword of *UNLIMITED: A London 2012 Festival Book.*

[Outdoor Work + Jenny Sealey]

A VISUAL HI STORY

'I have worked for Graeae for thirty years photographing numerous shows. I share their values and philosophy completely. It has always been a wonderful challenge to show the innovation, splendour and beautiful theatre that is included in everything that Graeae touches. An absolute favourite client.' **Patrick Baldwin**

[Bent]

[Blood Wedding]

[Diary of an Action Man]

[Blasted]

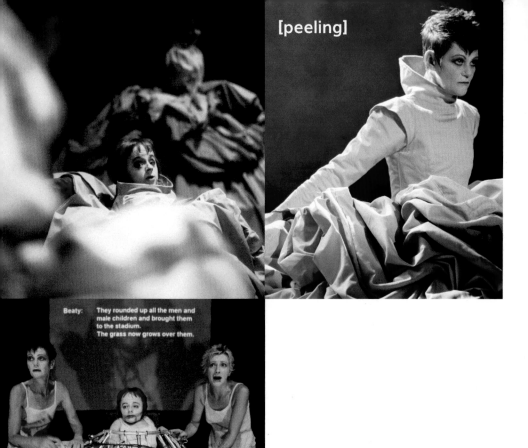

[peeling]

Beaty: They rounded up all the men and male children and brought them to the stadium.
The grass now grows over them.

[Prometheus Awakes]

[Reasons to be Cheerful]

[Romeo and Juliet + Bangladesh]

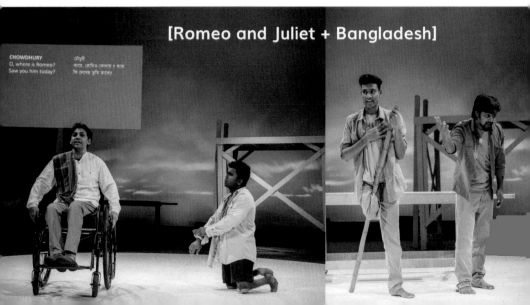

[Romeo and Juliet + Japan]

[Signs of a Star Shaped Diva]

[The Changeling]

[The Garden]

[The House of Bernarda Alba]

[The Iron Man]

[The Limbless Knight]

[The Solid Life of Sugar Water]

[The Threepenny Opera]

[Whiter than Snow]

Jack Thorne

Mike Kenny

Jonathan Meth

Chloe Todd Fordham

**Writing &
New Work**

Alex Bulmer

Carissa Hope Lynch

Jack Thorne
Writer

My first meeting with Graeae was at an open day. I was cowed, ill, and really struggling with my condition, an invisible disability called cholinergic urticaria. It was a beautiful day in South London. Jenny immediately got us relaxed by playing some strange games and then we talked about what shows interested us and what art we wanted to make. But the key moment for me was at lunchtime. I was slinking around feeling a bit self-conscious and I got talking to this woman called Alex Bulmer. I told her what I was going through and told her I wasn't sure I should be there, that I felt like a bit of a fraud. She said, 'but that sounds terrible, being in pain like that, of course you're disabled.' And that's the thing I love best about Graeae. I love the shows they make, I love the fact that I've had the opportunity to make two shows with them. But the thing I really love is that it's a community.

Theatres try to make communities all the time but very few succeed. With Graeae, you'll walk on marches with them, you'll make shows with them, you'll appear on panels with them, you'll fight with them and for them. I hope Graeae is always part of my life, I know my life is stronger with Graeae in it.

One of the shows I was lucky enough to make with Graeae was *The Solid Life of Sugar Water* which I think we made in the most Graeae way possible: writing without casting implications, casting without writing implications. We simply found the best actors we could for the roles, and boy were they good actors—Genevieve Barr and Arthur Hughes. We weren't going to rewrite the play at all for them at first. But then the great director Amit Sharma and I talked about it and decided Gen's deafness should be part of the story. I have to say, that rewrite was one of the most fun I've ever done. It transformed the play for the better and now the play will always be that way, Gen made that part deaf and it can never be different. We were originally destined to do a run at Plymouth and then Edinburgh. But then people started to get the show, to get the beautiful work Amit, Gen, and Arthur had done and so we were given a chance to do it again, this time on a tour that ended up at the National Theatre.

I wasn't aware at first that we'd be the first show from Graeae to make it inside the theatre (Britain's National Theatre of Disability should have been in there a lot sooner in my opinion) but I was honoured to be part of Jenny's charge into that building. Press night there is one of the highlights of any run, and that particular press night will always be one of the highlights of my professional life.

[Writing & New Work + Jack Thorne]

Mike Kenny

Writer

I've struggled to sum up my experience of working with Graeae. I'm finding it really hard. It feels impossible to say, 'Graeae is this'. So, I'll try to break down my experience.

The first time I worked with the company was on *Fittings: The Last Freak Show*. I'd seen the company many times before. I think I even saw their first piece, *Sideshow*. I also knew, and had worked with, quite a few members of the company in other situations. But I still remember feeling nervous when we began work. It seems strange to me now, but I think I felt afraid of being exposed as a total charlatan. I mean, everyone else in the room had earned their right to be there. I wasn't sure I had. After all, I was not disabled, 'yet!' intoned Mandy Colleran, brittle-bone dry. We got stuck in and work is a great leveler. You can either do it or you can't. And they asked me back. It can't have been that bad.

The thing about Graeae, which everyone who works in theatre could do with looking at, is this: given that theatre is all about communication, how do you ensure that everyone—on stage and in the audience—is getting it? All individuals have different challenges and impairments. They are united by a common humanity. That is the essence of theatre. In one sense, it's not hard to understand but sometimes it can be hard to achieve.

After *Fittings*, where we purpose-built the show around the individual performers, I went on to work on two children's shows with the company: *Diary of an Action Man* and then *Whiter than Snow*. They demonstrate that there's no single question, and definitely no perfect answer, about how to approach the work.

Action Man wasn't really 'about' disability at all. The family at the centre of the play was mixed in many ways. Both the children had mobility impairments and one of the parents had a sensory impairment. This affected the way in which the family communicated but it wasn't 'the problem', and it wasn't what the play was about. The story was about a boy who idealised his absent ex-forces father. The trouble in communication wasn't anything to do with anyone being D/deaf. The task I had to take on as a writer involved creating a text that could be 'read' by a mixed audience. I'd been finding ways of incorporating signing for many years. This was the first time I tried to incorporate audio-description (AD). It nearly killed me. The rule in plays is that people almost never say what they mean. You bury meaning in subtext for an audience to discover. I'd spent years cutting out text; AD requires that you use words to describe what is going on. It's hard to pull off. It's easy to overdo it. The late Tim Gebbels said to me around that time, 'I'm blind. I'm not stupid'. We ended up with a form of alienation of which Brecht would have been proud. In a play where their diversity was not the point, a diverse cast performed a play that deconstructed its own meta-levels of meaning as it went—and all this for children. Frankly, I needed a lie down.

[Writing & New Work + Mike Kenny]

To show how diverse the questions and answers can be, the next play, *Whiter than Snow*, was completely different. I had come across the true story of the Ovitz family, a family of Jewish 'dwarf' performers who were taken to Auschwitz, came under the wing of Josef Mengele, and yet survived. We had long discussions about casting. Gradually, Graeae had moved towards a policy where casting wasn't dictated by disability. The best person was cast, then supported to play the part. This play was about a family of dwarfs touring a production of *Snow White* who meet someone cloned to be 'perfect'. 'Who is the loveliest of all?' was the question hovering over the piece; whether genes are destiny. It seemed that the family had to be played by actors of short stature. Ironically, in a play which questioned whether someone of short stature could ever play *Snow White* we had to be really specific in the casting of these roles.

> **Graeae is often called a family. It feels more like a Tardis to me. It looks like a small thing from the outside, with not much room to move. Once you enter, it's an enormous world of possibilities that allows you to move through time and space. I love working with Graeae. Every time I work with the company, it's a challenge and a voyage of discovery. Plus, one of my kids said to me lately, 'Dad, Graeae is the coolest company you work for'. It's that too.**

Jonathan Meth

Project Dramaturg, Crossing the Line and Curator,
The Fence Network

In response to the lack of work being produced by disabled playwrights, writernet undertook research for the London Arts Board (LAB) guide for disabled theatre writers. The guide was intended to map existing provision and identify priorities. *Theatre Writing—A Guide for Disabled Writers* was ultimately published by LAB in March, 2000. Out of this research and in addition to the provision of information, advice, and guidance, there emerged a need to change the attitudes that discouraged the development of disabled theatre writers' work and to explore alternative ways to support their careers. This was demonstrated practically when writernet was later approached by Graeae to discuss the lack of good quality scripts emerging from disabled writers. The company wanted to place a greater emphasis on the commissioning, development, and production of new work.

This resulted in the first collaboration between writernet and Graeae. We undertook a year-long Disabled Writers Mentoring Scheme in association with New Writing North in 1999. The scheme matched nine disabled writers (mentees) with more experienced (and not necessarily disabled) counterparts, overseen by an advisory panel of experienced individuals and representatives from the new writing and disability theatre sectors. The mentors were: Patrick Marber, Mark Ravenhill, Lucinda Coxon, Sarah Woods, Philip Osment, Elizabeth Melville, Kaite O'Reilly, Ann Coburn, and Alan Plater.

[Writing & New Work + Jonathan Meth]

The scheme provided a vital opportunity for writers to learn and to work towards completing first drafts of material. Two writers were already under commission less than one month after the completion of the scheme, and Graeae produced and toured Peter Wolf's *Into The Mystic*.

Rather than simply repeating a successful scheme, writernet and Graeae elected to evaluate the next steps in terms of strategic implications. A range of needs emerged from the scheme, particularly in the final mentee evaluation meeting. Responses to these needs were synthesised into two projects following further consultation with the sector, including *Lemonia*: a week-long residency for ten emerging writers at Holton Lea, near Poole in Dorset, in the spring of 2003.

The second need that emergered from our consultation was for a project that would meet the needs of more experienced theatre writers. This call led to *disPlay4*, an apprenticeship for those writers who needed support to achieve fuller integration into theatre practice. It give writers both paid time and incentive to produce a draft that was ready for production consideration. This apprenticeship would extend beyond theatre to cover writing for radio and television through Soho Theatre's unique Writers' Centre.

Soho Theatre wanted writers on *disPlay4* to have the best shot at getting produced. At every stage, writers would have access to what was happening at Soho. The Attachment Programme, which playwright and tutor Lin Coghlan was running, would run as a sister course. The *Writers Festival* at

Soho Theatre at the end of November/beginning of December provided an important platform for the work via rehearsed readings by the *disPlay4* writers.

The dramaturg needed to be someone experienced. As well as a practicing and successful writer in a number of media, Kaite O'Reilly had worked as a mentor on the earlier writernet/Graeae project and drew on her wide experience of teaching on the MA degree programmes in Glamorgan and at Ty Newydd. She knew the context in which we were working and had experience of being disabled.

Kaite sums up the impact this project had: 'five people (including me) are now part of a strong community of writers; all of them are in a very different place. *Anniversary Waltz* will be on at Scarborough then touring to Filey. Angela and Danny are both writing sample scripts for *Doctors*; also both are contributing to the National Disability Arts Forum book. Danny's involved with *Flip the Script* at Manchester Contact and he's also being interviewed by Red Ladder/Half Moon Young People's Theatre. Jamie is consolidating his work at Graeae and writing a forum theatre piece. Kerry has an agent, a bursary, and is filling the stock cupboards. *Meeting Myself Coming Back* was produced by Soho Theatre and submitted to the Meyer Whitworth/John Whiting awards and Alan Ayckbourn is directing her next piece. She's got funding from the Peggy Ramsay Foundation, plus she's been invited to do a week-long workshop with Jack Bradley and Moira Buffini at the National Theatre Studio; and John Wright, who directed *Meeting Myself Coming Back*, wants

[Writing & New Work + Jonathan Meth]

to direct her next play, which she hasn't written yet but he liked the synopsis ... everybody's career has improved.'

As the third project born out of writernet's collaboration with Graeae, *Lemonia* benefited from the experience of the earlier schemes, both through a more evolved working practice and through established relationships with key practitioners. The Disabled Writers Mentoring Scheme made a strong case for a beginners' writing course for disabled practitioners: several of the mentees were in need of a more fundamental grounding in basic theatre writing skills. Where *Lemonia* differed from the earlier schemes was in the intense focus of a single week of introduction to theatre writing and residential aspect, unlike the Disabled Writers Mentoring Scheme and *disPlay4* which both took place over longer time scales (of at least one year) and were aimed at writers further on in their careers.

Our fourth collaboration was another, more targeted, mentoring scheme in 2007, this time in partnership with Apples and Snakes. Graeae and Apples and Snakes made nominations to the programme; it was decided not to make the scheme open access but to target resources on artists known to both companies and to whose trajectories this scheme would add value. The scheme ultimately delivered six monthly meetings.

Five mentoring partnerships were created for individual writer/performers—with a mentee-led approach. Partner organisations scoped and made initial recommendations of mentees at the partner meeting. We worked with mentees to find their preferred mentor where possible. This was successful in four cases. This was not possible for the fifth case and the steering group brainstormed a number of suggestions to yield a shortlist from which we were able to successfully select an appropriate mentor. The mentee/mentor partners were:

Liz Carr and Gordon Anderson
Joseph Coelho and Shan Khan
Pete Edwards and Robert Pacitti
Ju Gosling and Deborah Williams
Claire Williamson and Anna Murphy

Built around the core writernet team of Sarah Dickenson, Kaite O'Reilly, and Jonathan Meth, these four projects helped to generate a cohort of disabled theatre writers as well as embed new writing within Graeae, and helped lay the foundations for the writers' work over the following decade.

Chloe Todd Fordham

Literary Manager, Graeae Theatre and Writer

New Writing, 2013-2017—Write to Play Programme

When I joined Graeae in 2013, it was to work on a new programme for D/deaf and disabled writers called Write to Play. It was the only fully accessible year-long development programme reaching out specifically to D/deaf and disabled writers in the UK. The vision of Write to Play was to do two key things.

Firstly, it would train up early career writers in a supportive, inclusive environment. Writers would take part in craft-focused workshops. They'd work with a mentor. They'd write two short pieces (a monologue first, and then a duologue) and a full-length play. They'd have opportunities to explore their work in a rehearsal room with actors. They'd share their work in an end of programme showcase for industry. New voices would be nurtured. And these voices would feed the larger theatre ecology, an ecology that needed, desperately, to acknowledge, embrace and platform the incredible playwriting talent that exists within the D/deaf and disabled community.

The second aim of the programme was about sector development and sustainability. The majority of further training opportunities are not accessible. Many theatre buildings, especially those that showcase new work like pub theatres, are not physically accessible. Many shows are not BSL interpreted. Theatre buildings and theatre people can feel scary and unapproachable. And with so few D/deaf and disabled writers making careers out of playwriting, there was a shortage of voices already in the industry pushing for change. To truly diversify the playwriting world, we needed to initiate a sustainable change in culture and practice industry wide.

Excerpt from callout for writers

The programme offers five new writers each year the opportunity to hone their craft and explore their ideas in a supportive environment. The programme involves:

Playwriting 101: a five-day writing workshop led by leading practitioners, offering writers crucial foundation learning and space with peers in a supported environment.

Six half-day specialist workshops facilitated by theatre-makers working today, giving writers a unique insight into the various approaches to writing for performance.

Access to an individual **mentor** who will support the writer dramaturgically through all writing projects during the programme, offer pastoral support, and challenge and encourage the writers' individual practice and open up new ways of thinking.

Miniatures: writers will have the opportunity to develop a short monologue and a short duologue during the programme, to explore with their mentor the performance potential of the pieces in a workshop with actors, and showcase this work to a small audience and get feedback.

Writers will also develop two drafts of a new **full-length play**. There will be a public sharing of an extract from this full-length play at the end of the programme for an industry audience. The full-length plays will be considered for production by Graeae and our partners.

Writers will have the opportunity to take part in a two-week **placement** at one of Graeae's partner organisations, allowing writers to expand their network and skills base.

There will also be opportunities to see new work at our partner organisations across the year.

WRITE TO PLAY YEAR ONE

Not in my wildest ambition or imagination did I think I'd be sitting, writing my play *Context* in the Peggy Ramsay room at the Royal Court.
—Rosaleen McDonagh

For the first year of Write to Play, Graeae teamed up with three key new writing organisations in London: the Royal Court, Soho Theatre and the National Theatre Studio. Over fifty applications came through to us from playwrights across the country; a sure sign that there were playwrights hungry to develop their craft. After some difficult decisions, we settled on our first intake of writers: Nicola Werenowska, Tom Wentworth, Amy Bethan Evans, Sean Burn and Rosaleen McDonagh.

Five Things I Learned on Playwriting 101
by Tom Wentworth

1   **The first rule of writing is: ALWAYS talk about writing.**
Get writers in a room together and in five minutes
they'll be discussing the craft, their favourite plays
and how they actually go about getting words on
paper. The chance to chat with the other writers was
one of the most satisfying elements of the week.
Writing can be a lonely, soul-searching job so Write
to Play provided a unique opportunity to have a core
group of lovely, talented writers with whom we can
each share the ups and downs of playwriting.

2   **Graeae are brilliant and want to support us.**
From the first moment, the company was clear that
it was all about us—the writers. Chloe (Graeae's
Write to Play co-ordinator), Amit (Graeae's associate director), Alex and Paul couldn't have been
more supportive or encouraging. Plus we have free
reign when writing our plays—it's the play we want
to write. This year we will be supported through the
help of a mentor, receive notes on each draft and
have the chance to workshop extracts. It's a licence
to experiment and explore, challenge and excite—
all under Graeae's watchful gaze.

3   **Theatres are actively looking for new writers and plays.**
We had excellent talks from representatives of the
three Write to Play partner organisations (Soho
Theatre, National Theatre Studio and Royal Court
Theatre) who all spoke passionately about the way
new scripts are read within their theatres. To some
they may seem like mysterious places but I was really encouraged by the evident hunger to read and

[Writing & New Work + Chloe Todd Fordham]

produce new work, as well as wanting to strongly invest time developing new relationships with writers. I came away from each meeting full of hope.

4   **Theatricality is the word of the week.**
What makes a play different from TV? What makes a play a play? Much of our conversations revolved around this idea, plus we also tried some writing exercises which pushed us to our theatrical limits so ... watch this space!!

5   **Other people share my coffee addiction!**
It was such a relief to find that Write to Play consists of a group of other writers who also choose coffee as their beverage of choice and can't survive a first draft without it either. Thank goodness too that Graeae continue their generosity when it comes to hot drinks!

Many people are struck by their first interaction with Graeae—with the building, with the team, with the work. Creating a learning environment that is inclusive, where everyone can participate equally, where no one is feeling left behind or sidelined, where access requirements are in place from the moment you begin work—that is, sadly, a rare environment. Coming to Graeae, our Write to Play writers were able to just get on with the task of being a writer.

The writer's voices couldn't be more different, but each had their own unique identity. One of the proudest memories I have of the first year of Write to Play was the end of programme showcase. To see how far the writers had developed, to see the writers talk about their writing with confidence, to see our mentors and partners glowing with pride, to see Graeae learning. Write to Play really is a journey.

The writer development strand of Write to Play was, and continues to be, strong. What was more challenging, what was harder to measure by the end of Year One, was whether the wider industry was shifting its practice and culture to open its arms to D/deaf and disabled writers. Writers need time to grow, plays take time to write, theatres take time to programme. Write to Play Year One was clearly just the beginning.

WRITE TO PLAY YEAR TWO

Graeae has nurtured me this year, with a focus on process as much as outcome. As well as my fellow writers on the programme, I have met and learned from practitioners at the forefront of the UK theatre scene and I feel I've developed as a playwright in leaps and bounds.
—Karen Featherstone

Building on the success of the first year, and keen that the programme should have a national reach, we led the programme out of London in Year Two, to the North West. We partnered with new writing giants of the North West, the Royal Exchange Theatre in Manchester, Liverpool Everyman & Playhouse and the Octagon Bolton. This time we were looking for writers based in the North West. Our search led us to five new family members: Jackie Hagan, Danni Skerritt, Karen Featherstone, Helen Martin and Helen East.

<u>Write to Play</u>
an interview with Jackie Hagan and Amit Sharma by Tom Powell

The Write to Play programme is Graeae's writer development programme, now in its second year and this time around focused on the North West of England. I interviewed Amit Sharma in person at Graeae's Bradbury Studios and Jackie Hagan—currently enrolled on Year Two of the programme—via email while she's preparing to tour her one-woman show *Some People Have Too Many Legs.*

For Amit, it came about because they noticed a lack of D/deaf and disabled writers working in theatre. 'There are a few reasons for that—a lot of writing courses are inaccessible—the buildings are, or theatre companies don't know how to provide for disabled people.'

There's also, perhaps, an implicit notion that disability becomes the subject of drama—'we wanted to provide the freedom of being defined just as a writer. And to provide practical opportunities—dramaturgs, mentors, actors, and to bring in mainstream theatres as well.'

The first year of the course was open to applicants based all over the country, though it was run from London, and Amit was surprised they had no applicants at all from the North West. The solution? To target that area in Year Two of the course, to bring D/deaf and disabled voices to the fore there. They're partnered with regional powerhouses the Liverpool Everyman, Royal Exchange Theatre in Manchester, and the Octagon Bolton.

Jackie Hagan is a writer and performance poet currently touring her solo show *Some People Have Too Many Legs*. 'It's the story of how, last summer, I suddenly felt this off-the-scale, red-hot pain in my foot and went to A+E and then didn't leave that hospital for five months. When I finally left, I had lost my leg, my fear of failure and loads of emotional deadwood that had been hanging round in my head causing chaos since I was a moody teenager.'

Amit waxes lyrical about the impact of the programme, and its pairing with big regional theatres—'we're potentially really changing lives—it's something that cannot really go underestimated. As a playwright, they'll write and be mentored on a full-length play, and it's a fantastic opportunity, a platform to spring from.'

WRITE TO PLAY YEAR THREE

Write to Play has been a journey. It's taught me a lot about myself: who I am, what I can do, what I can write. This has been more than about just creating three pieces of new writing for me. I started this year a shy, anxious lad and, although still anxious, I have a lot more self-confidence. I can't even put into words what it's meant. Thanks, Graeae for an awesome year and thanks to ALL who have been part of it.
—Rick Poppa

The North East was the region chosen for Year Three. There had been hardly any applications over the first two years from writers based in the North East, so we felt we needed to take the programme there.

[Writing & New Work + Chloe Todd Fordham]

We teamed up with Live Theatre in Newcastle, Hull Truck and West Yorkshire Playhouse as partners, and began our search for North East writers. After much deliberation, we offered places to writers Rick Poppa, Sarah Jane Dickenson, Sarah Gonnet and Rebekah Bowsher.

Rebekah Bowsher's blog, 28 November 2016

Dear future Write to Players

When I sat down to write this blog. I didn't know what to say. I didn't know who to talk to. I didn't know what to talk about. I wasn't thoroughly convinced by blogging as a process or my ability to do it. And then I remember seeing one of the new Write to Players and I thought—what do I wish I'd known at the start of this adventure?

So Dear future Write to Player,

You are about to embark on a journey. A journey altogether too long and simultaneously too short. The days will feel endless and yet the months slip by. You can't imagine it, but in less than a year you will have sixty plus pages of a play. The scary thing for me was at this point I didn't even know what that might be yet. And it could be anything! About anything! About anyone!

You know you've got masterclasses, and several weeks of focused playwriting as well as sharings of shorter work. You know you're going be at different theatres. But, you feel sick because you don't know what you're going to write; you don't know who you're going to meet, or where any of these things are going to be. You're terrified that any minute someone will shout—'you are not a playwright, leave now.'

Except they won't. Because you're part of the Graeae family now. And Jenny (Sealey) took our band of nervous, scared and shy Write to Players and made us stand up on the first day and learn sign language, so now we're fluent (only kidding—sort of). And Chloe and Amit nurtured us and cheered us on. They helped us connect with mentors who got 'us' and what we were trying to write. And they took our sensitive fledgling work to the next draft.

I'm not gonna lie. We are still a band of nervous, scared and shy playwrights. But we are playwrights and we all own that name now.

Write to Play is an amazing opportunity. That's why I applied, and why Sarah, SJ and Rick all applied. I assume it's why you applied. And it's true. In one year, I don't think I could have made so many connections, networked, written as much as I have, and learnt so much about how this crazy industry works had it not been for Write to Play. All of those opportunities made all the fear worth it. But getting to be part of the Graeae Family? That is the real, but unexpected, bonus.

So throw yourself at the opportunities. Ask every little question and make connections. Write all those things you've been too nervous to write before. Learn. Grow. And most of all—enjoy.

Don't forget to invite me to your sharings next year!

With fourteen writers now graduated, and with

[Writing & New Work + Chloe Todd Fordham]

Graeae still continuing a relationship with all the writers in some capacity (the words 'our doors are always open' is said, and meant, at the end of every year of the programme) it was quite clear that the programme was snowballing. The number of enquiries we had from writers about how to get involved increased, and new writing organisations began to ask if they could partner with Graeae. Something was shifting, the industry was starting to sit up, some of the graduates were starting to get agents and commissions. It was clear Write to Play needed to broaden into a new writing strategy that could support playwrights at all levels of their career, and which could continue to provoke and challenge the sector on accessibility and inclusion.

Play Labs and the birth of Play Chats

Running alongside Write to Play, but predating Write to Play, was an initiative called Play Labs. Play Labs offered theatre-makers one day's R&D in Graeae's accessible studio space, support from Graeae in assembling a creative team, financial support, mentorship and creative advice. Play Labs began to serve as a natural progression route for Write to Play graduates, or for artists we met through Write to Play callouts. But there was still something crucial missing. Where were the accessible writing programmes for D/deaf and disabled writers who were just starting out? And if there was no entry point, how could writers advance their skills and experience to the point where they would benefit from the more advanced training offered on Write to Play?

We devised a companion scheme, called Play Chats.

Play Chats would offer a dedicated space to writers right at the beginning of their careers. It gave these writers the opportunity to get a flavour for writing, to be introduced to some of the craft, to share their ideas and get some feedback, and also for us to signpost individuals to other introduction to playwriting courses. The hope then would be to inspire a generation of writers to get writing, that—when the time was right—these writers might then apply for Write to Play or Play Labs. That on Write to Play they would develop their practice and write plays that—when the time was right—would be produced, and these writers would act as role models for the generation behind them, who would in turn apply for Play Chats ... and so on and so forth.

Cosmic Scallies

We're cosmic scallies, we dance on the off-beat, we're wonky shopping trollies, we're forgotten and trod on, we're gravy-stained and piss-sodden, we're the breath between coughing fits.
—*Cosmic Scallies*

Perhaps the biggest measure of success for any writing programme is when a writer has a work produced. Jackie Hagan joined the Write to Play programme in its second year. Describing herself as a 'working class, queer theatre-maker, live artist, stand-up comedian and committed community arts worker', Write to Play was Jackie's introduction into playwriting in the formal sense.

This is the first time I've written a play. I secretly dreamt of being Willy Russell but I had put playwriting on an impossible pedestal, 'not for the likes of me'. This scheme has made me get out of my own way and I'm realising the scope of possibilities this type of storytelling gives me and I'm dead, dead excited about what I am going to make happen in the future.

—Jackie Hagan

When Jackie delivered the second draft of her Write to Play piece, a three-hander called *Spurt*, we were excited. Jackie had loads to say about the world, her writing was funny and tender and raw, she was writing from the heart. But the play didn't work yet. With the dramaturgical and pastoral support of Jeff Young, playwright and Jackie's mentor on Write to Play, Jackie delivered a next draft a few months later. The play had changed a lot. It was now a two-hander. It was set exclusively in Skem (Skelmersdale). It was about a friendship and loss and belonging and being working class and disabled. It had a new title, *Cosmic Scallies*.

Cosmic Scallies was the first play written on the Write to Play programme that was professionally produced. It was co-produced by Graeae and the Royal Exchange Theatre, Manchester, in 2017.

Reviews of *Cosmic Scallies* from *The Scotsman*

Northern Stage at Summerhall (Venue 26) ★★★★

A place of concrete, roundabouts and housing schemes, it quickly became the town that time forgot. But there are plenty of people who harbour affection for 'Skem', among them spoken-word artist Jackie Hagan, as her first play proves. A graduate of Graeae's Write to Play scheme for emerging playwrights, Hagan has written a love letter to her home town, beautifully evoked by Bethany Wells' set of multi-level concrete benches. As Dent and Shaun find unlikely companionship in the concrete jungle of Skem the play opens up questions about leaving and staying, and admitting you need a helping hand in a world where 'you're not allowed to be broken'.

from North West End

Writer Jackie Hagan, who herself identifies as a working-class woman from the town *The Guardian* called 'a waking nightmare', has created a tender and funny portrait of her much maligned Lancashire home town, and of a friendship between a pair of odd balls—'wonky shopping trolleys' who, despite the different paths they've taken in life, still experience the same hopes and fears: of the dark, of being alone, of not repeating the mistakes of absent fathers.

As Shaun and Susie reconnect, filling in the gaps of their threadbare friendship, their conversation at points briefly touches upon wider social and political themes, such as austerity, discrimination, the pay gap, and the demonisation of the working classes.

But the play really sings when it focuses on the personal—Shaun and Susie sitting in the dark, wrapped in fairy lights, chomping on Space Raiders and necking Irn Bru.

[Writing & New Work + Chloe Todd Fordham]

WRITE TO PLAY YEAR FOUR, YEAR FIVE, AND BEYOND

Write to Play is the most inspiring and encouraging opportunity I have had as a writer. I have had access to workshops, mentors, and the Graeae team, all who have helped me to explore my writing in ways not possible before. Apply, it will change your life forever.
—Khush Chahal

With Jackie Hagan and *Cosmic Scallies* leading the way, the Write to Play programme was growing and growing. Year Four, a Midlands-based year in partnership with the Curve Leicester, the Belgrade Coventry and the Birmingham REP, attracted more applicants than ever before. In reflection of this, we gave places to six writers (instead of five). They were: Khush Chahal, Naomi Westerman, Mike Southan, Jessica Lovett, Hannah Torrance and Karran Collings. Running alongside this were plans for Year Five, involving a return to London and a callout for BAME D/deaf and disabled writers.

By the end of 2017, we will have worked with twenty-five writers. By the end of 2018, it will be thirty. For as long as the programme exists, the numbers will keep increasing. I for one hope the programme exists in ten years' time, and in twenty, and in thirty. But I also secretly hope one day Write to Play won't have to exist. For no other reason than it shouldn't have to. As I write, in 2017, it is not just a writing programme, it is one of the only barrier-free spaces for D/deaf and disabled artists to create. All writing programmes should be barrier-free. How far away are we from that future? I don't know, exactly. All I know is Graeae can't do that on its own: and neither should we. We're moving in the right direction. When I think of our writers I know we are definitely moving in the right direction. Until then, Write to Play is critical.

We remain hugely grateful to our primary funders, the Esmee Fairbairn Foundation, without whom none of this work would be possible.

Alex Bulmer

Writer, Actor, Director and Film-Maker

Dedicated in memory of Tim Gebbbels and Sophie Partridge, my much adored friends and artists.

My association with Graeae has a twenty-six-year history. In 1991, while studying as an international student in the advanced voice programme at Central School of Speech and Drama, I met Graeae artistic director Ewan Marshall, producer Steve Mannix and education officer Carolyn Lucas in a small and somewhat precarious portable structure, which I think, was called the Interchange Studios. It was a meeting that I can now say likely influenced most of my working life. They offered me a job. Soon I was working with the company as a tutor on a disabled youth theatre project led by visually impaired artist Ailsa Fairley. Admittedly, I started the job with hesitation. At that time, I was in the very early stages of sight loss, and somewhat uncertain of an association with disability. Then the art hit me. Throughout that project I experienced wheelchair dancing, heard a teenage girl toss aside her computerized speech device and go fully into free vocal expression (including many a glorious 'f--- yes!'), listened to the power of Deaf percussionist Evelyn Glennie, and devised a great piece of disabled-led theatre. My uncertainty about art and disability dissolved.

> Four years prior to that time, when I'd first been diagnosed with degenerative sight loss, I'd been advised by doctors to abandon any notion of having an artistic career, as no one would want to see a blind person 'tripping across a stage'. My week with Graeae in 1991 silenced those voices and my understanding of what is possible changed forever.

Fast forward to the year 2004 and I had returned to the UK and was once again working with Graeae, and had another changing moment. This time I was leading a voice workshop for performers with differing speech patterns. The term 'differing speech' evolved during the planning phase while in discussion with Jenny Sealey and Jamie Beddard (associate director) and Claire Saddleton (access manager). It was a defining term for the two weeks that followed, as I grew to understand the expansive diversity of expression within the human voice. All of the participants in the workshop, if referred to in medical terminology, would have been identified as having significant speech impairment. Working with these artists revolutionised my approach to voice work and inclusive learning. It became apparent that nearly any exercise or any performative use of voice was possible once the essence of the work had been identified and communicated. None of the participants could execute a tongue roll in order to open the back of the throat, but oh how they used their imagination to trigger sensations of space and vocal freedom.

I vividly recall the moment that participant Pete Edwards spoke Hamlet's *'To be or not to be'*; infusing the text with meaning as I'd never heard before because of his focus and commitment to every word. Pete went on to become an award-winning theatre artist and he and I continued to develop an exciting and rewarding relationship through voice work.

For a number of years I was a voice and text instructor with London Metropolitan University and Graeae on an actor training course called Missing Piece. *Blasted* by Sarah Kane was on the curriculum and I was asked to direct a recorded reading of it with a team of actors. As the reading was intended to give access to blind students on the course, I directed the actors to read their own stage directions (connecting them to character). At the conclusion of this reading we all agreed that speaking the directions transformed the piece. A year later, Jenny Sealey and I teamed up and a Graeae production of *Blasted* toured the country to great critical and audience acclaim. Yes, we did the play with spoken stage directions. The experience revealed how imagining audience and artistic direction can intersect. My artistic practice has since repeatedly been fueled by a process of imagining audiences beyond the sighted assumed.

In 2008, Graeae and BBC Radio 4 partnered to create an original production inspired by the classic Victor Hugo novel *Notre-Dame De Paris*. I joined writer Jack Thorne and dramaturg/producer Polly Thomas to scribe Part 1 of a two part series. I had written for stage and done smaller radio plays in Canada but this project pushed my skills and craft in all the best ways. The production won an AMI Media Award for best radio drama and I have since had the honour of working with Jack and Polly on other projects.

Somewhere between 2006 and 2010 I took on the challenge to develop a department of new work and new writing for Graeae. While in Canada I had been involved in numerous writing programmes and felt very strongly that there was a gap in the UK for development of original work by disabled artists. My objective for Graeae was to design and implement a series of opportunities that both supported early flashes of ideas as well as more structured schemes to develop craft, dramaturgy, and scripts.

I worked alongside literary assistant Carissa Hope Lynch and launched Play Labs, an incubation space supporting disabled artists to risk, fail, succeed, boil and percolate—essentially to play. The first Play Lab supported Clair Chapwell to explore ideas around epilepsy, identity and intimacy. The scheme, to my sheer delight, has continued to this day and has enabled so many artists and their many ideas. It is a creative birthplace.

We also seeded other more structured programmes, including Write To Play.

The Write To Play programme grew from what I observed to be a gap in the ecology of playwriting and theatre-making within the UK, and a need for the sector as a whole to support, develop and produce work written or created by D/deaf and disabled artists.

The programme, now in its fifth season, has succeeded to shift concepts of dramaturgy and play-making and has helped to launch writing careers and new creative companies.

I counted. I have been involved in some way in over fourteen projects with Graeae over the past thirteen years. Corned Beef!! What a ride.

Carissa Hope Lynch

Script Development

I'm going to be brutally honest. And this kind of honesty, well it's exposing. But it's the kind of thing that working with Graeae made me demand of myself and others.

I wanted to be one of the great and the good. Now, when someone who identifies as non-disabled says something like that to me, and then says they want to work with a D/deaf and disabled-led company to 'help out' and 'make a difference', one has to consider what that actually means. Who is that for? And why is that?

The answer is altruism. And the answer is me. And the answer is—so I didn't have to feel bad about how disabling and dehumanising our society can actually be.

So that I wouldn't have to feel guilty about how debilitating so much of city planning is. The ableist fascism of technology and design.

So that I wouldn't feel a part of the denial of basic human rights: education, communication, recognition, participation, presence. Work.

My journey with Graeae was one of change. But it was me who was changed in the process. Selfish I know, but you'll notice a theme here. Slowly but surely, I came to learn that my mindset wasn't helping—it was hindering. Patronising.

I was part of the problem. Indeed, I am still all too often a part of the problem. It's just less often than before.

I often talk about the unconscious bias I feel as a woman of colour from a lower economic background. A person who's had to fight to become 'upwardly mobile', whatever that means. But my journey with Graeae unlocked in me both ferociously and tenderly the realisation that I carry just as much bias towards many, as many do towards me.

My first real day at Graeae was the first time I ever properly worked with Jenny.

(If you haven't met Jenny, she is a gale force of nature. A force to be reckoned with. The beating heart of Graeae. The pulsing creative brains fuelling the fluid and fast-hive mind. I often use 'Jenny' and 'Graeae' interchangeably.)

We were devising *The Garden*. I was there, contributing and note-taking. I was an access proxy. I was a participant. I was listening. I drew pictures. Imagined images. Painted phrases in the air. The morning was a flurry of ideas.

Then we broke for lunch. We had the wonderful pick 'n' mix which I had come to know Jenny loves: olives, hummus, a selection of cheese, pita bread, salad, fruit, a pitcher of water, glasses for everyone, biscuits, teas, and a cafetière of marvellously muddy coffee to follow.

Then we jumped straight back into the conversation. But something in the air was different. There was tension. I can't remember between whom or why. I don't even think it was caused by anyone in the room.

[Writing & New Work + Carissa Hope Lynch]

I can't remember. But the gist of the conversation was support. The gist was communication. The gist was that access was going to be denied. And Jenny stepped out, breathing—in with the good, out with the bad. Tears. You see, in that moment none of us knew what Jenny had just learned which was that there would be cuts to sign language 'terps'. And this would massively—and detrimentally—change how not just Jenny, but the entire creative team could work throughout the process. And indeed, during future processes.

I ask myself, why is this the moment that I recall as my Graeae first?

I was asking myself, when we say 'access to work' what do we consider work? And is art, and the making thereof, also work? The work of an artist is the act of art-making. That is work. And artists—D/deaf, disabled, non-disabled, whatever—are the lifeblood of innovation and change. To cut that off is to sever society's potential ability to change. By god, do we need to change. And that is when it dawned on me.

To deny anyone the ability to work. Well that's not just disabling, it's dehumanising. Desocialising. It is to qualify that work as therapy. As an 'applied' or amateur practice. That is the complete opposite to how anyone I've ever come into contact with, who's ever come into contact with Graeae, has ever described their work. And Jenny is at the centre of that work.

To stop that work is to say that change is no longer necessary. That we're all doing ok already. That is simply not true. Any notion of equality today is a myth lived out by people who've grown fat off the status quo.

Here's the brutal honesty: it's not doing a great service to level out the playing field, especially if the role you play keeps people on the bench, or in the stands, or even outside the arena because hell, tickets to this game are expensive and it's sold out. Everyone has a right to play or contribute to the game. Every role participating in that game is important. Everyone plays those roles in their own way. The different ways we play should not be reprimanded, corrected, infantilised, or demonised. Nor should they be sanctified. But the truth is, this doesn't happen.

> The truth is that, however close we have been to reaching parity on and off the pitch, fundamental barriers are being built and reinforced, even as I write, that prevent that parity.

> I realised that day at Graeae that my attitude was all about insisting on playing the game in the belief that I was somehow creating equality. And the truth is, I wasn't. I was contributing to inequality.

> I've stepped away from Graeae but it lives on and thrives without me. No surprises there. The surprise came when I realised that, although Graeae doesn't need me, we certainly need Graeae.

> **As selfish as it may be, I am grateful for the change that Jenny and Graeae brought into my life. And you know what? If that is the great and good work of Graeae—to influence and change one selfish fucker and do-gooder at a time—then we can certainly say that the work is a force for change in this world. Because it has. It is.**

[Writing & New Work + Carissa Hope Lynch]

Jenny Sealey

Satsuki Yoshino

International

Jenny Sealey

CEO/Artistic Director, Graeae Theatre

International Work

The UK has long been at the forefront of the global disability arts movement. This is largely because we are fortunate to have an Arts Council that funds this work and (until recently) the government sponsored Access to Work scheme which supported the access requirements that enable disabled people to work. People internationally look to the UK as an inspiration, as the struggle to be a D/deaf and disabled artist in many countries is fraught with attitudinal barriers, lack of physical access to training, and no inclusive arts infrastructure. The arts are seen in many places as therapeutic or a nice little activity done to, rather than with, disabled people.

It has always been vital to Graeae to be a part the movement to develop a global disability arts movement because of our profound belief that theatre changes lives, both for the artist and the audience. The process of making and performing theatre is transformative and empowering for anyone who has previously been sidelined by society and treated as a second-class citizen. Theatre is the best way to challenge perceptions of disability in a consensual space—where the disabled artist gives permission to be looked at and makes a bold political statement on their right to lead in the creative act.

JAPAN

Graeae's international work has skyrocketed since our involvement in the 2012 Olympic and Paralympic Games, but it was previous work in Japan that created a real template for our international process and gave me my first experience of working across multiple spoken and signed languages.

The mission of Mr Ohta (Able Art Japan) and Satsuki Yoshino (an independent producer) is to use theatre to break down attitudinal barriers and to create a narrative of inclusion and equality in Japan. I found myself visiting Japan with my signer Jeni Draper twice a year from 2008 to 2011 to deliver one or two-week workshop residencies for large groups of D/deaf, disabled, and non-disabled people. The participants started to gain confidence over time and eventually became comfortable calling themselves artists. They made history at the end of the project by taking centre stage as the first disabled people to perform in mainstream theatre in Japan.

We had beautiful stages to work on: Setagaya Public Theatre for *Blood Wedding* and Saitama Arts Centre (the late Ninagawa's theatre) for *Romeo and Juliet*. Both productions proved to be extraordinary experiences.

I was riveted by the intense conversations about translating the name for the character of Leonardo in *Blood Wedding*, as we searched for a meaning that captured the spirit of the character. It became Hayato Kurokawa, Hayato meaning fast and nimble and Kurokawa being a family name meaning black river. We learned about the complex social interactions between men and women in Japan, for example the flirting rituals which avoid any eye contact. Even though there was a shared understanding of the emotional landscape the 'acting of this' flirtatious behaviour was still polite and restrained. This particular detail was something with which I struggled. I wanted to encapsulate the passion of love, lust, and grief in a visceral and exposing way but I knew that I needed to be respectful of cultural differences. I continued to give space and permission throughout rehearsals to let go of restraint and, in so doing, unearthed beautiful and intense performances, an authentic blend of Eastern and Western values.

Having a Deaf Bride and a blind Father in *Blood Wedding* allowed us to play with the Bride texting Hayato directly in front of her Father who could not see her actions. We were also able to explore the diverse behaviours of the Neighbour who used a different voice pattern when communicating with the Deaf Mother of the Groom. The Groom signed to his Bride but Hayato, being more confident and assured of his relationship with the Bride, believed his passion and the 'language of love' communicated everything.

Romeo and Juliet used a framing device that freed us to break various theatrical conventions: the play was imagined as taking place within an evening class studying Shakespeare. After playing with the first few scenes for a time, we decided to cast two actors as Juliet—one Deaf and one hearing—and to use the same convention for the Nurse. The Deaf Nurse also signed for Romeo but, as his love with Juliet blossomed, Romeo began to sign for himself. The play was also captioned in Japanese which was the first time this had ever been done in Japan. To complete the picture, our onstage actors/signers also wove a live audio description narrative between scenes.

> The production took place only months after the 9.0-magnitude earthquake in 2011 and so it was to a rather fragile Japan that we returned. I felt that I couldn't use the contemporary framing setting without referencing what had happened, as each day the actors mentioned the rising statistics of missing people. I asked one actor during rehearsals to write down the ever-growing number of the missing as part of her 'classroom' character. I promised that we would find a moment during the show when she would reveal what it was she was doing. The producers were unhappy with this choice because they felt it was too soon after the event and it would be upsetting for the audience. The actors were divided in opinion so, as a compromise, I had the 'teacher' character dial a number on her phone throughout the play saying, 'please pick up, please pick up', believing audiences would create their own response. Many did indeed make the link to the missing people, including a director who had lost friends and family in the disaster. He was an older man cloaked in grief but he said seeing D/deaf, disabled, and non-disabled people working together in the production gave him hope and said now there was light for the future. He then hugged me tightly and I bawled my eyes out in front of an entire audience.

[International + Jenny Sealey]

BANGLADESH

Bangladesh proved to be a vastly different experience to our time in Japan, where we had worked with people who had some experience of theatre. The performers we worked with in Bangladesh had no previous exposure to the arts. We encountered director, producer, and freedom fighter Nasiruddin Yousuf ('Bachchu'). In 2012 Bachchu directed *The Tempest* in London as part of the Globe to Globe season. Bachchu had been thinking about the absence of D/deaf and disabled people in Bangladeshi theatre. He contacted Graeae and suddenly we were going to Dhaka twice a year to deliver two-week intensive training workshops for large groups of disabled people. Many of these participants came to us through the Centre for the Rehabilitation of the Paralysed and others were sourced from Building Resources Across Communities (BRAC), a large NGO that supports the education of disabled people in rural communities. The D/deaf gang came from an organisation similar to BRAC. The workshops were supported by the British Council, National Theatre of Dhaka, and BRAC.

> The training was run at an outdoor canopied space next to a man-made lake at Savar, the BRAC conference centre. This was the only venue we could find where any sort of accessible spaces and bathrooms were available. I remember entering the space for the first time to find a large group of people with beautifully diverse physicalities asking me to pray for them and rid them of their impairments. My carefully constructed workshop plan immediately went out of the window and the sessions were reworked to explore ownership, awareness, and acceptance of self that led to the creation of protest songs and short scenes about human rights.

The initial long-term plan was for Bachchu and me to co-direct *A Midsummer Night's Dream* with a cast of D/deaf, disabled, and non-disabled actors. Bachchu and I quickly realised there would be a clash of egos in the rehearsal room so he agreed to produce the show alongside the British Council and I would direct. The next stage was to explain to our partners that the actors from our training workshops were completely new to performance and that to place them on a stage alongside trained actors from National Theatre of Dhaka would be extremely exposing for them.

I ultimately chose to direct *Romeo and Juliet* after reflecting on the early moments of the project. The themes of the play are universal and I could draw on my experience of directing the show in Japan to inform the process.

We shot a trailer film short with some of the Bangladeshi workshop team and the British Council to promote the production. *What is Love?* was launched online on 14 February 2014, (vimeo.com/134173868) and confirmed my belief that everyone has a right to love and be loved. I cast the R&J team with thirteen D/deaf and disabled actors, three blind musicians, and the wife of one of the musicians, all drawn from the last workshop we ran. In true Graeae style, I doubled up the key characters—Romeo, Juliet, Nurse, Tybalt, and Mercutio—with one disabled actor and one Deaf Bangla Sign Language user working together on each part so that we had the richness of both spoken and signed words. The blind musicians and the actor playing Benvolio delivered some audio description and the text was captioned in both English and Bangla.

[International + Jenny Sealey]

The play started with a cricket match; this was something the cast and crew did every night after workshops, making it feel theatrically and culturally right to include it in the show. It also allowed the audience to appreciate the agility of those performers who walked on their knees, walked on their hands, or walked on all fours. The women joined in the game and as each person caught the ball they would say their name and a short audio description of who they were. The last person to catch the ball dropped her book as she did so. The boys grabbed the book and the pages of Romeo and Juliet fell out. Morshed (who has the best smile in the world) read out the cast list and cast the show with himself as Benvolio.

> The prologue was spoken and signed which was a way for the audience to understand that this would be the ongoing convention for this production.
>
> Romeo and his gang gatecrashed the Capulet's party with brightly coloured head scarves; Romeo and Juliet shared their first kisses as they slowly unwrapped his scarf and then kissed behind it.
>
> I had to be sensitive to the concerns of the Deaf actor playing Juliet, that having a tactile relationship with the actor playing Romeo might damage her own arranged marriage process. The other actor playing Juliet had a love marriage and, as a result, had no contact with her or her husband's family. She was not fearful of being tactile with other performers so I had the best of both worlds and was able to explore multiple aspects of Juliet through touch and through sign language, which are both visual ways of conveying love and passion.

The actors playing Mercutio, Tybalt, and Benvolio all had floor-based modes of moving: walking on their hands or knees or with hands and feet. They had a substantial advantage in stealth and speed over their regular-height actors in fight scenes. Romeo, who used a bamboo stick as his left leg, used this stick as a weapon only for it to be finally used against him; Tybalt floored Mercutio by trapping him between his short but extremely powerful legs.

Directors Esha Yousuf and Dola Jahan Samiun worked with the actors on understanding and delivering the (spoken) text and we worked collectively to share this newly discovered understanding to support the translation into Bangla Sign Language.

It was an emotional experience seeing the cast emerge from their cocoons and become butterflies owning their stage and expressing pride in what they achieved. The stage, the National Theatre Hall of Bangladesh Shilpakala Academy, was not accessible but Bachchu had organised the knocking down of walls and the creation of a ramp to enable wheelchair users to access the auditorium. He had the dressing room bathroom doors widened and ramps installed backstage. For the first time in the theatre's history, we had an all D/deaf and disabled cast on stage, with D/deaf and disabled people rubbing shoulders with non-disabled audience members.

[International + Jenny Sealey]

BRAZIL

The work we undertook in Brazil is perhaps the greatest legacy of the London 2012 Paralympic Games Opening Ceremony (POC).

Graeae was invited to remount their production *Reasons to be Cheerful* as part of the Brazil British Council Transformations programme in 2013. The programme was designed as a lead up to the 2016 Olympic and Paralympic Games in Rio de Janeiro. An extremely excited group of cast, musicians, and crew arrived in Rio ready to rock 'n' roll. I had arrived earlier to take part in a series of handover talks with the Brazilian team and to share my experience of being a part of the 2012 games.

Artistic directors Junior Perim and Vinicius Damaus were in the audience for our performance of *Reasons* and invited me to see a show by Crescer e Viver, their social circus company. Based on that first meeting of minds and propelled by the fieriness of Junior and the ambition of Vinicius I found myself, along with Tina Carter (aerial choreographer for the POC) and five of our ceremony performers, in Rio working with five Brazilian D/deaf and disabled artists. The core purpose was to start the process of training the Brazilian artists and circus staff in ways of working with diverse physicalities and communication styles. Junior was keen for us to create work for their International Circus Festival in 2014 which was held in Rio and São Paulo. This was also the year in which The Roundhouse in Chalk Farm, London held a circus festival at which we were due to perform. Our stated theme for Brazil was 'belonging' because we did feel we belonged together.

We spent ten days with the Brazilian team but, in hindsight, we should have spent much longer working together. Not only would this have given the Brazilian artists a longer time in which to hone their skills, but it would also have allowed me the opportunity to more perfectly understand the language of circus, and for Vinicius and I to develop the narrative of the final piece face-to-face rather than by email supported by Google Translate. As a result, we created a piece that half-worked and was half-finished. We had to manage with a dress rehearsal run for our first audience because we were simply not ready (a first for me). Tempers frayed, bodies ached, details were forgotten. I was forced to take stock and remember that most of the Brazilian and some of the UK artists were still very new to this process. The decision to step back took the pressure off everyone and eventually cast and crew pulled it out of the bag. However, the subsequent performances at The Roundhouse circus festival continued to reveal holes in the piece. Vinicius and Tina kept working on the show for the final Brazilian performances. It continued to grow and, by the time they got to São Paulo, it was good show.

Vinicius and I underwent an intensive debrief on the show, agreeing that an overwhelming clash of egos, and my ego railroading his contribution, had led to difficulties. We also finally came to an understanding that he is the circus artist and I am not! I was truly and rightly put in my place. We concurred that we had not given ourselves enough lead-in time, we made the huge mistake of cutting corners to make the finances work, and we did not make time after each rehearsal to sit down with a beer or cuppa to do a daily debrief. We eventually hugged and started planning our next venture.

[International + Jenny Sealey]

And the next venture came soon. The wonderful legacy of our first Brazilian partnership emerged when Crescer e Viver and People's Palace Project (London/Brazil) set up Circo sem Limites (Circus without Limits), a new inclusive company which premiered the show *Prada Shakespeare* at the Brazilian Cultural Olympiad in 2016. I acted as artistic advisor for the project, working alongside Vinicius once again and with Zé Alex, another director.

> Despite a brutal economic climate in Brazil, Crescer e Viver and People's Palace Project have plans to continue working together and to get the message out there: being D/deaf or disabled is not limiting!

Satsuki Yoshino

Independent Arts Manager

I saw *peeling* by Graeae in April, 2002. It was an eye-opening experience for me; it completely changed my image of disability arts and made me start thinking about accessibility in theatre.

I organised my first workshops in Japan with Jenny in 2004. Although I was experienced in organising workshops, I realised there were many things I had to think about and do to make the workshop accessible for D/deaf and disabled participants. I was understandably anxious about this visit.

However, Jenny blew away my anxiety as she treated everybody in the room (disabled, D/deaf, and non-disabled people) equally and everybody focused on how we could make theatre together. The workshops provided a chance to think about the meaning of 'access' in theatre and how peoples' differences can lead to various theatrical expressions.

I have worked with Jenny many times since those workshops. We have conducted numerous workshops and produced two plays in Japan, *Blood Wedding* (2007) and *Romeo and Juliet* (2010). The participants of the workshops and casts of the two productions were always a mix of D/deaf, disabled, and non-disabled people.

Blood Wedding and *Romeo and Juliet* were both beautiful shows and these projects paved the way for making a new theatre form with integrated access in Japan. Over 100 people participated in the workshops and over sixty people (cast and creatives) worked on the two productions.

> There were over 300 applications for the auditions of *Romeo and Juliet* and Jenny gave workshop auditions for 200 applicants. She ran ten one-hour workshops with twenty people per workshop. Soon after the auditions in March, 2011, Japan had a big earthquake in Tohoku (East Japan) and an accident at the Fukushima nuclear power plant. I did not think the planned production of *Romeo and Juliet* would happen. Not only was this a severe situation in Japan but also, I thought in all reality that no one was likely to come to Japan under those circumstances. However, in October, 2011 Jenny and her interpreter Jeni came back to Japan for *Romeo and Juliet* and created a stunning show with our Japanese team.

> I had a memorable experience in the post-performance talk. We invited a theatre producer from Tohoku as a guest speaker. He had lost so much in the earthquake. At the end of the talk, he was asked the question, 'What is the theatre to you now?' He answered, 'Having seen this production and this way of working, theatre is the light of the future.' I was deeply impressed with what he said and happy that the light is still shining in Japan.

All this happened before the London 2012 Paralympic Games. We did not know at that time that the 2020 Olympics and Paralympics would be held in Tokyo. We now have a flourishing disability arts movements, started in the run up to 2020 in and around Tokyo. The many seeds Jenny planted have already grown in Japan as some of the participants have become leaders of the movement and are making those seeds bloom beautifully.

I hope Jenny and Graeae will collaborate with those who are inspired by them and will create hybrid flowers of disability arts between the UK and Japan in the near future.

[International + Satsuki Yoshino]

The Board
Adam Hemmings

Richard Matthews
Dr. Kay Hepplewhite

Behind the
Scenes

Jenny Sealey

The Board

Avis Johns, Co-Founder, Social Engine
and Jodi Myers, Arts Consultant, Jodi Myers Projects
Interview with Avis Johns (AJ), Jodi Myers (JM) and Jenny Sealey (JS)

JS	Thank you both for coming.
	Let's talk about your time on the board and the journey you took us on to get to where we are now: things that were good, things that were tough, and some of the decisions you had to make. Who was the chair in the beginning? Was is Steve?
AJ	We have had Theresa Veith, David Pain, Rena Sodhi, Steve Mannix and Dawn Langley!
JM	I suspect that the quick succession of chairs was reflective of a less stable time. We eventually came into that more secure time through the experience of the capital programme to secure the building. I think this marked a moment of maturity for the board. There was a 'shit or get off the pot' moment. That journey gave the board confidence which meant that, when the Paralympics came up, we understood that it was a big risk but we'd taken big risks before in securing the building.
AJ	It felt like everybody knew their roles and, although we were not a large board, everyone was active. I think that is why we felt comfortable when Jen was invited to co-direct the London 2012 Paralympic Games Opening Ceremony (POC). It was a challenge to the company but one we thought we could manage. As a board, we'd been together for several years and so there was a sense of stability.

JM	While we've had five chairs, that's almost irrelevant as we were trying different management models.
JS	We had Roger Nelson and I as joint CEO and he was the main leader on the first capital programme. I loved working with Roger. We worked hard together to raise the profile of the company within the sector. We then had SMT with the triumvirate of Judith Kilvington, Claire Saddleton and me.
AJ	Then you and Judith became joint CEO and she lead on capital. Then Judith was solely in charge in the period that you were away doing the Paralympics. We have tried lots of different ways of working. I think that gave us confidence that the company could deal with change and the board could deal with change.
JM	That is also a factor of being a responsive organisation. This organisation always seeks to see the talent, the opportunity in a situation. By exploring different management techniques, I like to think that the company is always able to respond to changing circumstances. I always celebrated the fact that everybody on the board got on together. We explored issues deeply, for example the decision on the building and discussing the challenges of Jenny being absent largely for a year.
AJ	We have been part of Graeae as the growing brand; that was a step change for the company.
JS	Avis, you were central to that change because of your communications and marketing background. You pushed an awareness of the growing brand and moved this agenda forward. That was when

communications and marketing started to become something we had to take seriously.

AJ   Because I'm not from the arts world, it was a joy to have had the opportunity to explore these issues with professionals. We all had different experiences, different roles on the board. The joy of immersing yourself in the professionalism and the experience of others was profound.

JS   You came from John Grooms (organisation of residential care homes for disabled adults), didn't you? It is a little-known fact that he gave jobs to disabled women to make artificial flowers for the rich so they had flowers in the winter!

And it was you who started the ball rolling with the play *Flower Girls* by Richard Cameron. This was your baby, wasn't it?

AJ   It was. My motivation in joining the Graeae board was to explore the social model of disability and certainly my personal motivation has always been focused on human rights and justice. The disability organisation I was working for used the medical model of disability. I had a desire to create and provide an opportunity for these women's voices to be heard through *Flower Girls* and as much as it was an opportunity to work with Graeae, there was also an opportunity for the project. These women were being written off as little old ladies, which is what they appeared to be in a care home. Yet they'd had the most fantastic sex with soldiers during the Second World War ...

I thought, good! Let's tell that story! And the stories were something that John Grooms needed to hear as well.

JS	I remember having meetings with John Grooms staff to reassure them that we wouldn't damage the John Grooms reputation. At the same time, we were clear that we were moving away from the medical model.
	I must re-visit that play because it's beautiful and I think we should record it as a radio play.
AJ	I agree and I think it's a treasure. Those people that bore witness to the Second World War are fewer in number every year. There is something important about capturing those stories. We need to hold on to the perspective of disabled women during that period in history.
JS	That production was our first time working with Nickie Miles-Wildin as an actor. And look at where she is now. She's directing for the National Theatre. It's brilliant. What a journey she's been on.
JM	*Flower Girls* was part of the step change in the company and the impact it had is important. In the time that we were involved with the company, it went from being a small-scale touring company to a national player. We didn't quite realise that at the time, we can only see it with hindsight. There were several contributing factors.
	One is the acquisition of the building because finally the company had a home. Second is the development of the aesthetics of access. That aesthetic changed radically in the period I was on the board: how we made sure that every piece was accessible. The third factor was the development of the outdoor work, the work of epic scale of which the ceremony was a large part. There were

all these strands of activity which I think raised the profile and set the company up to be something it had been working toward for a long period. It felt like things matured at the same time.

AJ   We talk about things changing and developing. You were the constant factor. The only thing that has been constant has been you.

Your journey as an artistic director and CEO is interesting, how you've navigated the changes, and become more confident. Your journey is absolutely synonymous with the establishment of the company and there's also an interesting legacy in the fact that Amit [Sharma] has developed in that period. The company feels bigger now and it feels a part of the theatre landscape.

JM   This is an organisation that has always taken risks. I think the ability to do that is made easier when you've got a mature infrastructure in the administration, in the finances, in the board. Once all of those process pieces are in place then the real magic hits.

AJ   It also gets more challenging. The context in which the company is operating is changing, with the threats to allowances and the economic pressure that disabled people are under now.

Expectations are also changing. We all thought that things were going to change after the Paralympics and some did, but a lot of change didn't last.

JS   Some of this is down to the government cutting allowances, it puts us all on a horrible downward slide. But Graeae is a company that has always needed to evolve. This is the moment we live in; these things have happened and we have to move on. We have to take the rough with the smooth. But bloody hell it is hard sometimes.

JM   I remember when we were an all-women board. There was the official business that we had to deal with and some hard decisions around financial risks in particular, but we always felt we could say, 'Hello. How are the kids? How's your working world, how are you coping?' We could make that space and time.

JS   When it was an all-women board the Arts Council said ...

AJ   'You've got to do something about it!'

JS   They told us we needed to think about the diversity of our board. We responded, 'but we really like it like this!'

There was a board meeting after you'd both gone when I felt that the company was being 'taken over' and we were losing our identity. I was trying to explain this situation to the board and how I was struggling and then I just burst into tears and wept. They let me cry and moved the meeting on. They did not judge me or think I was unprofessional. It was absolutely fine; they were behind me to help make the right decisions.

AJ   That is as it should be. Board discussions should be a safe space in which anyone can show emotion and share moments of concern. There is an extraordinary culture of support and care about Graeae and the board.

[Behind the Scenes + The Board]

JM	I've been on lots of boards and there is something distinctive about the culture here. Everyone is solicitous of everyone else. Everyone's looking after everybody. Maybe it is a feature of the disability sector, where people are more caring of each other?
JS	I think it's a combination of many factors. I remember hating board meetings during a period of the capital programme. Roger and I were on overload because of the sheer volume of work. He and I would leave board meetings at Holloway Road, go to our separate bathrooms and text each other. 'God that was awful. I need a drink. See you in The Coronet.' We'd both drink a very large gin and tonic and try and see the wood for the trees. Essentially all in all it was not the right project. I was heartbroken when he stepped down, but he did the right thing as it meant we could withdraw from it.

When Judith Kilvington became joint CEO, we embarked on a new capital programme. This one was a tough one too but she had learnt from Roger and was able to navigate it differently. She was extraordinary! She drove the capital project through with you two, Steve Mannix as chair and Jo Hemmant from ACE and the rest of the board. The building would not have happened if we hadn't had a strong board.

| AJ | It's amazing, sitting here now. You had so many planning conversations with the board about projects that were coming, things that we could do; so many years discussing whether we going to do an Ian Dury musical. And to now be triumphantly |

returning with *Reasons to be Cheerful*, it's such a joy. Such a reflection on the trajectory of this organisation.

JS What have we fucked up on?

AJ I think there are things that we've failed to do, but I wouldn't say that we fucked up.

JM That's it exactly—opportunities not exploited; not fucked up.

AJ There were times when tours should have come together better or more money should have been made but those are not fuck ups. That is just things not working in quite the way we wanted them to. It goes back to what we were talking about before—we expected attitudes to disability to change more than they did after the Paralympics. But that's not our problem alone, that's a much bigger issue. You can express disappointment in the fact that we expected certain opportunities for artists to be there that haven't been. But that's not a mistake. The time during which I was involved with the company was joyous. I'm not saying it was a joy all the time but overall it was because, by and large, things worked. Unless you kept things from us that we didn't know about?

JS Ha!! I think we have a real transparency at Graeae. We have to be transparent; it's public money if nothing else! Some directors demand a closed rehearsal room. I really question that ethos. If you are a public-funded organisation anybody should be able to come in and watch a rehearsal because it's taxpayers' money.

JM   That's something to do with the sector because the disability arts sector can't work unless it collaborates. There's a generosity about the sector that you don't necessarily find in other non-disabled parts of the theatre ecology.

AJ   The issue of intellectual property in the arts is an interesting subject matter. We've had quite a lot of discussions on this subject in the boardroom, haven't we? We pride ourselves that we've always been a generous and open company. We share our knowledge and expertise but sometimes I suspect we're being overly generous. It feels like people have taken advantage of our generosity at times. We need to find a balance.

JS   I have a clear memory of the moment immediately after I was offered the big job directing the POC. Judith was on a sabbatical and I'd gone through six horrendous interviews. Avis, I told you because I had to tell somebody on the board. You came straight to Graeae and got the ball rolling, talked to the team and board who quickly allocated funds from our reserves to start everything going in terms of PR, getting Amit onboard to act up and appointing Judith as sole CEO for the period. When poor old Judith came back, she had a lot of questions. It was all change!!!

JM   We couldn't have taken on that project had it not been board-driven. Sometimes the operations and board governance roles can get mixed up. But that was an example of when you had to involve the board.

JS   I will never forget the support of the board when I got the job doing 'Sports Day' [the Paralympics]

	but I was scared you might decide to ask me to leave.
AJ	I think that we were frightened you wouldn't come back!
JS	Where else would I go? I've been here for twenty years. I don't want to be anywhere else.
JM	You haven't shown any evidence of running out of steam. The company has developed consistently over the period that you have been here and you are developing the Amits and Nickie Wildins of this world.
JS	When Judith left Graeae, you allowed me some thinking space and time to plan our direction. That space gave me the opportunity to train the younger members of the team and now some of them are directors of their department and their wisdom and care keeps me grounded.
	Perhaps we should have an alumni board that meets twice a year to discuss programming and planning. What do you think?
JM	I've written about this in the past: boards don't use ex-board members as advocates. Graeae is good at keeping in touch with people but some boards don't keep in touch with members once they've left. As an ex-board member, I talk about Graeae all the time. It's important to recognise that people who have been associated with the company, either as employees or as board members, can do you a useful service.
AJ	The flip side is that ex-board members can think more creatively about what governance means to the company. The board has a distinct role to play

[Behind the Scenes + The Board]

but there are other ways of involving specialists and ex-board members in a way that can contribute to development. They can support and mentor new members and show them the ropes!

When we have recruited disabled board members, we have recognised that they haven't always had the opportunity to develop the skills that are required. In that respect, it's important that we are creative about ways to develop board members, formally or informally. There are many reasons why it makes sense for Graeae to use people with experience but also to help nurture talent, where that talent hasn't been allowed to shine before.

JS   I know that I've been a tick box for some of the boards that I've been on.

AJ   I can't imagine you ever being a tick box!

JS   Oh, but I have.

AJ   But you're so much trouble!

JS   Jodi, you mentored me and included training on how to become a better board member. I can still feel the benefits of that mentoring. Though I'll never be as good a board member as you two, ever.

JM   You're just too naughty.

JS   Naughty?

JM   Yeah.

JS   So maybe on that note we should shut up. A million thank yous and see you at *Reasons*!

Adam Hemmings

Writer and Activist

Graeae—A History in Language

Since Graeae's inception in 1980, the perception within society of both the company in particular and disability in general has undergone a drastic transformation. Leafing through old press clippings and news reports, it is striking how language itself has been tempered. Previously seen as a curiosity (and certainly not in the mainstream), Graeae has forged a path into the future based on tolerance, acceptance and sheer talent. This was not without its challenges, however; as the press grappled with a concept that they could not fully understand within their own framework of theatre.

In one of the earliest press mentions of Graeae in *The Stage* of 1981, the disabled company-members are contrasted with Richard Tomlinson, who is labeled 'able-bodied' and is the only named individual. Whilst the language is regressively standard for the time, it is disturbing that the focus is on the only non-disabled member of the company, as if this somehow lends credibility to its mission that would otherwise be detracted from by mentioning also Nabil Shaban, who was Graeae's co-founder and is disabled. Further dated language appears again in the use of 'handicapped' to describe the participants of a Graeae workshop.

A listing from the same year in *ILN's Guide to Events* for the production of *Sideshow* refers to Graeae as a company 'for the disabled'. Here, the language is again a relic of a different time, and suggests that at this point the purpose of the company was interpreted as less integrative and more exclusive than it came to be. Rather than a theatre company that advanced the right of D/deaf and disabled performers and production staff to be centre-stage in a deeply exclusionary industry, such language unhelpfully portrayed disability theatre as something separate from the mainstream.

> Graeae's own use of language in this early period also suggests conformity with norms of the period. An advertisement place in 1982 seeks a 'wheelchair-bound actress', revealing that at this time the company had not fully claimed the inclusive attitude for which it is now known.
>
> Jumping forward to 2002, some offensive language seems to still be entrenched in press coverage of Graeae. A review of *peeling* from *The Daily Telegraph* uses the term 'able-bodied' in reference to the audience (which as has already been pointed out is not an acceptable term), even though the reporter has no way of knowing whether all the audience is non-disabled. Two years later in its review for *On Blindness* (a collaboration between Paines Plough, Frantic Assembly and Graeae), *The Daily Telegraph* once again demonstrates that it is unable to talk of Graeae other than in the most fossilized and unimaginatively voyeuristic terms:
>
> 'While the blindness of Maria is an integral part of the plot, no one actually mentions the fact that the portrait painter is played by a Thalidomide victim with truncated arms. This seems odd, considering his occupation ... The play mysteriously ducks the very issues it ought to be exploring—the problems

disabled people face when it comes to sexual relationships, and the chasm that exists between the able-bodied and the disabled.'

Let us take a moment for this paragraph to sink in. Charles Spencer, the reporter, gazes upon the production that unfolds before him. He sees only questions, which have little or nothing to do with the quality of the work. He requires actors' disabilities to be marched out front and centre and explained to him. He wants to know how a 'Thalidomide victim' (note the terminology) could possibly ever be a painter (apparently the award-winning Alison Lapper slipped his mind). Moreover, he would quite like to know a bit about the sex the characters are having, because of course that 'chasm' means that it is probably not as good as the 'able-bodied' sex he is having, but he would not mind a peek. This is typically antiquated reviewing from an archaic newspaper at the dawn of the twenty-first century.

Ultimately, language and its usage is one of the primary domains of political power. Originally, this lexicon was controlled by those who held regressive views about Graeae in particular and disability in general, writing for an audience who may have shared many such views. Retaking ownership over language has been essential and Graeae is now routinely discussed in the media using the social model of disability as a starting point. Challenges linger, with some reporters insisting on residing in the Dark Ages. And yet, the words crafted by Graeae endure and remake that lexicon in our image to serve as a sign and a guide for the future.

[Behind the Scenes + Adam Hemmings]

Richard Matthews

Head of Marketing & Development, Graeae Theatre

Marketing to D/deaf and Disabled Audiences

Early on in my career, I remember attending a marketing seminar where one key principal stuck with me; that marketing and audience development should be inseparable; by marketing our work, we should always be aiming to reach an audience who are both new to our products or services, and to the sector. The idea made total sense to me. Our relationship with our regular, loyal audience can—and should—be a strategic one. While remembering that these friends of ours are a key factor for our box office targets, they can also be used to help advocate and endorse our offerings to a new audience. And as the term suggests, we should always be aiming to DEVELOP our audience. However loyal or regular our current bookers are, let's face it, they're not going to be around forever.

Furthermore, when we live in a society which is currently more divided than it has been for decades, I believe we have a moral duty as arts organisations—the cornerstones of our communities—to ensure our audience reflects the true diversity of this country.

Graeae's raison d'être for the last thirty-eight years has been to put D/deaf and disabled artists centre-stage for the work we tour nationally and internationally. We also build audio description, captioning and British Sign Language into the aesthetic of the production from day one of the artistic process, ensuring these features of accessibility aren't an 'add on' but deeply embedded into the soul of the piece. We come at marketing from the same place—we don't create marketing collateral and then create accessible versions, we ensure that everything we produce is accessible to as many people as possible. We do this through the choice of font, size, colour and layout, to name but a few. We also audio describe and caption all our promotional videos and trailers, and create BSL and audio collateral for D/deaf and blind/visually impaired audiences. We ensure our BSL and audio materials are always engaging and entertaining in their own right so they can be appreciated by all audiences, whether disabled, D/deaf, non-disabled or hearing.

Once we've created this collateral, we don't wait for people to find it. We make sure that we pro-actively target communities that will benefit from its accessibility, and ultimately the accessibility of the production. As such, a large part of the work we do in and around developing audiences is spent researching who (and where) the D/deaf and disabled people are within the regions we're touring to, and what networks they use. Once we've spent time finding these networks, we establish a connection with them. Building this connection means that we can then ask if they can help to disseminate the accessible information on the production, whether it be an audio flyer, BSL introduction or BSL synopsis, to their members and users. And as with all relationships, this needs to be two way. Think about what you can offer them in return for their help in spreading the word: complimentary tickets, or a post-show event with members of the cast.

The old marketing cliché of 'knowing your audience' is one we stick by at Graeae. We are careful to create several different versions of the material we send out to groups, so that the communication

[Behind the Scenes + Richard Matthews]

is targeted to the access requirement of the group we're talking to. Of course, we always work closely with the marketing departments of the theatres we're touring to as well, to ensure that we're communicating clearly to their previous and existing D/deaf and disabled audience members, and building on any existing relationships the venue has with networks and groups of D/deaf and disabled people locally.

Up until recently, we've mostly relied on electronic communication to connect with these groups and networks. This includes the powerful targeting tools that social media channels, including Facebook and Twitter, offer for reaching individuals and groups by location, interest, lifestyle etc, as well as the obvious benefit that Twitter offers for sharing information instantly through a single click of the mouse. However, we've always known that nothing beats face-to-face communication, especially when talking to a D/deaf or disabled (potential) audience, who may never have used the internet.[1] Though the usual pressures of limited time and resource has been our excuse, we're currently investigating how we can reach networks of D/deaf and disabled people across the country in a more people-centred approach, including building on the existing 'Agents for Change' model: nationwide ambassadors made up of D/deaf and disabled people.

There are some key design considerations to factor in when producing promotional literature. For example, avoid using text on top of images, ensure text used against a background colour is of clear contrast (printing first in black and white is a good test of this), use sans-serif fonts, avoid

[1] www.theguardian.com/technology/2015/jun/29/disabled-people-internet-extra-costs-commission-scope

hyphenation, use at least size 12 point and try to use 1.5mm line spacing. We always try to use the 'access logos' wherever possible, e.g 'CAP' or a wheelchair user icon in a black box on all print, as well as flagging that information is available in a variety of accessible formats, making clear how people can access this (email address and phone number), using this text in at least 16 point font size. Likewise with websites, ensure images have ALT text equivalents (descriptions of the image in text for visually impaired people), that your website works with a screen reader and has functionality to change colour contrast and enlarge the text size. We'd always recommend asking someone you know who is visually impaired to proof collateral or test your websites for you before going to print/going live, to ensure it is all as accessible as possible. Graeae can give further guidance on all of this, email access@graeae.org.

The three key pieces of advice I always give to participants at the accessible marketing sessions I run are as follows. **Firstly, include D/deaf and disabled audience members (both new to the venue and existing) as a target audience into the campaign messaging at planning stage. Secondly, research groups and networks locally of D/deaf and disabled people (remembering that any relationship needs benefit for both parties!) Finally, consult and involve D/deaf and disabled people in your campaign**—ensure their voices are heard and show you value their opinion by offering payment or equivalent. By following these key points, your audience development and marketing strategies will not only dovetail but will complement one another and ultimately become one and the same thing.

A version of this article was first published in *ArtsProfessional* in 2017.

Dr. Kay Hepplewhite

Senior Lecturer, Northumbria University

Acts of Translation—In Touch

Picture this: seated at the front of the rehearsal room at Bradbury Studios, Jenny Sealey and Ruslin Malikor share a directorial role, with an impressive twenty performers arranged across the stage area. They are polishing sections of the play *In Touch*, a collaboration between Graeae and Inclusion Theatre Company with Theatre of Nations, Moscow, to be performed at the National Theatre, London. Each director gives comments on the scene they have just watched. Not sharing a common language, they then pause for the Russian or English translation of everything each other says. Jenny's signer stands opposite her to interpret the English words being vocalised.

> Six of the actors are D/deafblind; they wait to hear the directors' notes, holding either both or one hand of their interpreters, dependant on their origin. Some interpreters are D/deaf, so watch either the Russian or English signers to communicate spoken words before passing the direction to the deafblind actors. Questions arising from all the actors—hearing and sighted or deafblind—are discussed, relayed back through the layers of translation. A further dozen members of the Russian and UK production teams listen and watch intently. The whole room is alive with a web of communication. This is a performance in itself.

'There are at least seven languages operating in that room' observed one of Graeae's signers during lunchtime. Many languages—British Sign Language and Russian Sign Language, Sign Supported English, Russian and English deafblind Hands On and Manual signing, spoken English and Russian—were drawn upon during the theatre-making process of *In Touch*. The multiple ways in which ideas were passed around during rehearsals were impressive but also sometimes challenging to effective or accurate exchange. The embodied visual and aural communication certainly enriched the final play, which was performed in The Dorfman Theatre on London's Southbank in October, 2017. Multiple communication methods provide creative opportunities, although it is possible that some of the rehearsal dialogues may have been lost in translation. Nuances of expression, concepts, and cultural issues don't always transfer well. However, the encounters arising from linguistic and community difference, foreign exchange, and recognition of universal connection was deeply enriching to the theatre processes, and to the performance witnessed by audiences. Graeae makes work from the experience of being D/deaf and disabled. Being a Deaf director, Jenny states that she enters the sensibility of the world in a different way from a hearing person. She felt an understanding and ability to communicate with the Russian deafblind actors even without sharing their sign language.

> Connections are sometimes based in humour. National Theatre's production manager outlined evacuation routes in a safety briefing before the technical rehearsals. The potential double meaning of the instruction, 'in case of fire, make your way to the river' was received by a series of laughs as it was translated to each language group. The signed images of fire, people walking, and river enhanced the comedic potential.

[Behind the Scenes + Dr. Kay Hepplewhite]

In Touch was first performed in Russia in 2015. This version of the project was set in motion several weeks prior to the London performance, when UK actors and signers spent time working with the Russian company. The existing play was shared and new material was generated through workshops under the direction of Jenny. The process aimed to further embed representation of deafblind experience in the play, and to enhance the potential accessiblity of the performance style. UK actors and interpreters were added to the Russian cast for the performance at the National Theatre.

> The play presented deafblind experiences and included personal material developed from all the actors' own lives. The performance style was highly visual, using ensemble choreography and direct narration to explore aspects of sensory loss, societal discrimination, adaptation, and support. The audience also witnessed experiences of love, the joys and challenges of everyday and family life, along with ambitions and dreams. Quotations from significant Russian deafblind figures—Olga Skorokhodova and Professor Suvorov—were narrated by English actor Jenny Agutter (also a Graeae patron) and Yevgeny Mironov (a leading Russian actor). The play tells how deafblind children were killed by the Nazis in the Soviet Union. It also discusses strategies of survival for those to whom society fails to give full access.
>
> Visual and sound elements of production were significant for *In Touch*. The stage design included a huge, suspended globe light and a potted tree to frame the stage. Apples and ropes were used as visual metaphors throughout. The changing apple-based colours of the lighting flooded the costumes

and theatre space, illuminating the two onstage harpists and vocalist that provided musical accompaniment and sound effects. Vibration and resonance from the electric harp allowed both audience and performers to share the impact of sensory experiences.

As the title suggests, touch is important for deafblind communication, and physical contact informed much of the material. An early sequence in the play showed deafblind actors tracing the contours of partners' faces. Other embodied senses such as speed and movement were represented in scenes showing the pleasures of swimming, dancing, and riding a motorbike, for example. The inability of others to be aware of, and accommodate, deafblind people in public and home spaces was also represented, with illustrations of blatant prejudice, neglect, abuse, and violent attack.

Signers, audio describers, and surtitles enabled a diverse audience to follow spoken, visual, and audio elements of the performance. For this show, the captions also translated dialogue for audience members not able to understand Russian. Creating appropriate captions is an artistic decision as well as a functional one, evidenced in one sequence exploring an encounter between two mothers.

The scene is like the centre of a rose, situated at the heart of the play. Captions and speech fall away for a sustained period of time. The gestural communication of the Indian/UK and Russian deafblind actors, placed within a still circle formed by the seated cast, explored the experience of motherhood.

[Behind the Scenes + Dr. Kay Hepplewhite]

The sequence lyrically related narratives of caring from birth onwards, the love and amazement that children bring. Projected text was sparsely used to communicate only the meaning of each daughter's names: Hope and Moonlight. The empathy between the two actors proved that actions and signing can communicate what words and text cannot.

Shadowing Sealey for the UK rehearsal and performances of *In Touch* (also assisting the Russian producer and dramaturg to prepare captions) offered rare insights for me as a theatre researcher. It became evident how Graeae's aesthetic of access is embedded throughout their collaborative production processes.

Jenny Sealey

CEO / Artistic Director, Graeae Theatre

2017 and Beyond

At the time of having to hand all this in to Oberon, we have just finished our revival tour of *Reasons to be Cheerful*. We opened in Coventry—the very place where Graeae began, so it feels like we have come a full circle and now we embark on the next cycle of Graeae's life!

2017 has been a rather monumental year for Graeae; we had two co-productions with the Royal Exchange Theatre, *The House of Bernarda Alba* in February, followed by *Cosmic Scallies* by Jackie Hagan in the summer, performed both in Edinburgh and Manchester. Next up was our beloved *Reasons to be Cheerful*, and then we collaborated with Naked Productions and BBC Radio 4 on *The Midwich Cuckoos*, in a brand-new adaptation by Roy Williams.

There was a week in October where we had *Reasons to be Cheerful* at West Yorkshire Playhouse, *Cosmic Scallies* in Manchester and *In Touch* at the National Theatre.

Not bad for a small company!

We are now in the thick of planning our 2018-2022 programme of work and how we will continue to grow as an organisation and, more importantly, will there be a reason for Graeae to exist after 2022?

Many of the same challenges that existed when I first started working in this field are still prevalent, especially the lack of inclusion in drama schools. We have been battling this issue since the company was founded. Through continuous engagement with most of the leading schools over the years, we are finally seeing some shifts in the overall climate but there is still a long way to go. Ramps on the Moon consortium members, and other major theatres including the National Theatre, are starting to offer regular work so I hope drama schools will finally realise that there are jobs for D/deaf and disabled people so it is worth training us!

We provide a good place for D/deaf and disabled actors, to learn about themselves, their craft, and where they can start to grow wings. We open doors for our artists to spread their wings and fly … to Birmingham Repertory Theatre, West Yorkshire Playhouse, and the other large regional theatres. It is the responsibility of those repertory houses to open even larger doors so that D/deaf and disabled actors can have real career progression. I look forward to the day that these talented performers do not have to start their career with Graeae but are immediately welcomed across the industry. When that day comes, I wonder what the purpose of Graeae will be.

But we are not done yet!

We too have to get through those larger doors. I want Graeae to collaborate with the National Theatre and Royal Opera House and to take on larger site-specific challenges. These are not impossible goals. We are in the early planning stages for a partnership with the Royal Opera

House, we also have *This is Not for You by* Mike Kenny, a big outdoor production with disabled veterans, and we hope to do *The Iron Woman* as part of Coventry City of Culture.

Graeae will continue its role within the global disability arts movement as well as growing its reputation on the UK theatre scene. To achieve this aim, we are currently working on a reimagining of *The Tempest* that will bring artists to the UK from Japan, Bangladesh, Brazil, and India, as well as planning our first major commercial venture.

The economic climate is brutal. Much of our funding is at a standstill and, twinned with cuts in Access to Work support, this feels like a double whammy. But it is vital that we do not thwart our ambitions in these difficult times. Each new venture we undertake is designed to take us out of our comfort zone and explore how we can create a truly accessible production. I have not managed to reach this ambition in twenty years. Maybe I will never achieve it but it is the quest that keeps the company going. As is ever the case, it is not reaching the destination that matters in the end— it is the ability and passion to understand the journey.

Graeae, governed and supported by past and present board members, employs some of the most talented and committed core staff, performers, writers, associates, creatives, crew, interpreters, and audio describers in the industry.

It continues to be my privilege to work alongside them. If the perfectly accessible play is out there, these are the people that will find it.

[Behind the Scenes + Jenny Sealey]

The Scripts

Reasons to be
Cheerful

SORRY

Paul Sirett

Writer

For many years when I first started writing 'serious' theatre I felt that I was carrying a terrible secret around with me. That secret was that I liked musicals. Not only did I like musicals, I really liked the idea of writing back catalogue shows, the reviled jukebox musical. The jukebox musical is a much-maligned form. Barbara Ellen, writing in *The Observer*, refers to the genre as 'sub-panto' and asks, 'who really wants this kind of thing?' Well, the answer, thankfully, seems to be quite a lot of people. Including me. And I also like panto.

In an article in *The New Yorker*, Sarah Larson suggests that good jukebox musicals come in two basic forms, the straight-up celebration of a body of music, without a significant plot, and the much trickier biographical musical. She also acknowledges that the show that popularised the genre in recent years was *Mamma Mia!*—a show that does neither of these things but links the songs of Abba with an original story penned by Catherine Johnson. I ended up going a fourth route.

When Jenny Sealey first asked me if I might be interested in writing a show for Graeae based on the songs of Ian Dury and the Blockheads (to which I agreed indecently quickly) my first thought was to write a show about the man and his music—the biographical musical. I did the research. I planned. I started to write. I called it *Sex and Drugs and Rock and Roll*. But it was slow going. It was hard. How do you capture the essence of such an extraordinary man?

[Reasons to be Cheerful + Paul Sirett]

Then I heard someone was writing a film about Ian Dury called *Sex and Drugs and Rock and Roll* so I change the title to *Hit Me*. But I still wasn't getting anywhere. Then I heard that someone was writing a play about Ian Dury called *Hit Me*, and I concluded that I needed to re-think the whole thing. So, I let the songs dictate a story and wrote a play about a group of Ian Dury and the Blockheads fans and called it *Reasons to be Cheerful*.

But writing a jukebox musical is only half the story. The most important thing about *Reasons* is that this is a jukebox musical for Graeae. Writing for Graeae means finding creative solutions to making a show that is fully accessible. Instead of being relegated to add-ons; captioning, British Sign Language and Audio Description are at the heart of the process and performance. The ambition at Graeae is that everyone should be able to access every performance of every show.

It has always been important to me that the things I write reach a wide audience. My family didn't go to the theatre and it was only by chance that I discovered how amazing theatre can be. Ever since, I have had the zeal of a convert and like to write stories for and about the kind of people you don't normally see in a theatre in the hope that someone will perhaps see something they can identify with up on the stage and become another convert. This happened with a wheelchair user in Brazil and a gentleman who came to see *Reasons to be Cheerful* in Ipswich who had never been to the theatre before and was only there because he was a fan of Ian Dury and the Blockheads. He subsequently booked for all the shows at the New Wolsey that season.

And here we are, a decade after I started work on the script, and seven years after we first performed the show at the New Wolsey and Stratford East, doing a third UK tour and having performed the show in various versions in theatres and at festivals in Europe and South America. (Did I mention that I also get to play guitar in the band? And just in case you're wondering, I had to audition).

Reasons is set in the early 1980s and looks back to 1979, when Thatcher won her first election. The play isn't about her, it's about music fans, but at the same time it is also about ordinary, working-class men and women, some of whom are disabled by the society they live in, trying to make ends meet in a country that didn't give a damn about them. It was a difficult time for those of us who believed in community; as far as Thatcher was concerned, society didn't exist. Well, it did, and it still does, but back then she was doing her best to erase any hope of building a fair society in which we could all participate regardless of wealth, privilege and social status.

By the time Reasons was first produced in 2010, the Tories were back in power, leading a compliant and complicit Lib-Dem coalition, and the process of dismantling welfare and social services had begun once more. Suddenly, a play that was about a time a quarter of a century earlier was just as relevant again.

By the time we mounted the second tour, in 2012, the escalation of Tory policies that sought to punish the poor and make life as difficult as possible for disabled people was in full flow and the play felt like a potent contemporary mirror held up to the Thatcher years.

[Reasons to be Cheerful + Paul Sirett]

Hard to believe that in 2017 the Tories are still in power and that society (the one Thatcher said didn't exist) is at breaking point. Cuts to benefits of all kinds have led to many of those disabled by the country they live in now being unable to reach their potential. Careers have been put on hold, or abandoned altogether. These are difficult times for too many people. Unbelievably, *Reasons* is more relevant than ever. Why is it so hard for us all to believe in a fair society that treats everybody as equals?

Reasons brings my passions together—creating popular theatre with a political heart and equality.

I hope that other writers who, like me, love theatre and popular music won't be afraid to innovate and take the form forward. And, while they're at it, perhaps think about how to integrate access into their shows as well.

Jemima Dury

Author and *Reasons to be Cheerful* Ambassador

I have been connected to Graeae Theatre Company since I was fifteen years old, when my father, Ian Dury, became a patron in 1984 alongside Sir Peter Blake and the founders Nabil Shaban and Richard Tomlinson.

My direct involvement with Graeae began when *Reasons to be Cheerful* hit the stage in 2010 and took the roof off the Theatre Royal Stratford East. I was knocked for six. The audience that night was full of students from Newham College. To see young people in the interval grooving and singing *Sex and Drugs and Rock and Roll* blew me away. Dad would have loved it. It proved what timeless music he and the Blockheads created forty years ago this September.

For me, the show symbolises a perfect marriage of past and future. I close my eyes and the power and vitality of the music takes me back to a Blockheads gig in the seventies when punk rock gave a rallying cry against economically and politically difficult times. I open my eyes and I'm looking at some of our finest performers, disabled and non-disabled, working together, sharing resources and supporting one another.

Reasons to be Cheerful is our rallying cry, to build a world where we accept our challenges and celebrate our differences, where everything is accessible and possible.

[Reasons to be Cheerful + Jemima Dury]

[Drawings from the original show]

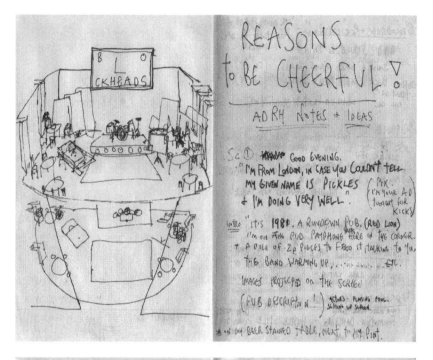

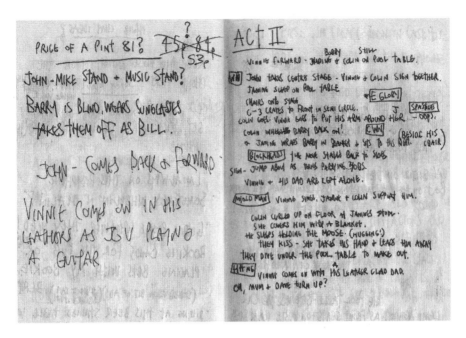

Reasons to be Cheerful cast (in alphabetical order by surname)

2010 tour:

Nadia Albina	Daniel McGowan
Stephen Collins	Wayne 'Pickles' Norman
Mat Fraser	Garry Robson
Robert Hyman	Nixon Rosembert
John Kelly	Paul Sirett
Stephen Lloyd	Karen Spicer
Jude Mahon	

2012 revival:

As above, with the addition of Paula Stanbridge-Faircloth who took over from Mat Fraser.

2017 revival:

Stephen Collins	Wayne 'Pickles' Norman
Joey Hickman	Nixon Rosembert
Beth Hinton-Lever	Max Runham
John Kelly	Louis Schultz-Wiremu
Stephen Lloyd	Paul Sirett
Jude Mahon	Karen Spicer
Gerard McDermott	Paula Stanbridge-Faircloth

REASONS TO BE CHEERFUL

By Paul Sirett

GRAEAE

UK Tour 2017
Version 2
(July 2017)

CHARACTERS

VINNIE BENTLEY
COLIN BRAVERMAN
JANINE WEST
PAT BENTLEY
BILL plays BOBBY BENTLEY
NICK plays DAVE HADDOCK
DEBBIE
PICKLES
…and MELVIN the Moose

The Band
COUSIN JOEY plays SANDRA
LOUIS plays GRAHAM
NIXON
PAULA
PAUL
JOHN KELLY

Script in bold indicates 'now' - 1981
Script in plain text indicates 'then' - 1979

TELEPHONE PIPS....
HELLO, I'M TRYING TO GET MY MONEY IN THE PAYPHONE
GOOD EVENING, I'M FROM ESSEX IN CASE
YOU COULDN'T TELL, MY GIVEN NAME IS
PICKLES & I'M DOING VERY WELL.
WELCOME, YOU ARE NOW LIVE & DIRECT FROM
THE RED LION HERE IN SUNNY SOUTHEND.
SORRY ABOUT THE NOISE, THE BAND ARE
SETTING UP & SOME OF THE REGULARS
ARE HANDING OUT TWIGLETS TO THE AUDIENCE.
(CHARACTERS COME TO THE PHONE
    AND DESCRIBE THEMSELVES.   )
    IMPROVISED CHAT!!

ACT ONE

1981. A rundown pub. An improvised set for a play written by Vinnie and his mates. A band's gear pre-set on the pub stage.

The play has a soft start with the actors and musicians checking their gear and chatting with the audience.

NICK and LOUIS are looking at Nick's holiday snaps projected on a screen at the back of the stage.

When we get the all clear, a slide of Nick in a car park is projected on the screen.

                    LOUIS
Where's that?

                    NICK
Yeovil.

                    LOUIS
You had a day out in a car park in Yeovil?

                    NICK
We stopped for something to eat.

                    LOUIS
And it was so good, you had to take a photograph of it?

                    NICK
It was a very interesting car park.

                    LOUIS
What was interesting about it?

                    NICK
Well, to start with, there were all these white lines that someone had painted really carefully on the ground.

                    LOUIS
Wow.

                    NICK
And some of them had cars parked in them.

LOUIS & NICK ARE
SHOWING OLD BORING HOLIDAY
SLIDES ONSCREEN. LIFE'S TOO SHORT,
I'D RATHER PULL MY TONSILS OUT!
WITH A STICK!
THAT'S A FEW MINUTES I'LL NEVER
SEE AGAIN.

LOUIS

That's very interesting.

NICK

See. Told you.

HERE'S COLIN, HE'LL SORT 'EM OUT!   COLIN crosses to NICK and DAVE.

COLIN

Right! Enough, you two. Put the slide of Vinnie's Dad up.

LOUIS PUTS THE OLD BLACK + WHITE   LOUIS puts up a slide of Vinnie's Dad,
SMILING PHOTO OF VINNIES DAD ON HIS   Bobby. Vinnie addresses the pub crowd.
WEDDING DAY UP ON SCREEN.

VINNIE

ROBERT JAMES   (Into microphone)
BENTLEY   One…Two…One-Two. One-Two. Hello. Is it working? Can you hear me?
1929-1979   Good. Right. Hello. Thanks for coming…Welcome to The Red Lion…

ALL

(Ad lib)
Weh-hey!!

VINNIE

My family's second home.

PAUL

First!

VINNIE

Thanks to Jean and Paul for letting us wreak havoc in their public bar
tonight.

All applaud.

VINNIE (cont.)

Today, as most of you know, is an anniversary and, er, this is a sort of
gig and play that we've put together for it. The script is by all of us, from
what we remember of what happened. Colin, here, the anarchist / made
the short films…

COLIN

Anarchy!   *HE RAISES HIS RIGHT FIST.*

VINNIE

My best mate Colin, here, the anarchist made the short films to go with
the songs, He'll be playing himself in the play tonight. Next to me here is
Colin's friend Debbie, she'll be signing, and she did the dancing.

OH, SHE WON'T LIKE THAT

HE TWANGS HIS RED
BRACES + FLINCHES.
THAT'S GOTTA HURT.

[370]

DEBBIE

Choreography.

VINNIE

Choreography.

DEBBIE

There is a difference! *told ya.*

VINNIE

Oh, yes, and on the screen behind there'll be slides and stuff for Colin's Mum, who's deaf but doesn't sign and, er, just in case we forget things. And, er, and on the phone to one of our mates who can't be here tonight is Pickles... *oh that's me*

PICKLES

Blind Derek says "Hello!" Ol Ol

ALL

Hello Blind Derek!

COLIN

Oi Oi!

VINNIE

Blind Derek, my dad's old mate, just moved to Yarmouth, so can't get here. He's made us promise to give him a blow by blow commentary on what's going on tonight.

PICKLES

He says he wants you to pop over for a chat when you get a chance.

VINNIE

Pickles sorted out the PA for tonight. Thanks, Pix. Oh, and he's the man to speak to if you want tickets for anything, if you know what I mean? ~ *don't tell 'em that, giving away all my secrets.* Janine over here who's doing some singing is also in the play as herself. She did all the decorations as well.

JANINE

Help yourself to the Twiglets by the way... *don't touch 'em they're mouldy*

VINNIE

And we've got a band! At the back on the keyboards is my Cousin Joey.

COUSIN JOEY

All right! *in his big coloured green shirt*

VINNIE

He's also doing some acting. He's playing Sandra. *he'll be wearing a red dress + blonde wig later*

[The Scripts + Reasons to be Cheerful]

VINNIE

This is my mate, Louis, who plays the sax. He's in charge of slides and all that. And in our story he plays Graham, Sandra's boyfriend.

HE'S ALL LEGS + BEARD, SIX + A HALF FOOT OF HIM

COUSIN JOEY

(*Sings a la Rod Stewart*)
"If you want my body, and you think I'm sexy"

LOUIS

Shut up!

VINNIE

On bass is Nixon who used to work at the council with my Dad.

BIT OF A DUDE IN HIS MUSTARD T-SHIRT Nixon plays a riff on the bass.
+ PORK PIE HAT — FUNKY!

ALL

Woah!!! Cool!!!

VINNIE

On the guitar, next to Nixon, is Paul. *GREEN TRACKSUIT TOP + FLAT CAP*

*Paul plays one note on the guitar
and raises his fist in triumph*

VINNIE

Rock and roll, Paul! And just behind me, on the drums, is Paula...

PAULA

A B C D Eviscerate the bourgeoisie!

COLINS GOING BONKERS.
BIT OF A DEBBIE HARRY LOOKALIKE OUR PAULA Paula drums very loudly ending with a beat
on the cow bell.

PAULA

Anarchy!

COLIN

Anarchy!

VINNIE

Thank you, Paula. And this is our vocalist, John.

A RIGHT MISERABLE SOD IN HIS RED Vinnie holds the mic out for John – John
ELECTRIC WHEELCHAIR (NOT A SMILE ON HIM) says nothing...
IN HIS PADDY T-SHIRT + RED NECK TIE.

VINNIE

Go on John, say hello – go on!

JOHN

(Pissed off)
Just get on with it.

VINNIE

Sorry about that. And, also playing a bit of guitar and keyboards
tonight, is a mate of mine from college, Nick.

A VAID BACK THESMAN IN ORANGE SHIRT

NICK

Evening.

VINNIE

SPREADS
HIS LEGS A
AKIMBO

He's also acting in the play. He's playing the part of my ex-boss at Fine
Fare, Dave. When Nick's got his arm on, he's Dave. And when he's got it
off, he's Nick. Louis, who's playing Graham, is Dave's brother, in the
play.

BILL

HE PUTS ON HIS FALSE
LEFT ARM, AND DEBBIE
PULLS IT OFF.

Keep it simple, eh, Vinnie.

VINNIE

Sorry. Basically, Dave is a bit of a twat...Not Nick, Dave. Is Dave here?

PAT

No, darling, he's not.

VINNIE

Down here, at her table, is my Mum, Pat. Pat's in the play tonight.
Playing herself. This is her acting debut.

IN HER FECTHING RED & BLUE TUNIC

Pub crowd cheer.

VINNIE (cont.)

So please be kind. You okay, Mum?

PAT

Not really.
(Indicating her drink)
Few more Bacardi and cokes and I'll be great.

WE'LL HAVE TO KEEP AN EYE ON HER
TONIGHT, SHE CAN PUT 'EM AWAY!

*Vinnie takes her drink away. Pat gets
another from the shelf under the
table*

VINNIE

And just behind Mum is Bill. Bill is Dad's best mate from the National Union of General and Municipal Workers

BILL

Well done, Vinnie. Power to the people!

VINNIE

Bill's playing the part of Bobby, my Dad. You'll know when he's Dad because he'll be in the wheelchair-

HERE'S LOUIS THE SAX PLAYER

LOUIS

I made for him, special for tonight. It's genius, look – chair sat on a hostess trolley, couple of dart boards for wheels-   CLEVER BASTARD

DEBBIE

Here's your Blue Peter Badge!

> Assorted comments like, "Yes, yes"; "Give it
> a rest"; "Here we go"; "Don't forget the
> sticky-back plastic" etc.

VINNIE

So, when Bill's in the chair and wearing shades he's Dad and when he's not, he's, well, he's Bill. You are a bit blind like Dad was. What's that thing you've got, Bill?

BILL

A detached retina. Amongst other things. I've got my white cane somewhere   THAT OLD GAG, WAP WAP WAP WAP.......

VINNIE

And I think that's everyone...

BILL

Thank Christ for that.

VINNIE

We've tried to squeeze in as many songs as possible.

JOHN

Blockheads!

VINNIE

Except for 'Blockheads' – which doesn't fit the story.

JOHN

Boo!!

[374]

NICK

John, shut up!

VINNIE

This show is called: Reasons to be Cheerful...

Music Cue
Drum intro to 'Reasons to be Cheerful, Part 3'.

VINNIE

Two years ago in August in 1979 Ian Dury and the Blockheads played
five nights at the Hammersmith Odeon. This single was released a few
weeks earlier...

COLIN

On July 20th, 1979.

VINNIE

Thank you, Colin.

COLIN

Making it to number 3 in the UK charts two weeks later...

VINNIE

Colin is a world expert on Ian Dury- COLIN GRABS THE MIC & GIVES MORE DURY FACTS,
WHERE HE WAS BORN ETC. WE COULD BE ~~Colin takes the mic...~~ HERE ALL NIGHT, WE NEED to START THE SHOW.

COLIN
Ian Robins Dury was born on
12th May 1942 in Harrow,
Middlesex. He later moved to
Upminster where he spent his
formative years. At the age of
seven, he contracted polio. He
nearly died...

VINNIE
Thank you, Colin...

VINNIE
Colin...Thank you-

COLIN IS STILL BANGING ON, OH WE'RE ABOUT to START

Vinnie takes the mic from Colin.

FOR THIS FIRST SONG WE ALL DO A NORTHERN SOUL FORMATION DANCE - I'M GONNA JOIN IN too.
REASONS TO BE CHEERFUL (part 3)   SPEAK to you SOON

VINNIE

I bought this single two days after it came out.

COLIN

I bought it the day it came out.

VINNIE

We were desperate to see Ian Dury and the Blockheads at the Hammersmith Odeon. My Dad offered to get tickets for me, him and Colin. Dad really liked Ian Dury. I think one of the reasons was because they were both such big Gene Vincent fans. My name's Vincent…

Song Finishes

VINNIE

Okay, I want you all to rewind back two years to the summer of 1979…

FLASHBACK, ONSCREEN A 1970'S LIVING ROOM ALL GREEN & BROWN.

COUSIN JOEY plays some "going back in time" music…

VINNIE (cont.)

It's July, a couple of months after the election and a couple of weeks before the gig at the Hammersmith Odeon. I'm on my way home from work; Colin's with me...

Colin joins Vinnie.

VINNIE (cont.)

Mum's in our sitting room giving Dad a shave. Our sitting room: Brown three-piece suite just here. Tele in the corner. Window here. Woodchip wallpaper-

COLIN

Don't forget Eric.

BILL GETS INTO THE WHEELCHAIR & PUTS ON THE SHADES

VINNIE

Eric the budgie. COLIN HOLDS UP A TOY BUDGIE

COLIN

They had an Ernie and all but he snuffed it.

+ DEBBIE SIGNS A DEAD ONE

Debbie and Colin make sign of cross over an imagined dead Ernie.

VINNIE

I get home from work…

Vinnie and Colin 'enter' and they step into the scene. Pat is shaving Bobby.

PAT

(To Vinnie)
Hello, darling.

VINNIE

Mum.

                        BOBBY

All right, mate.

                        VINNIE

Yes.

                        PAT

How are you, Colin?

                        COLIN

All right, thank you. Hello, Mr Bentley.

                        BOBBY

Hello, Colin. How's the Class War going?

                        COLIN

Very well, thank you.

                        PAT

        (To Bobby)
Keep still, Bob…
        (To Vinnie)
How was work?

                At the same time…

        VINNIE   COLIN

Fine.   Shit.

                        PAT

        (To Bobby)
There. Finito. Where's your pills?

                Pat gets bottle of pills from her table.

                        BOBBY

Not now, Pat.

                        PAT

You're taking your pills. 45p that prescription cost me.

                        BOBBY

I told you the Tories'd put up prescription charges…Bastards.

                        PAT

The Tories didn't give you cancer.

BOBBY
Yes they did! They give everyone cancer! Isn't that right, Colin?

COLIN
What?

BOBBY
The Tories – give you cancer…

COLIN
Yes.

BOBBY
See.

PAT
(Pat puts pills in Bobby's hand)
Vinnie, pass me that drink will you…

Vinnie passes glass from Pat's table. Bobby takes his pills.

VINNIE
(A thought...)
Mum…

PAT
Yes, darling.

VINNIE
Can you do my hair so it's sticking up?

PAT
What? Spikey?

VINNIE
Yes.

PAT
Come here…

VINNIE SITS ON A SMALL BAR STOOL
+ MUM SORTS HIS BARNET

Pat Brylcreem's Vinnie's hair so that it is sticking up.

BOBBY
Oi, Colin…SUMMER, BUDDY HOLLY, THE WORKING FOLLY

COLIN
GOOD GOLLY MISS MOLLY AND BOATS. Easy. 'Reasons to be Cheerful, Part 3'. One-Nil.

                        BOBBY

Bugger.

                        COLIN

KEEP YOUR SILLY WAYS

                        BOBBY

I know this! I know this!

                        COLIN

Clock's ticking.

                        BOBBY

Shit-shit-shit-shit-shit

                        COLIN

OR THROW THEM OUT THE WINDOW. 'Sex & Drugs & Rock & Roll'. Two-
Nil.

                        BOBBY

I knew that!

                        COLIN

Tough! Your turn…

                        BOBBY

I COULD BE THE DRIVER AN ARTICULATED LORRY

                        COLIN

I COULD BE A POET I WOULDN'T NEED TO WORRY

                        BOBBY

I COULD BE A TEACHER IN A CLASSROOM FULL OF SCHOLARS

                        COLIN

I COULD BE THE SERGEANT IN A SQUADRON FULL OF WALLAHS

                        BOBBY/COLIN/JOHN

WHAT A-

                        A bit of underscoring from the versatile Cousin
                        Joey.

                        BOBBY/COLIN

…WASTE

                        COLIN

Three-nil!

                              BOBBY/COLIN
WHAT A WASTE

                              BOBBY
I'll catch you out one of these days.

                              BOBBY/COLIN
WHAT A WASTE

                              COLIN
No chance.

                              BOBBY/COLIN
WHAT A WASTE

                              BOBBY
You just wait...

                              BOBBY/COLIN
BECAUSE I CHOSE TO PLAY THE FOOL IN A SIX-PIECE BAND-

                              PAT
You didn't though, did you! Too busy going out on strike all the time.

                    Pat finishes Vinnie's hair.

                              PAT (cont)
There you go.

                              VINNIE
Thanks, Mum.

                              BOBBY
What's it look like?

                              PAT
Very Sid Vicious.

                              COLIN
Sid Vicious lives!

                              PAT
You stopping for tea, Colin?

                              COLIN
No thanks.

                              VINNIE
Colin wanted to check with Dad about the tickets.

[380]

BOBBY

What tickets?

VINNIE

Ian Dury.

PAT

What's all this?

VINNIE

Dad's getting us tickets for Ian Dury and the Blockheads at the Hammersmith Odeon. All three of us.

PAT

First I've heard of it.

VINNIE

Aren't you, Dad? Dad?

BOBBY

Look, Vinnie, mate, I'm sorry. I forgot.

VINNIE

Forgot?

BOBBY

Sorry.

COLIN

What?

VINNIE

Dad forgot. COLIN DRAGS VINNIE to the SIDE

COLIN

They'll be sold out!

VINNIE

It's not my fault!

COLIN

What we going to do?

VINNIE

I don't know!

COLIN

You couldn't organise a piss up in a brewery!

VINNIE

It's not my fault!

BOBBY

Look, I'm sorry, lads.

VINNIE

It don't matter, Dad.

COLIN

Vinnie'll sort it out, won't you, Vinnie?

BILL TAKES HIS SHADES OFF + GETS OUT OF THE CHAIR

Music Cue
What A Waste

BILL

'What a Waste' was one of your Dad's favorite songs.

VINNIE

Yes.

BILL

He loved doing all the stuff he did for the union, but I think there was always a bit of him that wanted to be a rock n roll star…

WHAT A WASTE

VINNIE, COLIN, JANINE + DEBBIE SIGN THE SONG BEHIND BILL + JOHN
LATER THEY HOLD UP PLACARDS IN A PROTEST 'FUCK THE SYSTEM' 'THATHER OUT' 'STOP THE CUTS'

VINNIE

When Mum gave up work to look after Dad I got her old job at Fine Fare. That's where I met Colin. The morning after Dad told us he'd forgotten to get the tickets, I used the payphone at work to ring the Hammersmith Odeon…

VOCALIST/BILL

WHAT A WASTE

VINNIE

But it was no good.

VOCALIST/BILL

WHAT A WASTE

VINNIE

Totally sold out.

VOCALIST/BILL

WHAT A WASTE

VINNIE

Every night

VOCALIST/BILL

WHAT A WASTE

VINNIE

I tried some ticket agencies. Nothing.

VINNIE

I wasn't looking forward to telling Colin...We were in the storeroom surrounded by Pot Noodle and Golden Wonder crisps and rolls of Andrex... which he started throwing at me...

Colin does.

ALL

COLIN!!!! toilet Rolls EVERYWHERE *Song Finishes*

VINNIE

Eventually he calmed down...a bit...

COLIN

I'm going to chop your balls off!

VINNIE

Then Dave, our boss, came in...

Dave enters the scene.

DAVE

What's going on? Why is there stock all over the floor?

VINNIE

Now, Dave always wore trousers that were just that little bit too small for him. It looked like he had a giant toad squashed in his pants. It was really hard not to stare... HE POSES HIS BULGE to THE AUDIENCE

THE GIRLS HAVE A CHEEKY STARE

DAVE

What's all the noise about? ... I'm waiting...

VINNIE

I was supposed to get us tickets for Ian Dury.

                                 DAVE
You haven't got tickets?

                                 VINNIE
No. It's sold out.

                                 DAVE
I have.

                                 VINNIE
Yes, we know.

                                 DAVE
Fourth row….Gobbing distance…Clear this mess up. Now.

He clocks one of the boxes   *Dave picks up some stock and
                                       scrutinizes it.*

                           DAVE (cont.)
Hold on…What's this?

                                 Vinnie points Colin at Dave.

                           DAVE (cont.)
Colin! Have you been drawing circles round the 'A's on boxes of Andrex
again?

                                 COLIN
What?

                                 DAVE
Have. You…
        (Dave shows him the stock)
Look!

                                 COLIN
It wasn't me.   *Colin turns away + Dave grabs him*
                                 DAVE
Who else is it going to be?   *He see's another box*
        (He has seen something else written on the box)
What the! Right! That does it!

                                 COLIN
What?   *He picks it up + reads it*
                                 DAVE
        *(Reads out what Colin has written – one word on each of the four sides
        of the box)*
"Shit." "On." "The." "Cistern." I'm going to show this to Mister Patterson.

[384]

COLIN

Good! Sack me! See if I give a fuck!

Dave turns to leave. Stops.

DAVE

Oh, what's this I've got in my wallet? *HE SLAPS THE WALLET ON COLINS FOREHEAD*
(Dave produces some tickets from his wallet and puts them on the box)
Oh look…Four tickets to see Ian Dury and the Blockheads at the
Hammersmith Odeon on Saturday 11th August 1979. Row D, seats 13, 14, 15
and 16. For me, Janine and…oh, who else shall I take with me. I know!
I'll go with my brother and his girlfriend. They don't actually like Ian Dury,
they're more into Genesis and Emerson, Lake and Palmer, but they're such
lovely company…

HE PLACES THE TICKETS ON THE ANDREX BOX

THE BOYS LOOK TO EACH OTHER + THEIR EYES LIGHT UP

COLIN

Nazi!

DAVE

Fuck off!

COLIN

Fuck off!

DAVE

Fuck off!

COLIN KICKS DAVES PHOTO OF MAGGIE THATCHER OFF THE POOL TABLE + STAMPS ON IT, HE STORMS OFF.

*Colin storms out – tearing off a picture of
Thatcher stuck to the pool table next to a
picture of Farah Fawcett-Majors as he goes.*

DAVE

DAVE UNFOLDS IT, KISSES THATCH + PUTS IT BACK

Get back in here!
(Dave sticks the picture of Thatcher back up. To Vinnie)
If his Dad didn't work in head office I'd have his bollocks in a vice and I'd
squeeze till he…screamed his…Bastard!

VINNIE

You shouldn't wind him up.

DAVE

He's a fucking liability!

VINNIE

You should have let us take last Saturday off-

DAVE

To play at some poxy Rock Against Racism gig? Do me a favour.

[The Scripts + Reasons to be Cheerful]

VINNIE

You had the day off.

DAVE

It was on the rota.

VINNIE

There were two hundred people there, Dave.

DAVE

Why do you let him be in your band?

VINNIE

It's about attitude.

DAVE

Attitude my arse. He's deaf. Why don't you let me join the band?

VINNIE

We don't need another singer.

DAVE

I COULD BE THE DRIVER AN ARTICULATED LORRY

VINNIE

We've got a vocalist.

DAVE

WHAT A WASTE
WHAT A WASTE –
I could get us gigs…

VINNIE

What? At Tory garden parties?

DAVE

Don't knock it. You get some very hot totty down at the Conservative Club.
Hey, I bet you get loads of chicks hanging round at your gigs, don't you?

VINNIE

Not really.

DAVE

You would if I was in the band…
        (Sings into imaginary mic.)
WHAT A WASTE
WHAT A WASTE
BUT I DON'T MIND!

DAVE PUTS AN IMAGINARY MIC IN A STAND THEN BUGGERS OFF

Dave puts down imaginary mic and exits.
Vinnie sees he's left the tickets.

VINNIE

Dave, you left your tick...ets

VINNIE PICKS UP THE DURY TICKETS + STROKES 'EM

He picks up the tickets and strokes them lovingly. Dave re-enters.

DAVE

HE SNATCHES THEM BACK

Oi! Get off my tickets!
(Snatches the tickets back)
You seen that new bird Shelley on the tills? I had to sort out her float this morning. She is gagging for it.

HERE'S COLIN

Colin re-enters.

DAVE (cont.)

You are in deep shit.

COLIN

I'm so scared.

DAVE

I'm going to see Mister Patterson.

COLIN

Go on then.

DAVE

Clear this place up. And take that trolley down. No lunch for either of you until it's done.

OFF HE TROTS

Dave exits.

→ YEH, HE IS A KNOB!

COLIN

What a knob! Vinnie...Look...I didn't mean to kick off like that. I'll take the trolley down. No hiding.

VINNIE

I'm not gonna hide.

COLIN PUTS A BOX ON THE TROLLEY + GOES. BUT VINNIE DOES HIDE, UNDERNEATH THE POOL TABLE.

Colin exits. Vinnie hides under the pool table. Janine enters singing to herself. She goes to pool table.

JANINE PUTS ON HER BROWN OVERALL + ENTERS. VINNIE GRABS HER LEG

VINNIE

Yaaa / aaaaaaaaaaaaaaaaaaaaaarghhh! (Vinnie grabs Janine's legs.)

JANINE

Aaaaaaaaaaaaaaaaaaaaaaaaaaaaaaaaaaahhhhhhh!

VINNIE

Janine! Shit! Sorry! I thought you were Colin...Sorry!

> *Vinnie comes out from under the pool table.*

JANINE

Christ, Vinnie! You scared three sacks of shit out of me!

VINNIE

I'm really sorry!

JANINE

What were you doing?

VINNIE

It's this game me and Colin have...we hide and...I'm really sorry...

JANINE

My heart is...I'll get you for that!

VINNIE

I wouldn't have done it if I'd known it was you, would I.

JANINE

Whoa...
  (Calming down)
Have you seen Dave?

VINNIE

I think he's in the office.

JANINE

He's supposed to be taking me to the Red Lion for lunch.

> *Janine takes off her work coat and gets her boots from under the pool table.*

VINNIE

He was having a go at Colin again.

> *Janine gets a stool to put her boots on.*

JANINE

They're as bad as each other. What? They are. I know Dave can come across as a bit of a tyrant, but he's lovely when you get to know him. He's quite gentle really. He is. We've been talking about moving in together...

VINNIE

Seriously?

JANINE

Yes. We've been going out for six months. How's your Dad?

VINNIE

Same.

JANINE

Give your Mum my love won't you.

VINNIE

Yes.

> *Janine puts a foot up on the stool and pulls
> on her boots. Vinnie watches her,
> transfixed…*

VINNIE (cont.)

(To audience)
Janine had these shiny Docs with zips, she stood in front of me, slipped
a foot in one and slowly pulled up the zip…zip, zip, zip, zip…then she
saw a scuff mark or something and licked her fingers…and…started to
rub, and…rub, and- EVERYONE, INCLUDING THE BAND LEAN IN + LEER AT HER BOOTS

JANINE

Vinnie?   THEN TURN AWAY!

VINNIE

Yes?

JANINE

You all right?

VINNIE

Yes.

JANINE

I'm gonna get you back for frightening me like that!
          (Goes to leave - an afterthought)
I like your hair.

VINNIE

Thanks.

JANINE

See you later.

[The Scripts + Reasons to be Cheerful]

VINNIE

Yes.

JANING GOES BACK to HER TABLE.
VINNIE PUTS A TRAFFIC CONE ON HIS HEAD.
COLIN SEES HIM BUT PLAYS ALONG WITH HIS LITTLE GAME.

*Vinnie hides behind John, the Vocalist. Colin
re-enters. Colin looks around.*

COLIN

Vinnie? Are you hiding? You won't get me again. Vinnie?

*Colin investigates some boxes – looking for
Vinnie. He tries some discarded
packaging… nothing.*

COLIN (cont.)

Vinnie…

VINNIE

*(Vinnie puts a box over Colin's head, or hits him with loo rolls to scare
him)*
AAAAAAGHH!

COLIN

AAA / AAAAAAAAAAAAAAAGHH! Bastard! Bastard! Bastard!

VINNIE

I'm sorry, Col. Couldn't resist.

COLIN

Bastard!

VINNIE

I got Janine.

COLIN

Janine?

VINNIE

Yes. I thought she was you. I scared the crap out of her.

COLIN

What?

VINNIE

Janine.

COLIN

You fancy her.

VINNIE

No, I don't…

COLIN

Yes you do. You look at her funny. You go...   He MAKES A DROOLING SIGN.

Colin pulls a face.

VINNIE

No...Do I?

Dave enters.

DAVE

What's all the shouting about? I could hear you from the meat counter!

VINNIE

I was hiding...

Colin gets the giggles.

DAVE

What are you laughing at? This isn't primary school.

*Both Vinnie and Colin have got the giggles
now.*

DAVE

Christ, what did I do to deserve you two? Stop laughing. It isn't clever-

VINNIE/COLIN

Trevor!

They laugh even harder.

DAVE

Shut up!

VINNIE/COLIN
(Everyone in the pub and Vinnie and Colin start singing)
Knock me down with a feather Clever Trevor!

DAVE

No singing! You know Mister Patterson doesn't allow singing!

COLIN

Sorry, Trevor.

DAVE

Don't call me Trevor.

COLIN

What did Patterson say? Are you going to sack me...Trevor?

DAVE

Do. Not. Call. Me. Trevor.

COLIN

What did he say? Come on...

DAVE

He said to tell you...Don't do it again.

COLIN

Anarchy!

DAVE

Get lost.
(To Colin)
And take that earring out.

COLIN HOLDS UP HIS HEARING AID TO DAVES FACE

COLIN

Sorry, can't hear you, Trevor.

DAVE

I won't tell you again!

COLIN

(To Vinnie)
What did Trevor say?

DAVE

You fucking...fucking...

Music Cue

HE FUCKING FUCKS OFF...

Dave storms out. They perform a synchronized sung and signed routine to the song.

CLEVOR TREVER

COLIN + VINNIE SIGN + DANCE THIS NEXT SONG WHILE CLEARING THE MESS.
IT'S TOILET ROLL MAYHEM!

Vinnie and Colin getting ready to leave work.

COLIN

Are you coming to the pub tonight?

VINNIE

No money.

COLIN

It's payday.

VINNIE

I give it to Mum.

COLIN

I like your Mum. When she used to work here she used to give me a Walnut Whip every Thursday after we got paid.

VINNIE

Did she?

COLIN

Yes. I like Walnut Whips. Except the walnut. I hate walnuts. Your Mum used to eat the walnut. I might buy her a Walnut Whip.

VINNIE

Yeah, She'd like that. She's got a lot on her plate at the moment.

COLIN

She's got what?

VINNIE

A lot on her plate. With Dad... I keep thinking I want to do something for him...That's why I thought it was great he wanted to come and see Ian Dury with us, but... look...I'm really sorry about the tickets, Col.

COLIN

We could always nick Dave's.

VINNIE

He'd kill us.

COLIN

(A thought)
What about Pickles?

VINNIE

Pickles?

COLIN

Down the pub. He can get tickets for anything. He got my Mum tickets for Brotherhood of Man in Ipswich. They were like gold dust. I MADE A FEW QUID OUT OF THAT

VINNIE

Really?

COLIN

It'll cost us.

VINNIE

How much?

COLIN

Five-six quid…

VINNIE

Each! I can't afford that-

COLIN

I'll pay.

VINNIE

No-

COLIN

I've got money in my TSB account.

VINNIE

I didn't think anarchists had bank accounts.

COLIN

Do you want a ticket or not?

VINNIE

Yes. Course. I'll pay you back later. You're my hero! Come here!

Vinnie hugs Colin.

VINNIE HUGS COLIN,
THEY'RE GOING to SEE DURY. THE BOYS LOOK UP to THE SCREEN *Song Finishes*

VINNIE

What's next?........... Eventually he calmed down… a bit

COLIN

I'm going to chop your balls off!

VINNIE

Then Dave our boss came in… THIS IS AW A BIT DÉJÀ VU!

DAVE

What's going- What?

VINNIE

Stop! It's the wrong slide.

[394]

DEBBIE

Louis!

Louis HAS put the WRONG SLIDE UP

COLIN

Dickhead!

Colin's not HAPPY

LOUIS

Hold on!

Louis CHANGES the SLIDE

COUSIN JOEY

Typical.

LOUIS

Shut up!

DEBBIE

Here…

Debbie helps Louis.

VINNIE

What's next?

JOHN

Blockheads!

VINNIE

We're not doing Blockheads. John.

JOHN

Aaaagh!

PAT

Vinnie, it's me and your Dad.

VINNIE

Louis?

DEBBIE

Got it.

LOUIS

Yes. Right. Sorry.

VINNIE

Meanwhile, back home, Mum and Dad were at it again.

BILL SITS IN THE DARTBOARD WHEELCHAIR Pat and Bobby are mid-argument.
& PAT PUTS ON A YELLOW APRON

                    BOBBY
I don't want to buy the fucking house!

                    PAT
It's an investment!

                    BOBBY
It's a scam!

                    PAT
How is it a scam?

                    BOBBY
What do you think'll happen to council housing if everyone starts buying. It'll
be everyone for themselves. Before you know it there'll be no bloody council
houses left! Everyone in their own little fiefdom. What about community?

                    PAT
There's nothing wrong with wanting to better yourself.

                    BOBBY
Here we go! I'm all right Jack!

                    PAT
For Christ's sake!
        (Pat gets a bowl of Twiglets/snacks from her table)
Eat.

                    BOBBY
I'm not hungry.

                    PAT
You have to eat!   SHE HOLDS OUT A BOWL OF TWIGLETS

                    BOBBY
You're playing right into their hands.

                    PAT
I give up!

                    BOBBY
Fucking Tories! Fucking…Fucking… Fucking
BILL GETS OUT OF THE CHAIR + TAKES HIS SHADES OFF
PLAISTOW PATRICIA

                        BILL

    ARSEHOLES

    BASTARDS

    FUCKING CUNTS

    AND PRICKS

DEBBIE STANDS ON THE WHEELCHAIR & SIGNS
WE'RE ALL ON BACKING VOCALS, VINNIE & I ON THE POOL TABLE   *Song Finishes*
                        PAT
    I'm not from bloody Plaistow!

                        BILL
        No, you're from East Ham where it's soooooooooo much posher!

BILL GETS BACK IN THE CHAIR & PUTS THE SHADES ON
                        BOBBY
    Fucking…Fucking… Fucking

                        PAT
    For Christ's sake! I can't talk to you when you're like this.

                        BOBBY
    Fuck off out then!

                        PAT
    I don't want to go out.

                        BOBBY
    Plenty of blokes out there.

                        PAT
    What's that supposed to mean?

BOBBY GRIMACES IN AGONY   *Bobby is suddenly in great pain.*

                        PAT (cont.)
    Bob?

                        She goes to him.

                        PAT (cont.)
    Bobby?

                        BOBBY
    I've had enough, Pat! Put a pillow over me head. Strangle me / I don't care
    how you do it…

                                    [The Scripts + Reasons to be Cheerful]

                              PAT
Stop it! Stop it, Bobby!
        (Pause)
I can't take much more of this.

                              BOBBY
Don't then.

                              PAT
Bobby-

                    Vinnie enters.

                              VINNIE
Mum. Dad…Is everything-

                              PAT
Fine…

                              VINNIE
Colin sent you a Walnut Whip. Well…just the walnut.

                              PAT
Bless him.

                              VINNIE
Everything all right, Dad?

                    Bobby doesn't answer.

                    VINNIE (cont.)
I'm going to get us tickets for Ian Dury.

                              PAT
I thought it was sold out

                              VINNIE
We're gonna ask Pickles to get us some.

                              PAT
Pickles?

                              VINNIE
Yes. Down the Red Lion, the bloke with the "Love" and "Hat" tattoos / on his
hands…

                              PAT
I know who Pickles is

                              VINNIE
He can get tickets for anything.

PAT

And how much is that going to cost you?

VINNIE

Don't know yet. Colin's going to lend me the money-

PAT

No, Vinnie.

VINNIE

I'll pay him back.

PAT

How?

VINNIE

Please, Mum…It's for Dad

BOBBY

What?

VINNIE

You want to go, don't you, Dad?

BOBBY

I can't, mate.

VINNIE

It'll be great!

PAT

He can't, Vinnie.

VINNIE

He can!

PAT

You know how sick he is.

VINNIE

Dad?

PAT

No, Vinnie.

VINNIE

You have to let me take you! You have to!

                              PAT
Vincent, stop it! You're upsetting your Dad!

                              BOBBY
          (Shouting)
No, he's not!

                              PAT
          (Shouting)
What are you shouting for then!

                              BOBBY
          (Shouting)
What are you bloody shouting for!

                              A moment of silence.

                    BOBBY (cont.)
I need the bog.

VINNIE WHEELS HIS DAD OUT   *Vinnie goes to wheel his Dad out.*

                              PAT
No fags.

                              *Vinnie wheels Bobby out. Pat tidies. Vinnie
                              re-enters.*

                    PAT (continued)
Is he smoking?

                              VINNIE
Yes.

                              PAT
There's something we need to / talk about...

                              VINNIE
Why won't you let me take him?

                              PAT
I'm going to speak to the people at St Mungo's. The hospice.

                              VINNIE
What?

                              PAT
They can care for him properly in there.

[400]

                              VINNIE
No, Mum.

                                PAT
I can't do it no more.

                              VINNIE
I'll look after him.

                                PAT
Don't be stupid.

                              VINNIE
I could-

                                PAT
I want you to go back to sixth form and / get your 'A' Levels…

                              VINNIE
I'm not going back to sixth form. Please don't do this Mum…

                        Pat turns to go.

                        VINNIE (cont.)
Mum…Where are / you going?

                                PAT
I'm going to get your Dad.

                        *Pat exits. Pat re-enters with Bobby. Bobby
                        has been sick.*

                        PAT (cont.)
There you go. He's been sick. Why don't you clean it up seeing as how you're
so keen…

SHE THROWS A TOWEL AT VINNIE   *Vinnie goes to wipe his Dad's mouth.*
HE GOES TO WIPE HIS DADS MOUTH
                                        BOBBY
Get off!

HE THROWS DOWN THE TOWEL   *Vinnie throws down the towel and exits.*
+ STORMS OUT
                                        PAT
Vinnie! Come back!

                                        BOBBY
Has he gone?

[The Scripts + Reasons to be Cheerful]

                              PAT
Yes.

                             BOBBY
I'm sorry, Pat. I'm sorry for all this. I'm not dealing with it. I love you, you know
that.

                              PAT
I love you too.

                             BOBBY
Don't get soppy.

                              PAT
You started it.

BILL GETS OUT OF THE CHAIR, HE + PAT GO BACK TO THEIR TABLES

                             VINNIE
          (To audience)
We asked Pickles to get us tickets. No good. Even he couldn't get any. *I TRIED EVERYWHERE*
Come the day of the gig, Dave was insufferable…

DAVE STROLLS ON IN HIS YELLOW FLARED
CHORDS. IN THE NEXT SONG MYSELF, LOUIS,
JANINE + DEBBIE BECOME THE WOMEN.
IT'S ALL A BIT 'CARRY ON' USING MOPS FOR WIGS.
DAVE ADJUSTS HIS CODPIECE TO
THE AUDIENCE

Supermarket storeroom. The end of the
working day. Dave is preening himself in
front of a mirror held up by Debbie, getting
ready to drive to London for the Ian Dury
gig.

                    BILLERICAY DICKY

                              DAVE
          Good evening I'm from Essex
          In case you couldn't tell
          My given name is Dickie,
          I come from Billericay
          And I'm doing
          very well…

DAVE, JANINE + DEBBIE ROLL ONTO THE POOL TABLE.   *Song Finishes*
VINNIE RELUCTANTLY HOLDS UP THE MIRROR Vinnie enters and Dave thrusts the mirror
WHILE DAVE PREENS HIMSELF + SORTS   into his hands.
OUT HIS TOAD. AGAIN!
                              DAVE
          Ah, Vincent! How are we? Doing anything special this evening? No?
          Did I tell you I've got tickets to see Ian Dury and the Blockheads at the
          Hammersmith Odeon tonight? *ABOUT TEN BLOODY TIMES DAVE*
                    Vinnie ignores him.

DAVE (cont.)

(Preening)
Am I gorgeous or am I gorgeous? **NO YOU'RE NOT, YOU'RE A MUG!**

Vinnie doesn't answer.

DAVE (continued)
You know that bird Shelley on the check-out? Whuh-uh-oh…Ladies bogs after tea break. "Oh Mister Haddock, you're so good-looking…" Fucking Ada…Talk about Deep Throat! Then…then, half an hour later she's back for more. She can't get enough.

VINNIE
What?

DAVE
Twice. Tuh-wice. Not one gobble, but two. And she swallows.

VINNIE
Shelley?

DAVE
They all want a bit. What can I do?

VINNIE
What about Janine?

DAVE
She spits.

VINNIE
I didn't mean that! I thought you Janine were serious?

DAVE
With that arm? Do me a favour. She's just a sympathy shag. She don't half go, mind, so I might hold on to it for a bit longer. What? Look, I know you fancy a bit of it, but she's out of your league, mate. Even if she is a raspberry.
(Checks his watch)
Fuck, where is she? My brother and his bit of stuff'll be here in a minute…Did I tell you we got tickets for Ian Dury and the Blockheads tonight? Oh yes I have…Oh yes I have…Christ, my cock aches. See you later, masturbator.
(Sings as he goes)
Had a love affair with Nina, in the back of my Cortina… **TA LA YOU MUPPET**

JANINE SLOWLY EMERGES FROM BEHIND THE POOL TABLE, SHELL SHOCKED

Dave exits. Slowly Janine emerges from behind the drumkit where she has been hiding – waiting to get her revenge on Vinnie for when he frightened her. Her face is streaked with tears. Vinnie sees her.

                                          VINNIE
Janine...Were you hiding? Did you...

SHE RUNS BACK to HER TABLE   *Janine runs off, crying.*

                                          VINNIE (cont.)
Janine...Janine, don't go...

COLIN'S BACK   *Beat. Vinnie thinks about following her, but*
                                    doesn't. Colin bumps into Janine as he
                                    enters.

                                          COLIN
What's up with Janine?

                                          VINNIE
Dave was...It doesn't matter.

                                          COLIN
Tell me.

                                          VINNIE
Dave was boasting about Shelley giving him a blow job and Janine heard him.

                                          COLIN
She heard him?

                                          VINNIE
Yes.

                                          COLIN
She heard him getting a blow job?

                                          VINNIE
No. She heard Dave telling me.

                                          COLIN
Oh. Shit.

                                          VINNIE
I think she was hiding to get me back for the other day.

                                          COLIN
What happened?

                                          VINNIE
Nothing. He doesn't know she knows yet.

                                          COLIN
Double shit. You should...

[404]

                              VINNIE
I should what? Tell him?

                              COLIN
No. You should ask her out!

                              VINNIE
Me?

                              COLIN
Yes!

DURING THIS NEXT SONG, COLIN SMARTENS VINNIE UP   Music Cue
FOR JANINE. LEATHER JACKET ON, COLLAR UP + GREASED HAIR.

                    <u>CRIPPLED WITH NERVES</u>

                                        Dialogue spoken between lyric lines.

                              COLIN
If they split up…

                              VINNIE
No.

                              COLIN
Why not?

                              VINNIE
She wouldn't look twice at me.

                              COLIN
She might.

                              VINNIE
I'd just make an idiot of myself.

                              COLIN
Do it! … Go on! … On the rebound … Boing! Boing!

                              VINNIE
They haven't split up yet.

                              COLIN
Boing!

                              ALL
OO BOP, OO BOP OO BOP

Everytime Colin says 'Boing' he makes pelvic thrust gestures. He puts a couple of bog rolls down his t-shirt as fake boobs & bundles of lipstick on his chops. Now he flirts & dances with Vinnie as if he is Janine.

Vinnie is practicing talking to Janine. Meanwhile Colin is putting loo rolls down his t-shirt as fake boobs which he reveals to Vinnie. Vinnie takes over singing. Colin gets involved.

COLIN

Boing!
Boing!
Boing!
Boing!

Colin pulls Vinnies face into his cleavage

Colin buries Vinnie's face in his boobs.

Song Finishes

COLIN

Right. Pub. If I'm not going to this gig tonight I'm going to get well and truly hammered. Come on.

VINNIE

(To audience)
Then, out of the blue, Mum turns up…

Oh, she's not ready, she was about to light a fag.

Pat realizes she has missed her cue and runs on.

VINNIE

…in her best jacket…

Janine helps her into a brown leather jacket

Pat runs off and Janine helps her on with jacket.

VINNIE
…with giant shoulder pads and big hair…

Janine shushes her hair & gives her a little red leather handbag

Janine sprays Pat's hair.

VINNIE
…like she's Sue Ellen from Dallas or something… Ready?

Come on Pat, we ain't got all night *Pat enters.*

VINNIE

Mum?

She's nearly ready

PAT

Hello, love.

Pat walks towards pool table and spots Colin.

COLIN

Hello, Mrs B.

Colin hurries to remove the loo rolls.

PAT

Hello, Colin.

COLIN'S EMBARRSSED, HE TAKES OUT HIS FAKE BOOBS + SMILES AT PAT

Pat puts her bag on the table.

VINNIE

What are you doing here, Mum?

PAT

I've come to see Mr Patterson. See if I can get my old job back.

VINNIE

What about Dad?

PAT

Your Dad's going to the hospice tomorrow.

VINNIE

No, Mum-

PAT

We want you to go back to school-

VINNIE

No!

PAT

You are not going to waste your life. You are going to get an education if it bloody kills me!

VINNIE

But what about Dad?

PAT

He's going to the hospice.

SHE GOES, LEAVING HER BAG ON THE POOL-TABLE

Pat exits.

VINNIE

Mum! Shit!

COLIN

A hospice?

VINNIE

Yes...

COLIN

I'm sorry, Vin.

COLIN GIVES VINNIE A HUG
+ HERE COMES SOPPY BOLLOCKS

Colin gives Vinnie a hug. Dave enters with
his brother Graham (Louis) and his
brother's girlfriend, Sandra (Joey – in a
wig).

DAVE

Bum bandits!

VINNIE

Fuck off, Dave.

DAVE

Don't you tell me to fuck off! Oi Sandra, Graham get in here.

WITH HER DODGY BLONDE SYRUP, RED DRESS + HEELS

GRAHAM

Come on we gotta get going!

SANDRA

Yeah, we gotta get going

GRAHAM

Where's Janine?

SANDRA

Yeah, where's Janine?

DAVE

Where is she? Janine! Silly cow.

VINNIE

You don't deserve her! You don't deserve someone like Janine!

DAVE

(Mimics Vinnie)
"You don't deserve her!"

VINNIE

Fuck you!

[408]

ONSCREEN A PICTURE OF BRUCE LEE + THE WORDS 'KUNG FU MOMENT'
VINNIE + DAVE BOW TO EACH OTHER. IN SLOW MOTION VINNIE DOES A FLYING CHOP ONTO DAVE'S
RIGHT ARM. OH, IT'S FALLEN OFF. NOT SURE IF THAT WAS MEANT TO HAPPEN.
VINNIE GIVES HIM HIS ARM BACK + HE PUTS IT ON. BACK INTO SLOW MO, THE DRAGON STANCE.

                                    DAVE   DAVE PUNCHES VINNIE IN THE CHOPS,
Fuck you!   VINNIE TURNS + POKES DAVE IN THE EYES.
                                                COLIN POINTS TO DAVES TESTICLES. (SOUND
                                VINNIE/DAVE   VINNIE DOES A RUNNING KICK AND... EFFECT)
Fuck yooooooooooooooooou...   DAVE DOESN'T FLINCH, HE SHAKES HIS HEAD.

*Vinnie and Dave go into a slow-mo Kung Fu fight. Joey runs back to
his keyboards in slo-mo to play the Kung-Fu theme to underscore the
fight. The fight is deliberately exaggerated. Vinnie chops Dave's arm
and Dave's prosthetic arm accidently falls off. He puts it back on to
conclude the fight. When Janine enters we go back into real time.*

BIT OF A SCUFFLE REALLY, HANDBAGS & ALL THAT — JANINE BREAKS THEM UP [10]
                                    JANINE
        (Screams)
Stop it! Stop it! Stop it! Stop it!

                                    DAVE
Right! You're sacked! Both of you!

                                    COLIN
Yes!

                                    DAVE
Come on, we're going!

                                    JANINE
Get lost!

                                    DAVE
You what?

                                    JANINE
I said: Get! Lost!

                                    DAVE
What's got into you?

                                    JANINE
Why don't you take Shelley?

                                    DAVE
You what?

                                    JANINE
Bastard!   SHE SHOVES HIM IN THE CHEST
                                    DAVE
        (Referring to Vinnie)
What's he been saying to you?

JANINE

He hasn't said nothing. I heard it all myself.

DAVE

What? Come on-

JANINE

No! Didn't you hear what I said? Not. Going.

DAVE

Janine, look...Come on...
(Pretends to be a hypnotist)
You are under my power, you will remember nothing...

HE WAVES HIS HANDS IN HER FACE.
HE THINKS HES BLOODY ALI BONGO

Janine isn't amused.

DAVE (cont.)

Come on, babe... It's Ian Dury!

GRAHAM

It's Ian Dury!

SANDRA

It's Ian Dury!

DAVE

Babe. Babe. Come on...Babe...

JANINE

Find yourself another "sympathy shag"!

DAVE

I never said that.

JANINE

I heard you! Go on, fuck off! Go and get Shelley to suck your dick!

DAVE

I dunno what you're talking about.

JANINE

Your dick! Your willy! Your penis! At least I think it's a penis. It looked like a penis the last time I saw it...Only...much smaller... SHE TURNS TO THE AUDIENCE
(To audience)
Actually, I didn't say that, I only thought of it later...What I actually said was...
(To Dave)
Wanker!　　GO JANINE

                              DAVE
We'll go without you then.

                              GRAHAM
Yes.

                              SANDRA
Yes.

                              JANINE
Good. Go on.

                              DAVE
We will. We're going.

                              GRAHAM
Yes.

                              SANDRA
Yes.

                              JANINE
Go on, then.

                              DAVE
Right.

                              GRAHAM
Right.

                              SANDRA
Yes. Right.

                              DAVE
Come on.

THERE GO THE THREE STOOGES   *Dave, Graham and Sandra exit.*

                              COLIN
     (To Janine)
Aren't you going?

                              JANINE
What? With him? No way!

                              COLIN
So they've got a spare ticket...

                              VINNIE
Colin!

                              COLIN
What?

                              VINNIE
You're being a bit …insensitive-

                              JANINE
No…Hold on…

SHE REACHES INTO HER BAG   *Janine produces four tickets from her bag.*

                                                    Music Cue
                                          Sex & Drugs & Rock & Roll

                              VINNIE
Are they-?

                              JANINE
Dave's tickets, yes. Come on.

                              VINNIE
What?

                              JANINE
Let's go to the gig.

                              VINNIE
Us?

                              JANINE
Yes.

                              VINNIE
How?

                              JANINE
Have you got a car?

                              VINNIE
No.
        (A thought)   HE GOES TO THE BAG ON THE POOL TABLE
Mum has though.
        (He rummages in Pat's bag and finds them)
Car keys!

                              JANINE
Shall we?

[412]

                              COLIN
We're gonna see Ian Dury?

                              VINNIE
Yes!

                              COLIN
YAAAAAAAAAAAAAAAAAAAAAAAAAAAA! Kill the rich! Eat their babies! Come
On!

                              VINNIE
        (There's something else…)
Just…

                              JANINE
What?

                              VINNIE
Would it be all right to take my Dad?

                              JANINE
Why not? We got four tickets. Shame to waste 'em. Come on!

                              COLIN
Come on!

                              VINNIE
        (To audience)
**We were sprinting across the car park to Mum's orange Morris Marina.
Five minutes later we were at my place, Dad was in the back of the
motor and we were off down the A13…**

THEY JUMP ONTO THE POOLTABLE CAR   *Vinnie, Colin, Janine and Bobby in Vinnie's*
JOHN COMES FORWARD THEN WE   *Mum's car. The gang sing along as they*
ALL DANCE & SIGN BEHIND HIM   *drive along…*

                      SEX & DRUGS & ROCK & ROLL

                              DEBBIE
**Right I want to see all of you copying us – thrust your hips, pop a pill
and strum your guitar!**

SEX AND DRUGS AND ROCK AND ROLL

                                              Song Finishes

VINNIE
You've got about fifteen minutes to get some…sex…and drugs…and
rock & roll…See you in fifteen! Oi Oi!

End of Act One

AND I NEED to GET SOME MORE CHANGE FOR THE
PAYPHONE. IF I SEE YOU IN THE BAR I'LL HAVE
A PINT OF 'CREME DE MENTHE', I'M GAGGING!
SPEAK SOON.

PHONE PIPS.... HELLO
WELOME BACK to THE 'RED LION'
HOPE YOU HAD A CHEEKY BABYCHAM OR
CINZANO, I DID! THE BAND ARE
SETTING UP... BLA BLA BLA...
(MORE CHARACTER DESCRIPTIONS ON PHONE)
OH, HERE'S PAT, SHE WANTS A WORD
WITH YOU...

ACT TWO

The band and actors take up their positions in the pub. Pat goes to the phone to talk to Blind Derek. The band plays the riff from SEX & DRUGS & ROCK & ROLL...

VINNIE
(To audience)
Welcome back! I hope you had plenty of sex and drugs-

COLIN
We did!

Vinnie sees Pat on the phone.

VINNIE
Mum...Mum! Give the phone back to Pickles...

PAT
Blind Derek says, when are we going to do 'Blockheads'?

JOHN
Yes!!!!

VINNIE
We're not doing Blockheads!

JOHN
Boo!!!

VINNIE
Mum, we have to start! Right...Everyone ready?

Vinnie, Colin, Janine and Bobby return to their positions in the 'car'. They mime the movement of the car.

VINNIE
So...we were driving along the A13 to London when the car in front indicates to turn left, I go to overtake and then he turns right and I go straight into the back of him...

OH. A SMOKEY CLOUD EFFECT
OVER THE POOL TABLE

Music screeches and bangs to represent the crash. Silence.

JANINE
We only got as far as Stanford-le-Hope.

[The Scripts + Reasons to be Cheerful]

                              COLIN
I couldn't believe it.

                              VINNIE
The bloke driving the other car went mad.

                              JANINE
He tried to blame Vinnie.

                              VINNIE
We stood there arguing for ages.

                              COLIN
Then the pigs turned up.

                              JANINE
By the time all the details had been taken it was too late to get to the gig.

                              VINNIE
The car would never have made it anyway.

                              BOBBY
Radiator had burst.

                              VINNIE
And it was stuck in second gear. We had to drive back to Southend at 15
miles an hour with all this steam coming out…

                              JANINE
I fell asleep.

                              VINNIE
We got as far as the roundabout on the Thorpe Esplanade and it conked
out. Went urrrrrrrr….and died. Me and Colin got out to look at the
engine. I don't know why, we didn't know what we were doing. Then
Colin says…

THEY LOOK AT
THE POOL TABLE   COLIN
CAR. COLIN   Wake up and make love with me…
GIVES IT A   VINNIE
KICK.   What?

                              COLIN
They'll probably start with 'Wake Up and Make Love With Me…'
                    (Imagining the gig)
The lights go down…

                         The lights dim.

[416]

VINNIE

All you can see are the twinkly little red lights on the amps...

COLIN

The audience is up...

Fade up audience sfx.

VINNIE

Stamping their feet, cheering...

COLIN

You can feel the buzz...

VINNIE

Here comes Norman...

Cheering...

COLIN

And Chaz...

VINNIE

Micky, Davey...

COLIN

Johnny, Charley...The audience is going crazy...

VINNIE

Then we hear the piano chords from the start of the song...

And we do...

<u>Music Cue</u>
Wake Up and Make Love With Me

VINNIE (cont.)

. And here comes Ian...stick, dark glasses, braces-

COLIN

Razorblade earring...

VINNIE/COLIN/VOCALIST

Oi Oi!

WAKE UP AND MAKE LOVE WITH ME

JOHN COMES FORWARD, DEBBIE SITS BESIDE HIS WHEELCHAIR + SIGNS RATHER SEDUCTIVELY, ITS AWFULLY RUDE.

DEBBIE STEERS JOHN BACK to THE BAND   *Song Finishes*

BOBBY

Oi! Get me out the bloody car!

JANINE
(Drowsy, getting out of the car)
What's going on?

VINNIE

Car's broken down.

JANINE

Where are we?

VINNIE

Thorpe Esplanade.

BOBBY

Let's go down to the sea.

JANINE

What?

VINNIE

Why?

BOBBY

'Cos I want to. The only time I ever get out is to go to the bloody hospital. Come on, give me a shove...

VINNIE

(To audience)
We left the car on the side of the road and went down to the beach. I didn't mind. I didn't want to go home and have to face Mum. Dad wanted us to take him to a beach hut we used to go to when I was a kid. It was a bugger to get to 'cos the beach is quite shingly there, so we had to pick him up and carry him.

MULTI-COLOURED BEACH HUTS ONSCREEN *Vinnie and Colin move the wheelchair.*
COLIN PUTS DOWN A WOODEN CRATE OF BOOZE

BOBBY

We there yet?

VINNIE

Yes.

BOBBY

You sure it's the right one?

[418]

                    VINNIE
I think so.

                    BOBBY
Purple?

                    VINNIE
And white.

                    BOBBY
That's it.

                    JANINE
This your beach hut?

                    VINNIE
My aunt's.

                    BOBBY
Years since I've been here.

                    COLIN
        (Referring to the beach hut)
It's falling to bits.

                    VINNIE
So what?

                    COLIN
All right! Don't have a go at me!

                    JANINE
He never drove into the back of some nutter from Braintree.

                    VINNIE
It wasn't my fault!

                    JANINE
I know!

                    BOBBY
Boys...Girls...Deep breaths...Calm...That's better...

                    VINNIE
        (To Bobby)
Sorry. What am I gonna tell Mum about the car?

                    BOBBY
Bugger the car. There's more important things to life than the bloody car.

[The Scripts + Reasons to be Cheerful]

                                        VINNIE
It's just…Mum's gonna kill me.

                                        JANINE
Dave's gonna kill all of us.
             (Looks over to Bobby)
Is your Dad okay?

                                        VINNIE
Dad? You all right?

                                        BOBBY
Yes. I love it here.

                                        JANINE
I'm hungry.

                                        VINNIE
I'll get us some fish and chips later.

                                        JANINE
Did you say you had some booze, Colin?

HE GRABS A BOTTLE   *Colin gets his crate of Thunderbird from DS*
FROM THE CRATE   *area.*

                                        COLIN
Thunderbird!

                                        JANINE
Thunderbird?

                                        COLIN
"Shall I mourn your decline with some Thunderbird wine…"

                                        JANINE
Wine?

                                        COLIN
Fortified wine.

                                        JANINE
What's it "fortified" with?

                                        BOBBY
Anti-freeze. Here, I'll have some. Give it here.

                             Colin passes a bottle to Bobby. Bobby
                             swigs.

[420]

                    VINNIE
Dad, are you sure-

                    BOBBY
Wanted to take me out didn't you? Well this is perfect. Describe it to me.
Come on. I want the perfect English summer's day at the seaside. The sun is
shining…

                    The sun isn't shining. Colin and Janine look
                    at each other and shrug.

                    BOBBY (cont.)
The sea is…
          (Waits for a response)
The sea is…

                    At the same time.

          VINNIE   JANINE/COLIN
Blue   Brown.

                    BOBBY
     (Insistent)
The sea is blue! The sky is blue! and the sun shining.

                    COUSIN JOEY
Blokes with their trousers rolled up   EVEN THE BAND CHIP IN

                    PAUL
Handkerchiefs knotted on their heads…   BILL'S OUT OF THE CHAIR,
                                              THEY PUT A KNOTTED HANKY ON
                    NIXON   HIS HEAD + ROLL HIS
Sitting behind stripy windbreakers.   TROUSERS UP. A BLANKET
                                              COVERS HIS SHOULDERS.
                    JOHN
Grans fast asleep under crocheted blankets-

                    PAULA
Kids with buckets and spades.

                    BILL
Well done

TIME FOR A COCKNEY KNEES UP NOW AND I'M GONNA JOIN IN. *Music Cue*

                    ENGLAND'S GLORY

WE'LL BE DOING THE 'OKEY COKEY' + A CONGA
     EVEN HAROLD THE CHAMPY BOY BOX JOINS IN!

                    [The Scripts + Reasons to be Cheerful]

                              VINNIE
Meanwhile back on the beach

                              JANINE
Whose beach hut did you say it was, Vinnie?

                              VINNIE
My aunt's. The key is still under the bucket!

                              BOBBY
Dippy Deirdre. Pat's sister. Dyed-in-the-wool blue-arsed Tory. I wouldn't mind betting she's the one put voting for Thatcher in Pat's head.

                              JANINE
My ex is a Tory.

                              BOBBY
Is he a prick?

                              JANINE
Yes.

                              BOBBY
That explains it then.

                              JANINE
Wuh! It honks! What's that?

                              VINNIE
A moose head.

                              JANINE
What's it doing in there?

                              BOBBY
Used to be in their front room.

                              JANINE
A moose head?

                              VINNIE
Put it on your head Col.

HE DOES + CHASES JANINE   *Colin holds the moose head up to his head.*

                              COLIN
Mooooo!!!

JANINE

Suits you.

BOBBY BENDS IN PAIN

Bobby groans – he's in pain.

BOBBY

Vin? Got my tablets?

VINNIE

Yes. Here you go…

HE WASHES THEM DOWN WITH THUNDERBIRD

Vinnie gives Bobby his tablets. Pause.

JANINE

Now what do we do?

VINNIE

Hold on…

HE DASHES BACK & RETURNS WITH…

Vinnie dashes back into the hut. He returns a second later with a box.

VINNIE (cont.)

Monopoly!

JANINE

I don't think I can stand the excitement.

COLIN

Monopoly is a game for thieving capitalist bastards!

BOBBY

I know…MY OLD MAN WORE THREE PIECE WHISTLES

COLIN

HE WAS NEVER HOME FOR LONG. One-nil.

JANINE

You what?

VINNIE

The lyric game.

COLIN

IN MY YELLOW JERSEY…

VINNIE

I WENT OUT ON THE NICK.

                                BOBBY
I knew that!

                                COLIN
Two-nil.

                                BOBBY
That's not fair!

                                COLIN
Tough. Your turn.

                                BOBBY
        (Has a think, then...)
I'VE BEEN CHEATED BY YOU SINCE I DON'T KNOW WHEN

                                COLIN
That's not Ian Dury.

                                BOBBY
I'm branching out. What's the matter? Don't you know it?

BOBBY GOES TO MARK A POINT ON AN IMAGINARY CHALKBOARD
                                COLIN
SO I MADE UP MY MIND IT MUST COME TO AN END. 'Mamma Mia' Abba.
Three-Nil.

                                BOBBY
Bastard!

                                VINNIE
How do you know that?

                                COLIN
I move in mooseterious ways.

                                VINNIE
YOU'RE MORE THAN FAIR

                                COLIN
YOU'VE GOT A GORGEOUS BUM. 'B' side of 'Sweet Gene Vincent'. Four-
Nil. Braverman has the Bentleys by the balls.

                                BOBBY
WORKERS OF THE WORLD UNITE

                                COLIN
YOU HAVE NOTHING TO LOSE BUT YOUR RHYTHM STICK

                                VINNIE
HIT ME SLOWLY, HIT ME QUICK

[424]

BOBBY/COLIN/VINNIE

HIT ME! HIT ME! HIT ME!

They laugh.

VINNIE

You all right, Janine? I'm sorry about you and Dave.

JANINE

I'm not.

BOBBY

Vinnie, Col why don't you see if them deckchairs are still in there...

VINNIE

Col. Come on.

Vinnie and Colin go to look for the deckchairs.

JANINE

(Referring to the wine)
Give us a swig.

BOBBY

Where are you?

JANINE

Here.

Bobby holds up the drink. Janine takes it.

JANINE (cont.)

Ta.
(Swigs)
Christ that's rough.

BOBBY

It's lovely.
(Wants the booze)
Here...give it us back.

Janine hands him the wine back.

JANINE

Should you be drinking?

BOBBY

Doctor's orders.

                    JANINE
I bet.

                    BOBBY
Cures cancer this stuff. Not a lot of people know that.

                    JANINE
My Gran had cancer. Where's yours?

                    BOBBY
Every-bloody-where. Thanks for the ticket for tonight, Janine. I know they
were hard to come by…

                    JANINE
They weren't mine.

                    BOBBY
No?

                    JANINE
My boyfriend- my ex…they were his. I nicked 'em because he's a wanker.

                    BOBBY
The Tory?

                    JANINE
Yes.

                    BOBBY
Well done.

                    JANINE
He called me a sympathy shag.

                    BOBBY
He what?

                    JANINE
I'm a raspberry.

                    BOBBY
A raspberry ripple?

                    JANINE
Yes.

                    BOBBY
Like me?

JANINE

No. I was born like this.

BOBBY

What do you look like?

JANINE

Five foot two, eyes of blue.

BOBBY

Really?

JANINE

Nah...not really...I'm Spasticus!

BOBBY

No! I'm Spasticus!

EVERYONE COMES FORWARD AND SIGNS THE DEFIANT ANTHEM MUSIC CUE

SPASTICUS AUTISTICUS

VINNIE

Our vocalist, John, was so furious when he heard the BBC had banned 'Spasticus Autisticus' he wrote to them. What was it you said in your letter, John?

JOHN

Dear Director General of the BBC, You are a cunt.

All cheer.

JOHN

And he didn't even have the courtesy to reply.

Song Finishes

VINNIE

Meanwhile back on the beach-

JOHN

They were all singing Blockheads!

VINNIE

We're not doing Blockheads.

[The Scripts + Reasons to be Cheerful]

JOHN

Aaggh!

VINNIE

Back on the beach... Look what I found! A load of old LP's! Little Richard, Gene Vincent and the Blue Caps

JANINE

Let's see.

Janine looks through the records.

BOBBY

Those are mine. I wondered what your Mum had done with my records. Give me the...Gene Vincent Rocks the one where he's wearing the silk green shirt...that one...pass it over...

Janine hands him the LP.

BOBBY (cont.)

This it?

JANINE

Yes.

BOBBY

I love this album.

Bobby kisses the album cover.

VINNIE

I found some old leather gear and all...

BOBBY

Here...Give...

Vinnie gets the waistcoat and hands it to Bobby.

BOBBY (cont.)

I used to fancy myself as a bit of a Gene Vincent..
        (Sings)
WELL BE-BOP-A-LULA!

Bobby laughs as he clutches the gear. He wants to put the waistcoat on.

BOBBY (continued)

Help me put it on.

HE STRUGGLES GETTING INTO THE BLACK LEATHER WAISTCOAT

[428]

*Vinnie tries to help his Dad into the
waistcoat. But Bobby is in pain and it's too
much of a struggle.*

BOBBY (continued)

It's no good…
(To Vinnie)
You put it on.

VINNIE

Me?

BOBBY

Yes. Go on! **HE DOES, IT'S A PERFECT FIT**
WHAT DO YOU THINK DEBS? JANINE **DEBBIE: I WOULD**
Go on.

Vinnie puts the waistcoat on.

BOBBY (continued)

(To Vinnie)
Come here…Let me feel…

Bobby feels the waistcoat on Vinnie.

JANINE

You look like James Dean.

BOBBY

Gene Vincent, if you don't mind. I saw him play live seventeen times.
Followed him up and down the country one year.

VINNIE

I'll see what else I can find in there.

Vinnie exits to hut.

BOBBY

I wouldn't have minded being a rock 'n' roll star.

JANINE

What stopped you?

BOBBY

Life. Has this habit of getting in the way. What about you? What do you want
to do?

JANINE

Me? No idea.

                              BOBBY
Must be something.

                              JANINE
I don't know...I quite like art, making things, drawing and that.

                              BOBBY
Do it, then.

                              JANINE
You sound like my Gran.

                              BOBBY
Good for her. Will you get Vinnie for me?

                              JANINE
Sure.

                         She goes.

                              BOBBY
Col...Col...

                              COLIN
Yes?

                              BOBBY
Is there anything going on between them two?

                              COLIN
No. Vinnie's a coward.

                              BOBBY
Why don't we see if we can...you know...

                              COLIN
I've tried.

                              BOBBY
Come on, Col, let's make ourselves scarce; see what happens...

                              COLIN
I'll just get Melvin.

                              BOBBY
Who?

                              COLIN
The Moose.

[430]

                    BOBBY
Bloody hell!

            Vinnie joins them with Janine.

                    VINNIE
Dad, Janine said you wanted me?

                    BOBBY
I wouldn't mind a little nap, You too! (Col does fake yawn)
Come on Push me in the hut will you Colin.

COLIN OVERDOES THE YAWING + STREACHING   DEBBIE: REALLY MILKS IT!
                COLIN
            (Conspiring)
Vinnie...remember what I said...

                    VINNIE
What?

                    COLIN
Boing!

BEFORE COLIN TAKES BOBBY OFF   *Colin exits with Bobby.*
HE DOES THE PELVIC THRUST
SIGN AGAIN   *Music Cue*

                            *Vinnie looks over at Janine. 'Crippled with
                            Nerves' underscores. Vinnie shaking out
                            blanket and trying to make his move. Janine
                            sorting out LPs and pushing crates together
                            to sit down with Vinnie.*

                    CRIPPLED WITH NERVES (Reprise)

VINNIE + JANINE ARE LEFT ALONE.
THEY AVOID EYE CONTACT BUT THEN   *Vinnie finally sitting next to Janine stretches
SMILE NERVOUSLY AT EACH OTHER.   out an arm to put it around her...*
JANINE GETS A CRATE + SITS BESIDE
VINNIE, VERY CLOSE.   *Song Finishes*

                            *Music stops abruptly and Vinnie retracts his
                            arm sharply. Colin enters.*
                    COLIN
Yesssssssssssss

                    VINNIE
What?

                              [The Scripts + Reasons to be Cheerful]

JANINE

What?

BOBBY

What?

COLIN

Nothing!   OH, THEY NEARLY KISSED THEN, CHEERS COLIN!

JANINE

You all right Col?

COLIN

Yeah.

BOBBY

What's going on?

COLIN

Nothing!

BOBBY

Nothing?! Got any more of that thunderbird wine?

JANINE

Vinnie, what do you think your Mum'll do when she finds out?

VINNIE

I dunno.

BOBBY

She'll be all right.

VINNIE

You reckon?

BOBBY

Yes. Her bark's worse than her bite. I just wish I hadn't put her through all this.
Vinnie, I want you to promise me something.

VINNIE

What?

BOBBY

When this is over I want you to go back to school. For me and your mum

VINNIE

Dad. Don't.

JANINE
What 'A' Levels were you doing?

VINNIE
Maths, French and Theatre Studies.

JANINE
Theatre Studies?

VINNIE
I was going to do Drama at uni.

BOBBY
What do you mean "was"? Still are, aren't you?

COLIN
I can speak French and German: JE T'ADORE, ICH LIEBE DICH...

COLIN/VINNIE
HIT ME, HIT ME, HIT ME

JANINE
Say something in French.

VINNIE
Err...Mon coeur est à toi.

COILN
Did you just call her a twat?

VINNIE
...à toi.

JANINE
Mon cœur... ?

VINNIE
Mon coeur est à toi

JANINE
Mon coeur est à toi. I done French. I know what that means.

VINNIES BLUSHING

Vinnie is embarrassed.

COLIN
What? What does it mean?

JANINE
Vinnie?

                              VINNIE
          (Reluctantly)
My heart is yours.

                              COLIN
Wey-hey!

                              VINNIE
          (To Janine)
Sorry.

                              JANINE
S'all right. I didn't really know what it meant.

                              COLIN
Mon kerr ate a twat.

                              JOHN
I'm sick of this sentimental bollocks! Let's do 'Blockheads'!

                              VINNIE
We can't just do 'Blockheads', John!

                              JOHN
Want to bet? I-2-3-4-

                                              Music Cue

          Guitar Intro.

                        BLOCKHEADS
JOHN'S UP FRONT, WE ALL SIGN & DANCE BEHIND HIM
LIKE DRUNKEN HOOLIGANS. IT'S A RIOT!!
                                          Song Finishes

                              VINNIE
Meanwhile back on the beach...Dad was looking a bit tired... → TELL ME ABOUT IT.
          (Turns to Bobby)   I'M FUCKED AFTER
You all right, Dad?   JUMPIN ABOUT LIKE
                                                              A NUTTER!
                              BOBBY
Yes. I'm a bit knackered.

                              VINNIE
Do you want to go home?

[434]

BOBBY

No. No, I want to stay a bit longer. I'm not ready to go just yet. I wouldn't mind another little nap,

Colin and Janine move away as Vinnie gets a blanket and puts it around Bobby.

VINNIE

Let me get a blanket for you.   HE puts A TARTAN BLANKET OVER BOBBY'S LAP.
                                 & SITS ON A CRATE BESIDE HIM

BOBBY

Ta, mate. She's all right that Janine, eh?

VINNIE

Yes.

BOBBY

Did I ever tell you about the first time I went out with your Mum?

VINNIE

Didn't you know her from work?

BOBBY

Yes, but the first time I took her out was to the Speedway at Rayleigh. Some bloke told me she liked Speedway.
I'd been besotted for months and I finally saw my chance. So I asked her if she fancied it and she said yes.
Course I bloody hated Speedway. Turned out; so did she. We ended up in the Wimpy having a laugh about it...
She wrote some articles for a magazine once. She ever tell you that?

VINNIE

No.   HE TAKES VINNIES HAND

BOBBY

You look after her for me. Yes?

VINNIE

Course.

BOBBY

Now, bugger off and let me get some sleep.

VINNIE WHEELS HIM OFF, TAKES A MICROPHONE FROM A TRAFFIC CONE *Music Cue*
& LOOKS UP TO THE OLD PHOTO OF HIS DAD SMILING DOWN ON HIM.

<u>MY OLD MAN</u>

DURING THE SONG VINNIE GOES OVER TO COLIN SITTING ON THE POOLTABLE
WHO GIVES HIM A PINT & THEY BOTH RAISE THEIR GLASSES
TO THE PHOTO ONSCREEN.

COLIN
Later that night. Me and Melvin went to sleep on the beach

COLIN LAYS DOWN ON THE FLOOR
USING THE MOOSE HEAD AS A PILLOW.
JANINE SITS BESIDE HIM.

Janine and Colin take their positions DS.
Janine leaning on Colin's legs with a
blanket, Colin lying down.

JANINE
Nice here, init, Col. I used to walk along here when I was little with my Gran.
I can remember looking at these beach huts and feeling really jealous we
didn't have one. Maybe we should all club together and buy one. What do you
reckon, Col? Or would that be against your principles? Col?

HE'S FAST ASLEEP, SHE PUTS
A CROCHET BLANKET OVER HIM

Janine looks over at Colin – he is fast
asleep.

JANINE (cont.)
(American accent as in "The Waltons")
Good night, John-boy…

VINNIES BACK

She lays the blanket over him.

JANINE (cont.)
Your Dad all right?

VINNIE
Think so.

JANINE
Colin's out cold.

VINNIE
He does that. Don't matter where he is, if he's pissed he just kinda konks out.
There's no waking him. Watch…

HE GIVES HIM A BIG SHAKE,
NOTHING!

Leans over Colin. Shakes him…

VINNIE (cont.)
(Loud)
Colin!

Colin doesn't flinch.

VINNIE (cont.)
See.

JANINE
Come here you…

SHE GRABS VINNIE + SNOGS HIM

Janine grabs Vinnie. She kisses him. Pub crowd wolf whistle. They stop. Janine waits for Vinnie to kiss her again…

                    JANINE

Well…

                    VINNIE

Well?

                    JANINE

What you waiting for? I'm single.

                    VINNIE

Yes.

                    JANINE

Don't you want to?

                    VINNIE

Yes…

                    JANINE

So…

                    VINNIE

Is this really happening?

                    JANINE

Let's find out…PAULA!…

VINNIE PUTS A MIC STAND CENTRE STAGE FOR JANINE.   *Music Cue*
HE'S HANDS ARE ALL OVER HER.
LOUIS THE SAX PLAYER CLIMBS   *Vinnie and Janine…do their thing…*
ONTO THE POOL TABLE.

HIT ME WITH YOUR RHYTHM STICK

VINNIE + JANINE DANCE FLIRTATIOUSLY TOGETHER + I'M GONNA GET DEBBIE to
HIT ME WITH A POOL CUE WHILE I'M BENT OVER THE TABLE*Song Finishes*

WHY NOT!   *Pat finds Vinnie's "T" shirt that has been thrown out from behind the pool table.*

       PAT PICKS UP VINNIE'S T-SHIRT THAT HAS COME FLYING ACROSS THE STAGE.
                    PAT

Vincent!

*VINNIE & JANINE EMERGE
HALF DRESSED FROM BEHIND
THE POOL TABLE.*

Vinnie & Janine emerge from behind the
pool table.

PAT

Shall we get on with the story? The bit where I turn up. Come on, we
haven't got all night...

SHE THROWS HIM HIS T-SHIRT, HE PUTS IT ON & JANINE TIES UP HER HAIR!

VINNIE

Right. Sorry...It's the next day. Janine, you and Colin are fast
asleep...Me and Dad are in the hut...

Janine lies down beside Colin. They wait for
Colin to speak his line. Janine gives Colin a
shove. He doesn't move.

JANINE

Colin...
        (Shakes him)
Colin, it's your line...
        (Shakes him)
Colin!

VINNIE

What's the matter?

JANINE

I think he asleep. I mean, like, really asleep...   *HE'S SNORING AS WELL*

DEBBIE GIVES HIM A BIG KICK!   Vinnie joins her as does Debbie who does it
the 'deaf way' and kicks Colin awake.

COLIN

        (Sitting bolt upright - waking from a strange dream)
I want my Walnut Whip!

VINNIE

What?

COLIN

        (Confused)
Where am I?

JANINE

        (Indicating the audience)
We're doing the play.   *HE TURNS to THE AUDIENCE & REALISES WHERE HE IS*

COLIN

Oh...
        (Remembering where they had got up to)
HIT ME! Right, come on, let's do HIT ME!

[438]

VINNIE

We've done it, Col.

COLIN

Oh...

VINNIE

It's the next day. When you and Janine wake up.

*THEY LAY BACK DOWN &
SIT UP STRAIGHT AWAY*

*Vinnie re-joins Bobby. Colin and Janine lay
down in preparation for the scene. Colin
wakes.*

COLIN

Morning, Janine!

JANINE

Morning, Colin.

COLIN

I feel like shit. How do you feel?

JANINE

Like shit.

COLIN

Me and Melvin might go up the shops. Do you want anything?

JANINE

Crisps. And coke. And a Curly Wurly. And a Strawberry Mivi.

*VINNIE WHEELS IN HIS
BLACK LEATHER CLAD DAD*

Vinnie wheels his Dad out.

VINNIE

And here he is...Modelling the latest in rock 'n' roll leather chic...the one, the
only: Mister Robert James Bentley!

BOBBY

(With gusto)
WELL BE-BOP-A-LULA SHE'S MY BABY
BE-BOP-A-LULA I DON'T MEAN MAYBE

*BOBBY LOOKS REALLY
POORLY*

VINNIE

(His hangover hurts)
Not so loud...

BOBBY

Lightweight. Right! What's for breakfast?

[The Scripts + Reasons to be Cheerful]

VINNIE

Chocolate.

BOBBY

Excellent.

COLIN

I'm going up the shop...

Pat and Dave

PAT

Bobby!

OH NO, IT'S PAT + DAVE

VINNIE

Shit...

Pat runs over to Bobby.

PAT
(To Vinnie)

What the hell do you think you're playing at?

VINNIE

I'm not letting you take him to the hospice, Mum.

PAT

You bloody idiot! How dare you drag him down here!

BOBBY

Nice to see you, Pat.

PAT

Shut up!
(Noticing the leather waistcoat and trousers)
What the hell are you wearing?

VINNIE

Dad wanted to come here.

PAT
Don't talk rubbish! Look at him! He looks terrible!

BOBBY

I'm happy!

PAT
You shouldn't be out in this sun! You could have least put a hat on him.

She waves at Colin to get his attention to help her. Pat and Colin wheel Bobby into the hut. Vinnie sits, head in hands.

Dave crosses to Janine.

DAVE

We went to London. To the gig. Pat came with us. We've been driving round all night looking for you. We thought you had my tickets.

JANINE

I did.

DAVE

We waited outside. We didn't see you.

JANINE

We didn't get there. How did you find us?

DAVE

We saw the motor up by the roundabout. Look, Janine, I'm sorry about...you know...

JANINE

It's finished, Dave.

DAVE

Right.

JANINE

Dave, there's something else I need to tell you...

A look between Janine and Vinnie.

DAVE

What?

JANINE

I voted Labour...

Dave backs off. Pat and Colin push Bobby back out. A tea towel is draped over his head. He pulls it off. She puts it back on.

PAT

Vinnie, we're going.

VINNIE

Mum, don't...Mum...Can we just stay a bit longer? Just a few more minutes.

DAVE SLIDES OVER to JANINE

SHE SNUGGLES UP to HIM

HE PUSHES HER OFF IN DISGUST, DEVASTATED + REPULSED HE GAGS. I THINK HE'S GONNA BE SICK. HE RUNS OFF, TA LA BULLOKY CHOPS

Please...

                              BOBBY
I don't want to go yet.

                              Pause. Its Pat line, but she can't do it.

                              VINNIE (cont.)
Mum...It's your line...

                              Pat steps out of the scene.

                              Pause. Vinnie doesn't know what to do.

                              PAT
                  (Addresses an imaginary Bob)
We used to go down to that beach hut all the time –

                              VINNIE
Mum / we haven't finished...

                              PAT
Him in all that leather. Used to fancy himself back then. That black
leather glove he had. Just the one. With a bloody great fake ruby ring on
it. Bloody Gene Vincent. He was a bit flash, your Dad. I loved it. He was
quite a catch. I don't mind admitting it. Loads of girls round here after
him. But I had a secret weapon. I had one thing the other girls didn't
have...The key to a beach hut we could use on weekends. We had some
fantastic how's-your-father down there. Yes. It was good, Bob...

SHE TAKES THE SHADES OFF BILL & HE STEPS OUT OF THE CHAIR

                              *Pat gets her drink from her table and
                              raises it to everyone in the pub.*

                              PAT (cont.)
Lets raise a glass. Good times...   *WE ALL RAISE A GLASS TO THE
                              EMPTY WHEELCHAIR*
                              ALL
Good times!

                              VINNIE
Mum...

                              PAT
                  (Snaps back into the 'real' world)
What?

                              VINNIE
We need to finish the scene...

PAT

I don't know if I can, darling.

Pat goes to her table.

VINNIE

Okay...Don't...You stay there...
(To audience)
So...um...Mum wanted to take Dad home, but he wouldn't go without all
his old LP's so me and Mum went into the hut to get them for him. And,
er, yes, while we were in there, Dad was...Colin and Dad played the lyric
game, Dad caught Colin out using a lyric from an actual Gene Vincent
song. And Dad won. For, like, the first time ever. Then Janine and Colin
said goodbye and left and that was...Dave gave us a lift home. Pretty
decent of him really. And that's, sort of, it. We didn't get to the gig. But
somehow it didn't matter...All yours, Bill... VINNIE TAKES OFF THE CHAIR

BILL'S ALONE, ONSCREEN IMAGES OF GENE VINCENT + THE BLUE CAPS. *Music Cue*
THE GIANT GLITTERBALL SPINS HE GRABS A MIC, SPOTLIGHT ON HIM.

SWEET GENE VINCENT

VINNIE COMES ON AS GENE VINCENT, BLACK LEATHER TROUSERS, WAISTCOAT + GLOVE + GUITAR.
WE ALL SIGN + JIVE BEHIND HIM. *Song Finishes*

The End

*A picture of Margaret Thatcher comes on
the screen with the words: The End.*

CURTAIN CALL / ENCORES

Cast will take a bow, then the band will join them for their bow.

VINNIE
Do you want one more? Okay, John, What do you want to do?

JOHN
(Chants)
SEX & DRUGS & ROCK & ROLL

SEX AND DRUGS AND ROCK & ROLL

SEGUES INTO

HIT ME WITH YOUR RHYTHM STICK

Cast and Band bow and the final image of Maggie morphs into Theresa May with the words: This is not the end.

THE CROWD GO WILD, THEY ARE ALL ON THEIR FEET.

HOLD ON, IT'S NOT OVER YET.

'NOT THE END'

JOHN TURNS to THE AUDIENCE

JK: OUR NEW SONG
Let's 'AVE IT!!

This is where we do the new song written for Graeae by The Blockheads and John Kelly.

IF IT CAN'T BE RIGHT THEN IT MUST BE WRONG

ONSCREEN MAGGIE THATHER MORPHS INTO TERESA MAY.

[444]

SORRY
A Verbatim Play

Characters

Jenny Sealey (JS)

Amit Sharma (AS)

John Kelly (JK)

Jude Mahon (JM)

JS   I am Jenny Sealey. I am Deaf with speech. My careers officer told me I could be a librarian because libraries are quiet. However I am the artistic director of Graeae.

I will play me and amongst others I will be representing a Canadian gay blind woman, a black deaf gay man and various mainly male white non-disabled theatre directors.

AS   I am Amit Sharma. I have a mobility impairment or impairments. My careers advisor told me I probably wouldn't amount to very much but I think that was more my attitude than my impairment.

However I am the associate director of Graeae. I will be playing me and amongst others I will be representing a young deaf Asian woman, a white woman wheelchair user and various drama school personnel.

JK   I am John Kelly. I am a wheelchair user. My careers advisor told me I could possibly work in an office or be a French polisher.

However I am a freelance artist and I won best supporting actor in Graeae's production of *The Threepenny Opera* and Jude here won best supporting actor for her wonderful theatrical signing. I will be playing me and amongst others I will be representing a hearing general manager of a Deaf-led theatre company, an actress with Tourette's, an artistic director who is a mental health survivor and various audience members who commented on the aforementioned *The Threepenny Opera*.

JM   I am Jude Mahon. I am a fully qualified level 6 interpreter. I trained for seven years. I usually have a co-worker but these days ... things being what they are ...

[446]

JS   The following accounts are some of our own personal stories, as well as how D/deaf and disabled artists have responded to my request for sound bites about their dealings with Access to Work (ATW) and the Independent Living Fund (ILF). Some stories are from the SCOPE report.

AS   ATW is the government's best kept secret but what it is/was/is a fantastic scheme that allows D/deaf and disabled people to have their access requirements paid for so they can fulfil their role with full equality in the workplace. It funds interpreters, equipment, fares to work and support workers.

Let's look at the maths.

The government's budget for ATW is £108 million.

Around 37,000 people use ATW. When D/deaf and disabled artists are able to work they are also able to pay taxes. They receive fewer benefits and generate jobs for sign language interpreters and personal assistants who, in turn, pay their own taxes. Do you Jen? The Department of Work and Pensions (DWP) estimates that for every £1 that is spent on ATW, £1.48 comes back to the Exchequer.

ATW pays for our Jude here.

JK   The ILF was the Independent Living Fund which offered financial support to disabled people so they could live independently.

Esther McVey announced on 18 December 2012 that the ILF would be closed completely from June 2015.

All future funding for care and support to current ILF users will be met through their local authority. However, this money won't be ring-fenced as local authorities are generally having their funding slashed; it means they will not be able to meet the additional costs for a person living independently.

Let's look at the maths.

The current cost of ILF is £320 million a year and the average cost of ILF support packages is £346 a week, a tiny proportion of UK government spending. This also compares very favourably to costs in residential care. As an example, Winterbourne View (famous in the UK for residents being systematically abused) costs an average of £3,500 per week. The user base of ILF is mostly young disabled people with only 8.7% of ILF users being over sixty-five.

JM   Are you one of the 8.7% JK?

JK   Fuck off Jude.

Closure of the Fund has breached the human rights of disabled people as enshrined in the United Nations Convention on the Rights of Persons with Disabilities (CRPD), most notably:

- Article 19—right to independent living

- Article 28—the right to an adequate standard of living and protection

JS   Are we ready?

JK   I think I have said my bit but on that note I could do with a wee.

AS, JS and JM look at watches.

AS   You are not scheduled for your next wee until 1.35 pm.

JK   Dear Miss Sealey, I am sorry that your claim for thirty-five hours a week for ATW has been turned down. We will award you with seventy-two hours a month.

JS   We have had a four-year battle to get this overturned! Now we are fighting the £40k cap which will come into force April 2018 and again reduce my access hours by half.

AS   Dear Mr Sharma, I am sorry that your claim for Access to Work has been turned down. Can't you get a friend to help you out?

JK   Dear Ms Partridge, I am sorry your ILF will be cut.

PHONE CALL 0

JS   Hello Access to Work I am calling regarding access support for a colleague who has a differing voice pattern. Yes I will hold.

The phone stays on hold for entire show and ATW only come back at the end.

PHONE CALL 1

JK   Hello Access to Work I am calling about BSL (British Sign Language) provisions for some of our D/deaf actors.

JM   What is BSL?

PHONE CALL 2

AS   Hello Access to Work I am calling on behalf of my Deaf artistic director regarding her Access to Work. She runs our Deaf-led theatre company.

JK   Why are you phoning for her?

AS   She's Deaf and is a grassroots BSL user and doesn't use the phone and has asked me to make enquiries on her behalf.

JK   Why don't you just work with hearing people who sign?

PHONE CALL 3

JS signing and JM voicing over or signing with phone on crook of neck.

JS/JM   Hello Access to Work, I am calling as requested ... what is the issue with the hands-free headset?

AS   Yes I just wanted to find out why you needed a headset ... It's not clear.

JS/JM   OK so I use my interpreters to make phone calls. They are struggling to sign clearly because they're either using one hand to hold up the receiver or are propping it up with their shoulder.

AS   Riiight ... I still don't understand why they need the headset.

JS/JM   OK so you know how sign language works? The interpreters need their hands to sign?

AS   Yes ...

JS/JM   If one of your hands is being used to hold a phone receiver then ...?

[450]

AS   But why do they need the headset? Where does the headset come into play?

JS   Jude Mahon is a sign language interpreter who works with us a lot. Her first job was as rehearsal interpreter on our production of *Bent* by Martin Sherman—a play about what happened to gay men during the Holocaust. By day she was with us and by night she was out on various dates. She told one date all about *Bent* and how Graeae added a new layer as D/deaf and disabled people also suffered hugely under Hitler. His response was:

AS   I don't mean to be rude but don't you think Hitler had a point.

IN CONVERSATION

AS   You can come to drama school when you are cured.

JK   I thought all those disabled people busking in the foyer at the start of the show were just trying to raise some money for themselves. I did not think they would be in the show.

JS   Jenny darling you must see that people do not come to the theatre to be reminded of the tragedy of being handicapped.

AS   Dear Mrs G, we are sorry but we will be changing your lip speaking requirements from twenty-three hours a week to twenty-three hours a year.

AS   *(Lip speaking.)* Dear Mrs G. We are sorry but we will

JK   *(Lip speaking.)* be changing your lip speaking requirements from

[The Scripts + SORRY]

JS	*(Lip speaking.)* Twenty-three hours a week to twenty-three hours a year.
JK	I am A. I can no longer attend any meetings when various governments and NGOs ask me to be part of their various consultation plans. The end of ILF means I now have no social life and no longer volunteer at a primary school to assist children to do drama and reading.
AS	Dear Miss C, we suggest you get the cheapest indirect flight which unfortunately does have three changes but is cheaper than the direct flight. You are able to transfer from your wheelchair so we do not envisage this will be a problem.
JK	Dear Mr E, I appreciate that you need an accessible room with space for your hoist and that accessible accommodation is more expensive. We therefore suggest either your PA shares your room or they stay at a cheaper hotel.
JS	A director auditioning a Deaf actor for a Deaf character who is a first language BSL user.
	Lovely audition!
	Can your interpreter act too?
	The interpreter got the job.
JK	Was that you Jude?
JM	Fuck off John.
AS	You don't look blind.
	Oh shall I put on a crappy Mac, get some dark glasses and a white stick and take my make-up off? Oh please would you!

JK	I think you should get proper directors in at Graeae. It will raise the profile.
	Oh Jen I bet that one hurt!
JS	It did. But not as much as one of my actors, my darling Sophie was hurt with a review which read 'her torso is the same size as her head'...

PHONE CALL 4

AS	What's his disability? Oh OK, that's good, I just needed to make sure he wasn't Deaf.

PHONE CALL 5

JS	Hello RNIB (Royal National Institute for the Blind)? My guide dog has managed to detach the cone he has been wearing as result of an ear operation. He has been scratching his wound and I think there is blood everywhere. I don't know what to do.
	Sorry what did you say?
	There is a phone number on his collar.
	How do you expect me to read that I AM BLIND.

HELLO, HELLO, HELLO

AS	What did Access to Work say to a wheelchair user going for a job interview?
	'How would your life have been if you had not been this disabled?'
JS	What did Access to Work say to a wheelchair user who was a trainee?

[The Scripts + SORRY]

'Give us some examples of how having this disability compares with your peers who are not disabled at all?'

AS   What did Access to Work say to a Deaf theatre practitioner working with Graeae on an R&D project?

'Well you're Deaf not disabled and you can read and write after all. So you can write to each other.'

JK   Until now Access to Work have always been quick and efficient. Their support enabled me to keep working when my tics first intensified and when my mobility and independence suddenly deteriorated three years ago. The results of ATW's massive lack of communication and stupid systems have impacted on me financially and emotionally.

- Two non-profit organisations have been left carrying the cost of my support—now running into thousands of pounds

- I've been left terrified by the financial burden this has placed on them, and what it means for their cash flow while they continue to pay my support workers

- I'm spending hours of work and spare time trying to resolve this situation

- When the £40K cap on Access to Work comes in I will be buggered. So will you Jen—you and me both down to work three days a week and having to censor what we do artistically and meeting-wise.

DID YOU KNOW?

AS   Did you know that a surgeon told a man who had heart surgery that he needed to stop working on medical grounds? Later the man had to go in front of a panel to be means-tested for work. He was asked why he did not work and he said pointing to the very same surgeon: 'You told me I could no longer work.'

JK   Did you know that a panel asked a nurse who had to stop working because she started losing her sight if she could catch a bus unaided? She replied yes and declared fit for work and they took away all her benefits. She took her own life.

JS   Did you know that a woman who had her foot amputated has to go back to the panel every three months to check she is still disabled?

AS   What, do they think her foot will grow back?!

JS   Did you know that a Deaf actor who now has a hearing dog for the Deaf is not allowed a sign language interpreter anymore!

AS   Do they think her dog can sign?!

JK   Dear Jenny, I just found out that my Access to Work application was turned down due to the fact that I only pay Class 2 NI contribution. Freelance artists generally earn less than £20K a year and most of us pay NI Class 2 and this is NOT a criteria to stop Access to Work.

AS   Dear Jenny, I just found out that my Access to Work application was turned down due to the fact that I only pay Class 2 NI contribution.

JS   Dear Jenny, I just found out that my Access to Work application was turned down due to the fact that I only pay Class 2 NI contribution. THIS IS THE ONGOING CRY FROM DEAF ACTORS.

[The Scripts + SORRY]

AS   I am M—I have seen what my care package would look like without the ILF contribution.

Per day, I would receive support for a carer to sleep over, then:

one hour support for lunch
one hour for tea.

Per week would be added:
seven hours for social activities
ninety minutes for shopping
forty-five minutes for housework
twenty minutes ironing
two support slots of fifteen minutes each for showering.

With nothing but a local authority care package I will be sitting in my wheelchair from quarter to eight in the morning until half past ten at night with only two breaks, at lunchtime and at teatime.

Without support to go to the toilet between visits from a care assistant I would be wet, so when the care assistant did come for the hour at lunchtime and tea time would need to be taken to clean me. I would also get a sandwich, a hot drink and be toileted.

At teatime instead of a sandwich I would get a warmed-up meal, which would have to be a microwave meal because no time would be allowed in my support package for cooking.

By the time the night staff came on at ten, I would be wet again and need to be washed and changed as well as be given a hot drink and put to bed at half past ten.

Being left wet for so many hours every day would lead to open pressure sores, which would need to be treated by a nurse on a regular basis.

My day would be nothing more than me sitting in a wet pad, just being fed and watered, no freedom to do anything I wish. My home will be my prison.

JS   Dear Miss H, now that you've got a cochlear implant, why do you need an interpreter?

JK   Dear Mr E, you typed this email by yourself without an interpreter? Well, your English is clearly good enough that you don't need an interpreter for your work.

JS   Dear Mr J, you weren't available when I phoned before, and your Manager told me you only went to one team meeting per week, so your interpreter support is cut from thirty hours per week to three hours per week.

AS   Dear Ms M, well we don't agree that you deserve access support because you may well have a brain injury and mental health issues but you are fully aware of this.

IN CONVERSATION

JK   I really need a wee.

AS   Only twenty-six mins to wait till you PA comes.

JK   AHHHH!

JS   Let's just get on with it.

JK   As J's manager if you sacked your Deaf employee then the interpreter could do the job just as well couldn't they?

[The Scripts + SORRY]

JM   Don't go there John!

AS   There are not enough plays which have disabled characters so there seems to be little point training disabled people because there will not be enough parts for them in the world of work.

JK   If I had known there were disabled people in *The Threepenny Opera* I would not have come to see it.

JM   Dear Jenny, you are only allowed to use two interpreters in exceptional circumstances.

AS   We only provide Level 6 interpreters to scientists.

      Your work is not jargon based.

JM   Hang on. This is a typical policy meeting with Jen.

AS   Ready Jude?

AS reads very fast. JD signs.

AS/JM   The DCMS is just one of a number of discrete government departments that implement policy relevant to the ecosystem as a whole, distribute public funding and commission work and research. BIS, DfE, DCLGA, DoH also have a stake in the ecosystem. Beneath Government Departments there is another layer of intermediaries and arm's-length bodies with a stake in the CCI which are in themselves siloed and intended to serve different sub-sectors of the CCI. These include BFI, ACE, HLF ...

JM   Ok Amit. I think they have got the point.

JS   Audiences need to know that normal people are playing the disabled characters. You must see that it makes it more palatable.

AS	Lorca did not write *Blood Wedding* for you people to be in it.
JK	Don't you have your own theatres to go to?
JS	November 2012: Jenny, congratulations on the Paralympic Games Opening Ceremony. Please can you recommend disabled artists from your professional and volunteer cast to be in our amazing Channel 4 programme: *The Undateables*.
AS	Jen we are so bored of you going on about that. Let's have some gems from the last few months.

GEMS FROM THE LAST FEW MONTHS

JK	After being at *Act for Change*, someone working at a big drama school said to his team: 'Disabled artists are the "next big thing!"'
JS	A producer said to me last week: 'Graeae needs to grow up and stop broadcasting the fact that when the £40K cap comes in you might have to go down to three days a week. Graeae needs to have a budget to cover this cost.'
AS	An agent said: 'Oh you don't look very disabled can you make your voice sound more disabled, more thick, you know what I mean? Otherwise no point us having you on our books.'
JK	A director said: 'Mate with that hand you have been given a golden ticket. You will get funding like that.'
AS	A producer said to me: 'I think you should not mention anything to do with disabled actors in your publicity.'
JS	A York Theatre Royal customer said to me (a wheelchair user associate helping with programmes): 'It is so nice that they employ people like you.'

[The Scripts + SORRY]

JK   Dear FB,
A sad day for me, a CEO of a major Disability Arts organisation having to go to the bank to close my ILF account, and the cashier said: 'What is ILF?'

AS   Dear FB,
Just clarifying you all understand that this ILF thing is ongoing? Yes I have successfully managed to cross from ILF to local authority covering payments BUT THAT IS ONLY TILL MARCH 2016. Not quite sure if a trip to Lourdes will do the trick between now and then!

JS   Dear FB,
I am an up-and-coming theatre director ... or maybe I need to rethink my career ...
This is the final week of my Independent Living Fund. I lose the majority of my daytime care and three of the best support workers I've ever had. One of whom I've had since university. This is a worry and a tragedy that impacts on care workers' job security, families and those reliant on such funds just to be able to exist as ordinary members of society ... a silent cut for those who struggle with the most basic tasks. Let alone fight ...

Hackney pay the agency £14 an hour for my morning and evening care and pay the workers £6 something. I have been awarded ten hours a week for independent living. Originally fifty-five hours a week was cut to twenty-eight, now ten. They will not pay my current Independent Living Agency rate who pay their workers properly. A shortfall of £1 an hour for ten hours. And they refuse to pay the ten quid.
£37.49 for a monthly overnight as carer's respite.
£37.49! Slavery. Paying a professional that is an insult. The reality of adult social care is this ...

Meeting with my local Labour MP in mid-October to discuss ILF. I'm gonna fight this shit for the eighteen thousand of us!

PHONE CALL 0

JS   Yes I am still here. Yes this is a request about someone with a differing voice pattern. You need to put me through to someone else? Yes I will hold ...

JK   Dear Jenny, in response to your request for Access to Work soundbites:
DON'T GET ME STARTED.
I WANT TO KILL.
I AM HAPPY TO DO THE TIME.

THANK YOU

Nadia Albina

Geof Armstrong

Rachel Bagsahw

Jamie Beddard

Daryl Beeton

Jodi-Alissa Bickerton

Liz Carr

Dr. Tina Carter

Dr. Colette Conroy

Jeni Draper

David Ellington

Willie Elliott

Chloe Todd Fordham

Kellan Frankland

Mat Fraser

Professor Anna Furse

Lyn Gardner

Lewis Gibson

Ray Harrison Graham

Alison Halstead

Adam Hemmings

Dr. Kay Hepplewhite

Dr. Claire Hodgson

Christopher Holt

Cherylee Houston

Kathryn Hunter

Rachel Hurst

Avis Johns

John Kelly

Mike Kenny

Judith Kilvington

Dawn Langley

Sofie Layton

Milton Lopes

Carissa Hope Lynch

Steve Mannix

Ewan Marshall

Richard Matthews

Jonathan Meth

Steve Moffitt

Elspeth Morrison

Grant Mouldey

Jodi Myers

Caroline Noh

Rufus Norris

Maria Oshodi

Kaite O'Reilly

Caroline Parker

Pete Rowe

Nabil Shaban

Claire Saddleton

Jez Scarratt

Sarah Scott

Jenny Sealey

Amit Sharma

Rebecca Sweeny

Jack Thorne

Nickie Miles-Wildin

Satsuki Yoshino

Also thanks to Adam Hemmings, Paul Margrave, Rena Sodhi, Andrew Mitchelson and the late Helen Cadbury for editing and heartfelt thanks to all Graeae core staff, board members past and present – and to our Access teams, funders and collaborators.

And a big thank you to Konstantinos Vasdekis and George Spender from Oberon.

First published in 2018 by Oberon Books Ltd
521 Caledonian Road, London N7 9RH
Tel: +44 (0) 20 7607 3637 / Fax: +44 (0) 20 7607 3629
e-mail: info@oberonbooks.com
www.oberonbooks.com

WWW.OBERONBOOKS.COM